# The Ecology of Place

# The Ecology of Place

*Planning for Environment,
Economy, and Community*

Timothy Beatley
Kristy Manning

**ISLAND PRESS**
Washington, D.C. ● Covelo, California

ISLAND PRESS is a trademark of The Center for Resource Economics.

Library of Congress Cataloging-in-Publication Data
Beatley, Timothy, 1957–
    The ecology of place : planning for environment, economy, and
community / Timothy Beatley, Kristy Manning.
        p.    cm.
    Includes bibliographical references.
    ISBN 1-55963-478-2 (paper)
    1. City planning--Environmental aspects--United States.
2. Sustainable development--United States.  3. Urban ecology--United
States.  I. Manning, Kristy.  II. Title.
HT167.B43  1997
307.1'216'0973--dc21                                        97-15863
                                                               CIP

Printed on recycled, acid-free paper  ⊛

Manufactured in the United States of America

10 9 8 7 6 5 4 3 2

# Contents

# Acknowledgments

We would like to thank a number of people who helped create this book, most notably David Brower, of the University of North Carolina at Chapel Hill, who was instrumental in shaping its early content and direction. Without his guidance and enthusiasm, the book probably would not have come to fruition. At Island Press, we would especially like to thank Heather Boyer, who has provided tremendous encouragement and advice at many points along the way. Thanks also to Christine McGowan for her patience and support during the production process.

Timothy Beatley would also like to acknowledge the generous facilities and warm support provided by the Department of Physical Planning and Rural Development at Wageningen University in the Netherlands. It was during a sabbatical year there that much of his portions of the book were written. Special thanks are due Professor Hubert van Lier, who was generous with his time and insights, and who did much to illuminate the impressive model of spatial planning and sustainable land use policies that the Netherlands represents. While this book is devoted primarily to the practice of sustainable development in U.S. communities, many of the lessons of the forward-looking Dutch approach to land use, cities, and environment are implicit in the recommendations that follow. Thanks also go to the School of Architecture at the University of Virginia, and especially Dean William McDonough and Associate Dean Ken Schwartz, for its generous support (financial and moral) for this sabbatical year of research and writing.

This book draws upon the substantial earlier work of the authors. Chapter 2, "Envisioning Sustainable Places," is a modified version of a commentary written by Timothy Beatley and published in a special issue of the *Journal of Planning Literature* (Beatley 1995a). Dr. Beatley served as the guest editor for that issue, and portions of his introduction (Beatley 1995b) have also been used in Chapter 1. This special issue of the *Journal of Planning Literature* was devoted to the subject of sustainability and was one of the first efforts to systematically address the topic in the mainstream American planning literature. The journal's founder and editor, Kenneth Pearlman, deserves considerable recognition and thanks for supporting the development of this special issue, and indeed, the early genesis of this book.

It should be noted that the following chapters largely represent a synthesis of ideas, concepts, and case examples that have been implemented and discussed elsewhere, in one place or another. They illustrate the efforts of citizens, planners, and elected officials from around the country who are striving to create more sustainable and livable environments within their own communities. We would like to acknowledge the many innovative and exemplary initiatives that are emerging from these communities; hopefully, over time such efforts will become easier to implement and, ultimately, more common. We have tried to document many of these efforts, but this book is but a sampling of the good work and creative labor occurring around the country at the local level.

*One*

# The New Planning Agenda

The problem of the 21st century is how to live good and just lives within limits, in harmony with the earth and each other. Great cities can rise out of cruelty, deviousness, and a refusal to be bounded. Livable cities can only be sustained out of humility, compassion, and acceptance of the concept of "enough."

—Donella Meadows, "Can Los Angeles Learn to Live with Limits?"

Our nation and its communities are at a critical juncture in terms of how they will grow, evolve, and deal with increasingly urgent environmental and social concerns. American communities, and indeed the American people, have important choices to make about the types of places they wish to inhabit and the kinds of environments they hope to leave their children and grandchildren.

In many ways, this dilemma stems from competing visions of the future. One path continues the status quo by simply projecting our current patterns of development into the future. This scenario is one of continuing to accommodate the march of low-density, auto-dependent, sprawling growth; facilitating the loss of natural landscapes that sustain us and other life on the planet; perpetuating our irresponsible patterns of waste and consumption; and witnessing the continuing decline in the bonds of community and the quality of our living conditions.

But there is an alternative vision, one that imagines a different future. This future is one in which land is consumed sparingly, landscapes are cherished, and cities and towns are compact and vibrant and green. These are places that have much to offer in the way of social, cultural, and recreational activity, where the young and the old are not marginalized, and where there is a feeling of community, an active civic life, and a concern for social justice. In these communities, the automobile has been tamed, many transportation options exist (including public transit and walking), and fundamental human mobility and freedom are enhanced. These are communities in which the economic base is viable as well as environmentally and socially restorative. This vision of place emphasizes both the ecological and the social, where quantity of consumption is replaced with quality of relationships. In short, the vision is about creating places citizens can be proud of—places of enduring value that people are not ashamed to leave to their descendants.

This book introduces an expanded vision of what places can be, and of how we might plan for them. It builds on the ideas and power of recent concerns about ecological sustainability, but transforms those ideas in some important ways. First, the vision explored here is one that celebrates place. It recognizes that questions of ecological sustainability are fundamentally and inextricably tied to patterns of human settlement—to metropolitan regions, cities, towns, and villages. These patterns are directly influenced by natural processes and forces, including rivers, topography, and natural disasters. Just as they themselves are impacted, so do human settlements exert tremendous pressures on ecosystems, from the generation of pollution and wastes to demands on resources for food, electricity, and water. Perhaps most striking, at least in terms of the clarity with which its progress many be monitored, is the consumption and destruction of ecological capital through the conversion of natural landscapes and farmland to urbanized uses.

However dire its anticipated consequences, in this fundamental recognition lies the hope and promise of places that can actually support and help to achieve long-term ecological sustainability, rather than work against it. Land use and growth patterns can be shaped to minimize resource consumption; development needs can be focused onto already committed and degraded lands; and the processes of urbanization and community building can be used to repair and restore rather than degrade and destroy.

At the same time that this alternative vision explicably connects human settlement patterns to ecological conditions, so too does it emphasize the needs of humans and the quality of human communities. Environmental advocates are sometimes accused of showing concern for the ecological integrity of the planet to the exclusion of the needs of humans. The vision of sustainable places, or sustainable communities, presented in the following pages is explicitly human. Just as it seeks to protect, sustain, and restore the environment, it also strives to create livable, inspiring, enduring, and equitable places—regions, cities, and towns where the quality of life and the long-term quality of human existence will be enhanced rather than degraded. Hence, there is a unity of purpose in the vision of sustainable places that is at once environmental and ecological, as well as social and human, in its orientation.

To realize fully the potential of such a vision, Americans must begin to rethink in fundamental ways their approaches to planning, designing, and managing place. Such an approach seeks a way of living on the planet that respects the limits of its ecological health—the finiteness of land, biodiversity, and other natural resources—while finding hopeful alternatives to the many ways in which current approaches to planning and place making are unsuccessful at meeting human needs and desires.

## Understanding Sustainability

The vision presented in this book is about creating and nurturing sustainable towns, cities, and regions—"sustainable places." As the underlying basis for the new approach to planning, the notion of sustainability is fundamental to the many strategies that this volume will describe and advocate. A clear understanding of this concept is therefore a necessary starting point for creating sustainable places.

To many, *sustainability* and *sustainable development* are just the latest buzzwords to make their way into the planning field—another set of trendy phrases. There is no question that these terms are used increasingly to describe what planners do and what their professional mission is. Their meanings are not immediately obvious: sustainability and sustainable development require definition and elaboration, as do terms such as freedom, justice, or quality of life.

There is a general sense that sustainability is a good thing (and that being unsustainable is a bad thing), but will we know it when we see it? This ambiguity will likely remain, but the very fact that planners and citizens are questioning what is or is not sustainable, and exploring what the idea means and calls for, is a very positive sign. It opens opportunities for critical dialogue and serves as an important catalyst for thinking clearly and systematically about the future we wish to create.

Sustainability finds many of its roots in biology and ecology, and specifically in the concept of ecological "carrying capacity"—the notion that a given ecosystem or environment can sustain a certain animal population, and that beyond that level, overpopulation and species collapse will occur (for a detailed discussion of the history of sustainability, see Kidd 1992). Central to this concept is the idea that certain physical and ecological limits that exist in nature, if exceeded, will have ripple effects that bring population back in line with capacity.

The meaning of sustainability is perhaps clearest when applied to renewable resources such as ocean fisheries, forests, groundwater, and soils. Terms such as optimal sustainable yield have been explicitly incorporated into, for example, U.S. fisheries management law (Kidd 1992). The growing advocacy for sustainable use of a variety of renewable resources—sustainable forestry, sustainable fisheries, sustainable agriculture—is premised on the idea that these resources can be harvested and used in a manner that allows them to renew themselves and that preserves their long-term productivity (Aplet, Johnson, Olsen, and Sample, eds. 1993). Sustainability is also a useful concept in planning for the use of nonrenewable resources, the waste-assimilative capacities of the earth, and the natural service provided by the environment (e.g., climate regulation; Jacobs 1991).

The use of the term *sustainability* in environmental planning and policy circles is relatively new. It began appearing in the literature in the early 1970s and emerged as a significant theme in the 1980s. The term of preference became *sustainable development,* which focused on how human interventions—especially international development programs and projects—failed to respect the integrity of the natural systems in which they were sited. Projects of international development agencies such as the World Bank were highly criticized as the antithesis of sustainable development. Sustainability has since been strongly embraced by such nongovernmental organizations as the Worldwatch Institute and World Resources Institute (Brown et al. 1994; WRI 1994), governmental organizations such as the U.S. Agency for International Development, and a number of international study groups (Kidd 1992). Most recently, the President's Council on Sustainable Development has examined the role of sustainability in American communities as well as its implications for the future of the nation (PCSD 1996).

Particularly in the last decade, there have been a number of attempts to define sustainable development formally. Probably the most frequently cited definition is that put forth by the World Commission on Environment and Development (WCED), also commonly known as the Brundtland Commission, which defined sustainable development as that which "meets the needs of the present without compromising the ability of future generations to meet their own needs" (WCED 1987, p. 8). More recently, the National Commission on the Environment has defined sustainable development as

> a strategy for improving the quality of life while preserving the environmental potential for the future, of living off interest rather than consuming natural capital. Sustainable development mandates that the present generation must not narrow the choices of future generations but must strive to expand them by passing on an environment and an accumulation of resources that will allow its children to live at least as well as, and preferably better than, people today. Sustainable development is premised on living within the Earth's means (National Commission on the Environment 1993, p. 2).

These definitions share an emphasis on certain important concepts and themes. They stress the importance of living within the ecological carrying capacities of the planet, living off ecological interest, and protecting future generations. They envision a society that "can persist over generations, one that is farseeing enough, flexible enough, and wise enough not to undermine either its physical or its social systems of support" (Meadows, Meadows, and Randers 1992, p. 209).

## Community Planning in the Context of Global Environmental Crisis

The urgency of current environmental trends clearly necessitates a new approach to living on the planet—one that sustains our basic biological and ecosystem functions while offering opportunities for a meaningful quality of life to all. In the United States, we lose some 3 billion tons of topsoil yearly, extract groundwater faster than it is recharged, and continue to harvest the few remaining old-growth forests (Bouvier and Grant 1994). We have filled and destroyed more than half of the wetlands that existed in pre-Columbian times and continue to destroy and degrade the few that remain. The global loss of biodiversity is astounding—some predict that by the year 2020 we will have lost as many as one-quarter of the species that existed in 1980 (Wilson 1992)—and fisheries are being depleted throughout the world.

Moreover, humanity is modifying the very functioning of the global ecosystem. The ozone layer continues to diminish in size, accompanied by increases in ultraviolet radiation and a variety of ecological ripple effects. Anthropogenic increases in carbon dioxide and other greenhouse gases will likely lead to a significant rise in global temperatures and its attendant effects, such as sea level rise and changing precipitation patterns (Houghton, Jenkins, and Ephram, eds. 1990; see also U.S. Office of Technology Assessment 1993).

Most daunting, perhaps, is the exponential growth of the human population. While predictions vary, we are poised to move from a current global population of more than 5.8 billion to some 8 billion in 2025 and to 9 to 10 billion by the year 2050 (WRI 1994; Population Reference Bureau 1997). The population of the United States is projected to rise from 260 million to nearly 400 million by the year 2050 (Bouvier and Grant 1994). These projections raise real questions about not only future environmental degradation, but the ability to feed, house, and otherwise sustain future population increases (Ehrlich and Ehrlich 1991).

The global trend toward more and more immense "megacities" underscores the urgency of the population problem and of the need to adopt new planning and urban management approaches. The World Resources Institute reports that rates of urbanization continue to rise much faster than rates of absolute population growth, such that by the year 2000, more than half the global population will live in urban areas; by 2020, this figure will rise to 60 percent (WRI 1996). With the United States a leader in the global economy, the rapid growth of cities around the world has tremendous implications for sustainability in our country, and vice versa.

## The Unsustainability of Current Development Patterns

By almost any measure, our current use of land and resources is unsustainable. Contemporary land use patterns do not acknowledge the fundamental finiteness of land, air, water, and biological diversity. Nowhere is this tendency more conspicuous than in the sprawling growth of urban and suburban areas throughout the United States, where low-density development is literally eating up natural landscapes.

One striking measure of this trend is the amount of land consumed for development or converted to developed uses. In the Chicago metropolitan area, for example, while residential population grew by only about 4 percent between 1970 and 1990, the amount of land devoted to housing during that period rose by 46 percent. During this same time frame, the city of Los Angeles grew 45 percent in population but nearly 300 percent in size of the developed area (Leinsberger 1996). Such land-consumptive sprawl is evident throughout the United States, with dramatic examples including South Florida, Southern California, and Phoenix, Arizona, among others. Meanwhile, nationwide, some 1.3 million acres of farmland are converted to more developed uses each year (Zero Population Growth 1996).

Aside from the fact that the country's land base is in finite supply and ultimately cannot accommodate such growth, our sprawling development patterns manifest themselves in a range of economically and socially disturbing ways. To the majority of citizens, traffic congestion is perhaps the biggest obvious inconvenience. For those individuals who are too young, too old, too poor, or otherwise unable to drive or own a car, participation in many everyday activities—whether shopping, school, employment, or entertainment—is often impeded. As development marches out beyond the urban fringes, new infrastructure and services must be provided, often at the expense of higher property taxes levied on long-time residents. Meanwhile, the infrastructure that is left behind, particularly in the inner city, is left to decline, as are the income-generating powers of local businesses, residents who cannot afford to commute to jobs in the suburbs, and municipal governments that see their tax bases shrink (Bank of America 1995).

Few places around the country are immune to the destructiveness of sprawl. A recent series of articles in the *Kansas City Star* documented the host of problems brought about by the tidal wave of sprawl there. While population growth in Kansas City increased by less than 30 percent between 1960 and 1990, land devoted to housing and development rose by 110 percent. The study documents a dramatic shift in the "golden ring" of the region's most valuable homes; since 1970, every two years the location of the highest-valued homes has moved two miles farther away from downtown. There are always short-term winners in this sprawl process, particularly developers, builders, and owners of speculative land. At the same time, however, there are a multitude of losers, including businesses in older suburbs and "inner-ring" communities. Existing homeowners often experience the greatest losses: as their property taxes rise to fund the necessary new infrastructure and services, they may see their property values stagnate or decline (Lester and Spivak 1995).

Contemporary land use and development patterns also damage the natural environment and undermine important ecological systems. Wetlands, riparian areas, and natural habitats of all kinds continue to be sacrificed or degraded. Increasingly, these losses occur less through dramatic large-scale projects than through the insidious whittling away of resources, or what the late ecologist Bill Odum used to describe as the "tyranny of small decisions": the filling of several acres of wetlands for a roadway, the loss of a small area of natural beachfront, or the gradual rise in the imperviousness of surfaces in the watershed. While the impacts of any individual decision may be small, the cumulative effects are substantial. These losses are particularly evident where population and land use pressures are the greatest. In fact, a large proportion of development pressures in the United States are occurring in the most environmentally sensitive and ecologically productive places. As just one example, it is estimated that population in coastal areas will have grown by 60 percent between 1960 and 2010 (Culliton et al. 1991).

And we are losing and degrading many of our most precious landscapes, our secular "sacred places," to borrow from Native American culture. These are the places of both magnificent beauty and ecological subtlety—they impart to us wonder, peace, connectedness to "other," and ecological and cultural wisdom. In many important ways, these landscapes sustain us, whether spiritually, visually, or aesthetically. These landscapes include such areas as the Virginia Piedmont, the deserts of Arizona and Nevada, the Texas Hill Country, and the Outer Banks of North Carolina, among many others.

The ecological impacts of the American lifestyle, and of the infrastructure needed to support that lifestyle, extend well beyond the physical manifestation of decentralized land use. The economic and industrial base of our communities can be extremely destructive, for example, particularly in terms of waste and pollution generation. Over the past fifty years, some 70,000 new chemical compounds have made their way into our environment, very few of which have been tested for human toxicity (Landrigan and Needleman 1994). In the United States we generate some fifty tons of solid waste per person each year (Meadows, Meadows, and Randers, eds. 1992).The recent study *Our Stolen Future* (Colborn, Meyers, and Dumanoski 1996) indicates that in the normal course of production and consumption, emissions of dioxins, PCBs, and many other substances are implicated in high rates of breast cancer, declining sperm counts, and the decline of amphibian and other species populations. These findings represent only a small sampling of data that suggest the urgency of finding a different, more restorative economic foundation upon which to build our communities.

Contemporary building and development practices characterized by heavy auto use, abandonment of existing infrastructure and buildings, and lifestyles of high material consumption and waste generation are also unsustainable. American homes and businesses consume large amounts of energy, both directly—for example, through heating and cooling—and indirectly, most notably in terms of the "embodied energy" expended through materials generation, transportation, and the construction process. The construction and operation of buildings account for 40 percent of the materials entering the world's economy and for about one-third of the world's energy consumption (Worldwatch Institute 1995).

Our development patterns, and the lifestyles and consumption patterns they reflect, have environmental impacts and cause resource depletion well beyond the boundaries of their local and state jurisdictions.William Rees's profoundly important concept of the "ecological footprint" suggests that our shelter, energy, food, and other resource demands can be translated into estimates of the land and water areas needed to meet them (Rees 1992; Wackernagel and Rees 1996). The average North American has a very large ecological footprint, each person requiring about five hectares of land to support food, housing, transportation, and other consumer needs. Some quick calculations lead to the conclusion that North American lifestyles are supported in no small degree by appropriating the carrying capacities and resources of other regions and countries.We are, in essence, living beyond our ecological means, and it is in large part a function of the wasteful ways in which we grow and develop and inhabit the spaces in which we live.

As ecologically unsustainable as our communities are, they can be equally unsatisfying emotionally. As older cities continue to lose population to their suburban fringes, they are becoming economically dysfunctional and are home to a high proportion of the poor and disenfranchised. According to a recent study by the *Dallas Morning News*, 60 percent of the population of our nation's urbanized areas reside in the suburbs, and 42 percent of the poor live in cities (as cited in Kelley 1996). Our highly dispersed patterns of suburban and exurban development necessitate a heavy reliance on the automobile, resulting in increased traffic, longer commutes, and diminished time, opportunity, and energy for face-to-face social interaction. These patterns encourage the physical separation of land uses as well as the social segregation of demographic groups. Their "cookie-cutter" design results in largely sterile environments lacking in character and a sense of place. In short, as a number of recent and telling critiques of current development patterns argue, our singular quest to "develop" has come at the expense of the creation of enjoyable, livable, quality communities (for the best of these, see Kunstler 1993, 1996; Calthorpe 1993; Langdon 1994).

As these trends evolve, contemporary American land use is increasingly characterized by the ascendancy of the private over the public. While cities and towns of the past had a strong public dimension to their physical design and layout, contemporary developments have focused inward, causing one recent commentator to lament "the rise of the new walled cities" (Judd 1995). While the "walled" nature of such developments has traditionally been limited to golf course, resort, and gated retirement communities—the ultimate in "getting away from it all"— citizens are increasingly retreating to gated communities to make their primary residence. Blakely and Snyder (1995) estimate that approximately 4 million people are sequestering themselves in gated communities to escape the afflictions of urbanization, particularly crime. They document a rapid increase in this kind of "forting up," which, as is explored in later chapters, carries with it a distinct neglect of many important aspects of the public realm—aspects that are critical to the creation of functional, sustainable communities. While the rise of gated communities is perhaps an extreme manifestation of our increasingly divided ways, Blakely and Snyder view this tendency as a microcosm of the larger pattern of segregated land use in America.

Natural disasters dramatically illustrate the ways in which contemporary land use and development patterns are not sustainable in the long run. They tell us in some of the most graphic and striking ways that we are not living wisely on the planet. Community land use patterns are not sustainable if they allow or encourage the exposure of people and property to significant risks from natural hazards, and if alternative settlement patterns are available that would avoid such exposure. The dangerous combination of explosive urban growth and reckless land use patterns in locations that are susceptible to serious natural hazards is evident in many places. Consider the seismic risks of Southern California, development along the Wasatch front in Utah, and development on the Outer Banks of North Carolina and the Florida

Keys. Many of the places experiencing the highest growth rates, and the most sprawling development patterns, have recently suffered the consequences of severe natural hazards; examples include the devastating impact of Hurricane Andrew in South Florida, extensive damage in Los Angeles and San Francisco from recent earthquakes, and the destruction of coastal communities in the Carolinas in the wake of Hurricane Fran. Rather than retreat from these vulnerable areas, residents continue to rebuild directly in the path of future damage.

## The High Cost of the Current Approach

There are tremendous costs associated with current growth patterns and approaches to community building. Many of these costs are economic, including the escalating expense of car ownership and the ongoing investment in highways and infrastructure. Other costs, while ultimately manifesting themselves in economic terms, are more difficult to measure: the expense of mitigating pollution, time lost through commuting, or a community's inability to attract tourism or business due to diminished natural and social amenities. While there remains a relative paucity of data on the long-term economic costs associated with low-density, dispersed development patterns, the analytic work that exists has reached disturbing conclusions.

Beginning with a groundbreaking 1974 study by the Real Estate Research Corporation entitled *The Costs of Sprawl*, some twenty years of research yield a consistent message: that low-density, sprawling development patterns are very expensive, particularly in terms of the costs of such public infrastructure as roads, water and sewer systems, and schools (Real Estate Research Corporation 1974; Urban Land Institute 1989; for a good review and summary of these studies, see Diamond and Noonan 1996, pp. 35–40). For example, analysis conducted by the Urban Land Institute estimates that public infrastructure costs for lower-density development of three units per acre are some $8,000 per unit higher than for densities of twelve units per acre (ULI 1989, as cited in Diamond and Noonan 1996). Several other studies have effectively demonstrated the economic costs of residential growth and the fact that it rarely pays for itself.

One of the most illustrative recent "cost of growth" studies was undertaken by a group of researchers at Rutgers University. They compared the likely costs of implementing New Jersey's new comprehensive plan—which attempts to control sprawl and to guide growth to designated growth centers—with the perpetuation of current sprawling development patterns throughout the state. The study predicted that over a twenty-year period, planned development would save some $1.4 billion in public infrastructure costs in roads, sewer and water lines, and schools (Young 1995; Burchell and Listokin 1995). From 20 percent to 45 percent less land would be consumed under the plan, including at least 70,000 fewer acres of sensitive natural land and farmland (and some 174,000 fewer acres consumed overall) (Burchell et al., as cited in Diamond and Noonan 1996; and Young 1995). A more recent literature review, also conducted by the Rutgers group, determined that findings for New Jersey were similar to studies for communities around the country. Specifically, the review found that as compared to traditional sprawling trends, planned development consumes only 40 percent as much land overall and 60 percent as much agricultural acreage; is less expensive with respect to roads, utilities, annual municipal budgets, and schools (including annual budgets and capital expenditures for school districts); and does not increase housing costs. In some cases, the study found, planned development can result in modest costs savings for housing (Burchell and Listokin 1995).

An Australian study, focused on the cost savings realized by replacing American-style sprawl with transit-oriented urban villages over a twenty-year period, reached similar conclusions. Substantial savings in public infrastructure costs are predicted, as well as major reductions in per capita energy use and other social and environmental costs (air pollution, traffic accidents, and noise) associated with auto usage (Newman and Kenworthy 1992).

The findings of *Beyond Sprawl* (1995), an important study of growth trends in California, represent a strong condemnation of the impacts and costly nature of scattered development patterns. The report was sponsored by an unlikely coalition of interests: the Bank of America (the study has come to be known as the Bank of America study), the California Resources Agency, the Greenbelt Alliance, and The Low Income Housing Fund. Its conclusions are that sprawling patterns of growth threaten not only the state's environmental resources and its overall quality of life, but also its long-term business climate. *Beyond Sprawl* is one of the clearest statements to date of the relationship between land use, quality of life, and long-term economic vitality:

> California businesses cannot compete globally when they are burdened with the costs of sprawl. An attractive business climate cannot be maintained if the quality of life continues to decline and the cost of financing real estate development escalates. People in central cities and older suburbs cannot become part of the broader economy if sprawl continues to encourage disinvestment, and the state can neither afford to ignore nor fully subsidize these neglected areas.

> California must find a new development model. We must create more compact and efficient development patterns that accommodate growth, yet help maintain California's environmental balance and its economic competitiveness. And we must encourage everyone in California to propose and create solutions to sprawl (Bank of America 1995, p. 8).

Other impacts noted include the high cost to taxpayers of maintaining sprawling infrastructure, the costs of dealing with the environmental and social problems created by sprawl, and the permanent loss of agricultural land and productivity. The study also highlighted the loss of 95 percent of the state's wetlands, the highest number of candidate and listed species of any state, the worst air quality in the country, 40 of 350 groundwater basins "seriously overdrafted," and a 2- to 8-million-acre-foot water supply deficit predicted by 2020 (Bank of America 1995). In conclusion, the report states, "The sponsors of this report . . . believe that California cannot succeed unless the state moves beyond sprawl" (p. 8).

*Beyond Sprawl* offers a number of recommendations for minimizing these trends over the long term, including the need to: delineate with greater certainty where future development will and will not be able to occur; make more efficient use of already developed land (e.g., maintaining and enhancing older neighborhoods); streamline permitting where development is to be allowed and ensure that it pays its full marginal costs; enact more coordinated, less competitive land use policies (e.g., through joint powers authorities); and "forge a constituency to build sustainable communities" (p. 11).

A study of urban growth in California's Central Valley reinforces the conclusions and concerns of *Beyond Sprawl*. Over the next forty-five years, the Central Valley—which includes the cities of Fresno, Sacramento, Bakersfield, and Modesto—is expected to triple in population, from approximately 4 million to 12 million residents. The study shows that current, sprawling, land development patterns would consume 1 million acres of farmland at a loss of $5.3 billion per year to the state economy. This trajectory is likely to cause a 20 percent shortfall in city and county budgets and an overall deficit among local governments of $1 billion per year (Arax 1995).

Current development patterns require expensive and inefficient public investments that extend well beyond infrastructure costs. Sprawling growth often leads to the creation of costly new governmental units, including a variety of new special districts dedicated to sewers and water, libraries, and fire protection, among others. Local governments in the Kansas City area, for instance, were reported to cost some $3 billion in 1987, or almost $5,000 per household (Lester and Spivak 1995). In Johnson County, one of the

fastest-growing counties in the Kansas City region, the 1980s saw a 60 percent per capita rise in its budget; as the *Kansas City Star* points out, this increase is some four times greater than spending increases at the federal level.
Much of this type of growth does not pay its own way, and property taxes
are often increased substantially to compensate for shortfalls. Meanwhile,
outward growth is leaving behind schools, public buildings, and infrastructures that are underutilized at the same time that suburban and exurban
communities are frantically building new such facilities—a phenomenon
the *Star* describes as the region "cannibalizing itself" (Lester and Spivak
1995).

The foolhardy exposure of people and property to the forces of natural
hazards, in addition to being life-threatening, can result in extremely high
costs. Recent damage levels were almost unimaginable a decade or two ago:
$18 billion in damages from the 1993 Midwest floods, $20 billion from the
Northridge earthquake, and perhaps as high as $30 billion for Hurricane
Andrew. These events have caused an insurance crisis as some companies
have gone out of business and many others are significantly curtailing coverage. Projections for the future suggest even higher damage levels, again the
result largely of building in the wrong places, building shoddily, and devot-
ing insufficient attention to protecting the qualities of resilience provided
by the natural environment. Moreover, many parts of the country, such as
South Florida, are reaching the limits of their ability to evacuate and to ensure that people are able to escape from hurricanes and other natural events.

The maintenance and support of an auto-dependent landscape is also expensive. Subsidies and expenses (beyond what is paid in taxes and fees) associated with roads and automobiles are estimated to exceed $100 billion
per year, or anywhere from $4,000 to $9,400 per car (Nelessen 1994). And
if the full environmental and social costs of the auto are taken into account,
these costs together comprise some 5 percent of U.S. gross domestic product (a conservative estimate; Mathews 1996).

Our dispersed development patterns also contribute substantially to the
cost of everyday life. It has been estimated that the average two-car household spends nearly one-quarter of its after-tax income, or $9,000 per year,
on maintaining and operating automobiles (Langdon 1994). As a nation, we
are driving more—up to 2.5 trillion miles per year—and with cars that are
increasingly less fuel-efficient. Nationally, the number of miles driven is increasing three times as fast as population or job growth (ALT-TRANS
1995). Meanwhile, transit ridership is dismally low—about 5 percent compared with 35 percent in the 1940s.

There are many additional costs associated with our current spatial con-
figuration and consumption patterns. As a society we are highly dependent
upon fossil fuels. Energy-wasteful forms of transportation, and energy-guz-

zling buildings and development, raise real concerns about the energy and economic security of our nation. Nearly 60 percent of the oil we use in the United States is imported from the Middle East and elsewhere. The Gulf War illustrated vividly the pitfalls of such oil dependence (Pimental and Giampietro 1995). From solid waste disposal to water consumption to non-point water pollution, current practices usually involve the reaping of short-term economic benefits at the expense of much larger long-term costs.

There are health care costs as well. These stem from exposure to pollutants, from excessive chemicals in food and in working and living environments, and from the physical layout and spatial configurations of cities and towns. The negative health implications of auto-dependent lifestyles are particularly troubling, especially in that a high percentage of the population gets little exercise and is overweight

Finally, the long-term impacts of current development patterns on the social fabric of our society, though perhaps more difficult to document, are equally as serious. As Peter Calthorpe and Henry Richmond observe:

> Our land use patterns are the physical foundation of our society and, like our society, they are becoming more and more fractured. They increasingly isolate people and activities in an inefficient network of congestion and pollution rather than joining them in diverse and human-scaled communities. Our faith in government and the sense of common purpose essential to any vital democracy are eroding in suburbs designed more for cars than people, more for market segments than communities. Local zoning laws and development patterns designed to separate and segregate us make it difficult for Americans to work together on the social issues facing the country (Calthorpe and Richmond 1993, p. 700).

Sprawl breeds social isolation and undermines a sense of community and respect and appreciation for "otherness." As Philip Langdon states in his book *A Better Place to Live,* "Disconnection or fragmentation undermines the social ties that give individuals pleasure and invigorate community life" (Langdon 1994, p. 14).

## Current Development Patterns as a Matter of Ethics

The evolution of our built environment, and the ways in which we modify and interact with the natural environment, are themselves a manifestation of our societal values. While it is unfair to paint with too broad a brush in characterizing current land use and development trends, certain patterns of behavior are evident.

First, the dominant land and development ethic is increasingly parochial and atomistic, often reflecting a general lack of concern for the interests of the broader public. Widespread NIMBYism ("not in my backyard") reflects this attitude, in which individuals act to protect their own economic interests at the expense of public needs and values. The private property rights movement exhibits a similar belief that one's primary obligation is to protect personal benefits without concern for the impacts of individual actions on others, or on the general public. Ultimately, this value manifests itself as a failure to take responsibility for the broader implications of one's actions, decisions, and behaviors concerning land use.

Decisions to live in gated communities reflect a lack of concern for the future of our society at large. This "forting up" phenomenon and the privatization of many of the functions of traditional government (private security guards and road maintenance) suggest a serious narrowing of our social contract:

> What is the measure of nationhood when neighbors require armed patrols and electric fencing to keep out citizens? When public services and even local governments are privatized and when the community of responsibility stops at the subdivision gates, what happens to the function and the very idea of democracy? In short, can this nation fulfill its social contract in the absence of social contact? (Blakely and Snyder 1995, p. 3).

The greater our separation from the broader public, the easier it is to believe that we have few ethical obligations to others. This despite the fact that many of our public and private actions have significant environmental and social impacts "beyond our borders," affecting people and environments beyond our lot lines, beyond our community boundaries, and beyond our national borders.

Many of our most common land use practices have long-term consequences that are not commonly taken into account, thereby reflecting a degree of shortsightedness. Wasteful land consumption represents, among other things, an eating away of the ecological capital upon which future generations will heavily rely. Whether it manifests itself in a region overdrawing its water supply or a farmer producing crops with little concern for the long-term loss of soil, short-term thinking is prevalent. If we believe, as we seem to, that we have little moral obligation to consider the future, such practices seem economical and even practical.

Especially in the United States and other industrialized nations, values about land and development reflect a commodity-based view of land and life, illustrating the materialistic tendencies that permeate much of society as a whole. Land and property, for example, are considered among the most common forms of economic investment. In seeking to protect that investment, homeowners have an incentive to oppose any land use activity or policy—even if that change will benefit the broader public—that might diminish their financial return. Communities behave similarly, determining the legitimacy of land use decisions primarily by considering the tax base and tax monies to be generated by it.

The trend toward building increasingly larger homes, with more and more amenities, is perhaps the most obvious demonstration of our consumption-based values. It is ironic that the average home size in the United States has been rising at precisely the same time that the average household size has been declining.

Much of the physical landscape we have created serves to reinforce the "commercial" nature of land use. With commercial strip zones, gas stations, fast food restaurants, and car sales lots—and their accompanying signage—dominating the landscape, it is perhaps little wonder that we tend to think of land and place in terms of what can be bought and sold and consumed. Philip Langdon calls this a "sellscape." And according to Alan Durning, "All that matters, in this type of landscape . . . is whether a driver can recognize a place of commerce from far enough away to get into the turn lane" (Durning 1996, p. 28).

Theodore Steinberg, in his book *Slide Mountain: Or the Folly of Owning Nature,* talks of how we have "de-physicalized" the land (Steinberg 1995). That is, the average homeowner has very little sense of being connected in any real physical, environmental, or ecological sense to anything else. Most people do not know which way the water runs, what the prevailing wind patterns are, whether they are in a floodplain, or what species of bird is nesting in the eaves. Absent this sense of connection, we have manipulated nature, filling in wetlands, paving over farmland, destroying species and habitat, and attempting to channel the flow of rivers—all with a belief that the impacts will be manageable and that technology will protect us from the worst calamities.

Finally, our dominant land and settlement ethic exhibits a strong degree of anthropocentrism. It judges the moral correctness of land use decisions and policies against a decidedly human metric: how actions or policies will help or harm or otherwise affect humans. Consideration of other life forms, and indeed of the environment itself, is secondary. In a host of ways, from the destruction of natural lands to the depletion of water and nonrenewable resources, we exhibit an ethic that says, in effect, that *Homo sapiens* have moral value and that other life forms have very little.

Each of these values is difficult to separate or disentangle from the others, and they combine and interact to form a value structure that manifests itself in public policies and individual choices. Individualism and greed in land use decisions are reinforced and condoned by a relatively limited definition, temporally and geographically, of the moral community to which we have ethical duties and obligations. The challenge, in part, is to confront the ethical dimensions of the current sustainability crisis and to fashion and shape a new ethic that nurtures sustainable places.

## Sustainable Places: The New Planning Agenda

Environmental destruction and social dysfunction are occurring at a number of different geographical scales, from global to micro-local. Anyone involved in the sustainability movement has confronted the question of what the appropriate geographical scale of analysis or action is, or should be, in which to make a difference in the world. Many of our more serious and threatening environmental trends, from global climate change to fisheries depletion to biodiversity loss, appear to occur at global scales that seem beyond the influence of local citizens, neighborhood groups, or the actions of one's city council. There are undoubtedly a number of appropriate and potentially effective geographical levels at which actions and policies could be taken that will help to move us in the direction of sustainability. This book emphasizes the importance and potential of local and regional efforts and the need to understand the interconnectedness of local or regional actions with a wide range of unsustainable outcomes and conditions at a number of geographical levels.

The application of sustainability concepts to the field of urban and regional planning is a relatively recent phenomenon—in many ways a slower and more incremental process than global efforts such as the United Nations Conference on Environment and Development or national initiatives such as the President's Council on Sustainable Development. Until only recently, there have been few holistic efforts to translate the broad concepts expressed in the Brundtland Commission's report and elsewhere into local and regional planning and development policy.

In recent years, however, examples of sustainability initiatives at local and regional levels have become more common, led by cities such as Seattle and Chattanooga, which have begun to organize their planning efforts around sustainability. Two recent major expressions of support for the notion of sustainable communities or sustainable places can be seen in the 1996 Habitat II meeting in Istanbul, which had sustainable cities as a major theme, and the final report of the President's Council on Sustainable Development. Chapter 4 of the President's Council report, entitled "Strengthening Communities," is a strong statement recognizing the criticality of local efforts (PCSD 1996). The report also lists, as part of its national agenda, a goal specifically addressing sustainable communities: "Encourage people to work together to create healthy communities where natural and historic resources are preserved, jobs are available, sprawl is contained, neighborhoods are secure, education is lifelong, transportation and health care are accessible, and all citizens have opportunities to improve the quality of their lives" (PCSD 1996, p. 12).

In many respects, the agenda of sustainable places is the next natural progression in the evolution of planning history. In the last several decades the planning field has seen a gradual expansion of the notion of planning, from more narrow considerations of land use and zoning to the broader set of concerns addressed in the emphasis on "growth management" that blossomed in the 1970s. During this period, known as "the quiet revolution in land use control," communities began to examine the causes and impacts of community growth more systematically, ultimately adopting more comprehensive approaches and strategies for managing or controlling growth. The "stars" of this period included places such as Petaluma, California; Ramapo, New York; Sanibel, Florida; and Boulder, Colorado—all of which have adopted unusually stringent growth management tools and techniques, including phased development ordinances, impact fees, and annual development caps (Godschalk, Brower, McBennett, Vestal, and Herr 1979; Porter 1989; DeGrove 1984). The 1970s and 1980s also witnessed considerable activity at the state level as a number of states became active in mandating local planning and growth management requirements, the prime examples being Oregon and Florida, which required local consistency with statewide plans and standards.

Despite this increased level of activity, the accomplishments of communities engaged in growth management have been modest at best. Although growth containment has been an objective of many of these programs, it has truly been accomplished in only a few places, including Portland and other Oregon cities, and Boulder (Beatley, Brower, and Brower 1988; Knapp and Nelson 1992). Moreover, the growth management movement might more aptly be described as growth accommodation—enacting policies and mechanisms for marginally guiding growth, mitigating growth effects, and spreading the costs of growth in more equitable ways through mechanisms such as impact fees (Nelson 1988). Given the existing system of subsidies, incentives, and social myths that tend to work against it, it is no surprise that real growth containment has been difficult to accomplish in the United States (see, e.g., Katz 1994; Kunstler 1993; Jackson 1985).

While the development of growth management programs marked a very positive shift in the planning field, and while many of these programs are explored in later chapters, the agenda of sustainable places is, necessarily, more ambitious. It represents both an evolution in the spirit of growth management and an expansion of the subjects of concern. It is a change in spirit in the sense that its objectives, while not antidevelopment, question the accommodation of traditional patterns of development and growth. It is an expanded agenda in the sense that it takes a more holistic and comprehensive view of planning and of communities; it is not simply concerned with the way a parcel of land is used, or whether certain infrastructure exists to accommodate growth. The paradigm of sustainability views the community in its entirety: its environmental impacts and how they can be minimized; how well its citizens are living and how programs and policies can be coordinated and implemented to enhance quality of life; its resource needs and how they are being met; and the environmental and social impacts of meeting those needs.

Under this new planning agenda, traditional land use and growth management concerns remain important and primary, but they are not the only policy spheres. Equally important are a city's energy and procurement policies, the ways in which resources and services are priced, its economic development strategies, its housing programs, and its community institutions. In this sense, the agenda of sustainable places goes beyond land use planning to consider, from a holistic perspective, a much larger set of ways in which cities and communities are organized and operate. There has been considerable interest in recent years in the subject of urban ecology—that is, in understanding cities both as the generators of environmental impacts (through the consumption of resources and generation of wastes) and as intrinsically embedded within a larger ecosystem and set of natural processes upon which they depend. An understanding of urban ecology has implications for community land use patterns, but also for a host of other planning issues, including the kinds of industrial and economic activities at work in the community, the ways in which homes and buildings are designed and built, and the programs, policies, and strategies employed by the community for addressing its waste and resource needs.

The approach presented in this volume is clearly distinguished from that of the "New Urbanism." This movement, which initially was called "neo-traditionalism," grew primarily out of the profession of architecture (Katz 1994), driven by a few influential architects, especially Andres Duany, Elizabeth Plater-Zyberk (1991), and Peter Calthorpe (1993; see also Mohney and Easterling 1991). The thrust of the New Urbanism is a belief in the need to return to the design principles embodied in traditional American towns. The qualities and features that are emphasized include, among others, a return to the traditional grid street pattern; mixed-use, pedestrian environments; and public spaces and civic architecture. A number of development projects have been built according to neo-traditional principles, and many communities around the country have adopted ordinances to permit neo-traditional development. The first major project to gain national attention was Seaside, Florida, designed by Duany and Plater-Zyberk. Other notable projects include Kentlands (outside Washington, D.C.; see Fig. 1.1), Laguna West (in Sacramento, California), and Disney's Celebration (near Orlando, Florida).

There is no question that the New Urbanists have contributed much to the critical dialogue and assessment of contemporary development patterns. They have been courageous critics of sprawl and have succeeded in articulating and implementing a compelling alternative vision. In fact, many of the physical and social attributes and qualities advocated in this volume, under the label of sustainable places, are similar to those of the New Urbanists. These include support for compact, higher-density settlements;

Figure 1.1 Kentlands, a New Urbanist development outside Washington, D.C., in Gaithersburg, Maryland.

transit- and pedestrian-oriented developments; and the importance of civic and public space, among others.

But the New Urbanism movement also presents serious concerns that could have long-term implications for planning in the United States. The first concern is that the New Urbanism is not particularly urban. In fact, the most highly touted New Urbanist developments are located in suburban or exurban areas. While these projects certainly represent improvements over standard development practices, they do not address land use and development patterns within the larger municipalities and regions they inhabit. And while the proponents of New Urbanism espouse regional solutions, their projects and practice are essentially about building new developments in places that frequently work against sustainable regional growth patterns.

Second, the New Urbanism is not strongly environmental in orientation. The design features of many New Urbanist developments do have the effect of supporting certain environmental goals. But most New Urbanist projects may involve only one or two supportive aspects—for example, the creation of a more pedestrian-friendly neighborhood (although usually for nonenvironmental reasons, and the benefits achieved may often be canceled out because of an inappropriate location). More fundamentally, with just a few notable exceptions, such projects typically are not designed or conceived in ways that substantially reduce the overall ecological footprint, or impact, of the development and its residents on the environment (e.g., by designing buildings that dramatically reduce energy consumption and use of toxic materials). Environmental sustainability is at best an afterthought and, where incorporated, can be viewed skeptically more as a marketing ploy than anything else.

This volume offers a more holistic, comprehensive, compelling approach to repairing and enhancing communities, one that extends well beyond the reach of traditional architecture and urban design, and beyond simply tinkering with the physical layout of a development. This approach recognizes that the seriousness of our environmental and social problems requires reform at a number of levels and in a number of societal spheres. It recognizes that communities must examine the ways in which they educate, produce goods and services in the marketplace, and provide public services. Addressing these concerns requires questioning "business as usual" in many parts of the community and via many avenues for reform and innovation. The agenda of creating sustainable places emphasizes, for instance, fundamentally modifying the ways in which local governments function by reforming the methods by which they purchase and procure, deliver services, manage their building stock, and budget their resources. It means reconceptualizing the local economy so that it is restorative and sustainable. It means understanding in a comprehensive way the resource needs and flows of the community—where its energy, water, and food come from, and how its wastes are dealt with. It emphasizes a host of actions and programs that support and enhance the social life and vitality of the community.

The vision of sustainable places moves beyond urban development patterns to address a variety of public policies and practices, from the community's economic base to its transit options to the ways in which streets and public spaces are managed. The venues through which this vision may be realized extend beyond the drafting table, the design firm, and isolated, mixed-use development to a community's schools, social organizations, local government, business sector, and public realm as a whole. In exploring these various spheres of influence, this book examines the wide range of programs, policies, and creative ideas that might be brought into service on behalf of the vision of sustainable places.

Finally, this vision also implies a new agenda for environmentalism. Mainstream environmentalists frequently operate from the premise that what is natural, and what is worth saving and protecting, is beyond the urban realm. Cities are seen as polluting and cancerous (Pepper 1996). The agenda of sustainable places shifts environmental thinking to viewing cities as part of the answer to our environmental predicament, rather than a cause of it. Moreover, the perspectives embraced in this book view the potential of human places as restorative and regenerative; the vision and ideas presented here emphasize creating, enhancing, improving, and repairing. This includes everything from restoring urban wetlands to reducing the amounts of energy used in public and private buildings to "greening" urban environments through the planting of trees and gardens. This view emphasizes that many of the issues that have historically concerned mainstream environmental groups—such as endangered species, wetlands and habitat protection, and wilderness and national parks issues—are intimately connected to patterns of urban development and growth.

## Objectives of This Book

This book has several specific objectives. First, it seeks to develop and explore an alternative vision of place and community—one that unifies concerns about the environment, the quality of human life, and the distribution of social and economic opportunities. This alternative vision has its roots in the writing and thinking of many people and in the experiences of many communities. The attempt here is to bring together these many strands of thought and practice into a tangible, realistic vision of future place building.

In exploring this alternative vision, this book is intended to provide a more "holistic" and complete policy agenda for community planning. While it does not cover all subjects, or all aspects of community sustainability in great detail, it begins to identify a guiding structure—a set of sustainability spheres, or venues, that are essential for taking a holistic or comprehensive approach.

There are several different dimensions to the holism advocated here, and the book offers at least a sampling of the key ideas and planning actions that relate to each of these. One dimension involves scale. The following chapters take a "multiscale" approach, since it is essential to consider community sustainability (and to take actions to promote it) at a number of geographical levels, including the building and site, the neighborhood, the city, and the region or bioregion. In this sense, the book reflects an equal concern about what might be called "vertical" sustainability (the sustainability of a particular building or development project) and "horizontal" or "spatial" sustainability (e.g., the location of people and activities over space; the sustainability of patterns of mobility).

Another dimension of sustainability is one that might be called sectoral. Issues of sustainability typically arise in a host of community policy arenas, including transportation, land use, economic development, and housing, among others. A successful effort at creating sustainable places will require concerted (and coordinated) effort in each of these sectors. The chapters that follow, and the ideas and recommendations they offer, attempt to touch upon all of these different policy sectors.

Yet a third dimension involves the venues, or spheres, of influence. The agenda of sustainable places will require actions and innovation in a number of different places in the community—in the administration of government, in the schools, and in the civic sphere, among others. In exploring these areas, the book provides a uniquely holistic perspective on the subject.

While it is difficult in this brief volume to provide extensive case study discussions and analyses, the book offers examples and ideas from many parts of the country of tools, strategies, programs, and policies that can be utilized in pursuit of more sustainable places. It reports on the work and ideas of many different people and places. Much of what is presented, then, has been gleaned from others and represents the collective wisdom of many in the sustainable places movement.

It is important to emphasize that this book is concerned primarily with the experiences of North American communities, particularly those in the United States. Most of the examples, experiences, and insights are drawn from communities in this country. Occasionally, examples are cited from European cities, but the volume does not draw too heavily from experiences in other parts of the world, since some readers may too quickly dismiss such experiences as "not relevant here" or "possible there, but not here."

What follows is not intended to be an exhaustive or comprehensive study of current local practice. Rather, examples are used selectively to illustrate possibilities. Certain cities and places are perhaps overrepresented—for example, the book discusses and refers extensively to Portland, Oregon. Portland is unique in the United States for the range and extent of its efforts to forge a new path and to implement a vision that is similar to the one advocated here. As a result, Portland and a handful of other places are considered to be especially instructive, offering many examples of the strategies and practices advocated in this volume. There are relatively few other places (at least in the United States, at this time) that are taking such a holistic approach to planning.

In short, this book offers a vision and ideas for creating sustainable communities. It is intended not so much as a complete toolbox or step-by-step instruction book, but as a catalyst for innovative thinking about how cities and communities can be organized in the future.

## The Chapters to Follow

This introductory chapter attempts to explain the nature and magnitude of the crisis of place that our society currently faces—a landscape and development pattern that is unsustainable in some very fundamental social and environmental ways. It demonstrates that how Americans settle and inhabit the land, and the kinds and forms of the communities we create, are not unimportant or small questions. Rather, what is at stake is considerable, and the costs associated with continuing the present course are great. The following chapters sketch out a different settlement pattern for the future, an alternative vision for our regions, cities, and towns built explicitly on the concepts of sustainability.

The contours of this vision are laid out in Chapter 2, which discusses the conditions, qualities, and circumstances that might characterize what a sustainable place can be. The chapter presents a series of principles that, while certainly not definitive, represent the minimum list of factors that should be taken into account.

Chapter 3 begins the substantive discussion of how to move in the direction of creating sustainable places—what actions, programs, policies, and strategies can be undertaken, and what experiences can be drawn from within this country and, to a lesser degree, from around the world. Specifically, this chapter discusses urban form, arguing that sustainable places must be compact and contained, and identifies the key elements essential for bringing about the compact place. It also identifies a number of obstacles and impediments in the U.S. context and discusses ways to overcome or counterbalance them.

Chapter 4 discusses the ecology of place and argues for a holistic ecological view of cities and regions. Urban areas are fundamentally embedded in an ecological landscape, and the production and consumption activities that occur in human settlements have tremendous environmental and resource impacts. This chapter argues, among other things, that cities must live within their regional ecological limits and fundamentally reduce their impacts and demands beyond their regions, that they must protect and conserve their ecological infrastructure and capital, and that they must become safer and more resilient in the face of natural forces such as floods and hurricanes. It reviews ecological policies and actions at a number of scales, from the level of individual buildings to the regional landscape.

Chapter 5 examines local and regional economic development from the standpoint of ecological and community sustainability. First, it explores strategies for supporting business activity that is environmentally benign or restorative rather than polluting and degenerative. Recognizing the importance of a vibrant, compact downtown as the prime antidote to sprawl, the bulk of the chapter focuses on tools and techniques to foster or maintain downtown economic activity and to nurture local businesses, thereby providing the added benefit of encouraging a long-term investment in the local community. Implicit among these strategies is the importance of local products, labor, and services in supporting community sustainability, as well as the recognition that a community's environmental amenities and natural/historic heritage are among its most valuable economic assets. Chapter 5 introduces a variety of practical techniques that build upon these key ideas.

Chapter 6 explores the nexus between land use and community planning techniques and the concepts of civic involvement and social "connectedness," to borrow a term from Tony Hiss (1990). Beginning with a discussion of the isolating elements of current American development patterns, the chapter puts forth a variety of strategies for designing and managing a community to encourage human contact and to instill a sense of connectedness to, and investment in, a community's special qualities. Chapter 6 also explores the enhancement of cultural and social diversity in communities, with an emphasis on ensuring an adequate supply of affordable housing to accommodate residents across the socioeconomic spectrum. The chapter also briefly considers a variety of current patterns of development—from flourishing urban areas to New Urbanist developments to gated communities—in an attempt to create the various elements of civic life and demonstrate how to foster greater caring, participation, and face-to-face interaction within a community.

Chapter 7 discusses the next logical steps in promoting more sustainable places—where to go from here. It does this in a number of ways and at a number of jurisdictional levels. It begins with some thoughts about how to go about changing or modifying the prevailing ethic of land and land use. It identifies the elements of a new ethic of environment and community and the short- and long-term actions that might promote such an ethic. It then moves to a discussion of more specific actions that can be taken at local and regional levels to begin to move in the direction of sustainable places, including such things as establishing a system of indicators of sustainability, visioning strategies and other techniques to engage the public in a dialogue about the future, different types of strategic intervention, and suggestions for building partnerships in support of sustainable places. The chapter also identifies a number of potential policy changes and initiatives at the federal level that would assist localities and regions in moving in the direction of sustainability. These initiatives include reforms in the tax code, adjustments to federal subsidies and financial incentives, environmental policy reform, and demonstration projects, among others. While these are not discussed in great depth, it is important to acknowledge that part of the work must be done at the national level and to identify the essential elements of a long-term national agenda of sustainable places.

## Two

# Envisioning Sustainable Places

How do concepts of sustainability translate into a vision and plan for sustainable places? What is a sustainable place? What does one look like, and would we know one if we saw it? What would be the distinguishing characteristics of such places? What follows is an initial exploration of these questions and an attempt to visualize what sustainability can mean at community and regional levels.

## Sustainable Places Acknowledge Fundamental Ecological Limits

Whether they are called "green communities," "green cities," or "ecocities," sustainable places seek to limit environmental impacts and the consumption of natural resources. Cities and urban developments have tremendous ecological impacts, and the seriousness of the environmental crisis to which they contribute suggests the need for a fundamentally new governance and management approach—one that acknowledges and implements a new ecological paradigm. As Mark Roseland observes in *Toward Sustainable Communities*, "Cities provide enormous, untapped opportunities to solve environmental challenges, and local governments must and can pioneer new approaches to sustainable development and urban management" (Roseland 1992, p. 22).

Concern for environmental protection and conservation are not new to the planning and design fields, and the creation of sustainable communities builds on these concerns. Important early examples include Ian McHarg's groundbreaking *Design with Nature* (1969) and the attention paid to carrying capacity, protection of sensitive lands, watershed planning, and ecological land planning (e.g., Schneider, Godschalk, and Axler 1978; Godschalk and Parker 1975; Spirn 1984; Steiner 1991; Marsh 1991; Thurow, Toner, and Erley 1975; Salvesen 1990). What is new, perhaps, is the commitment and priority given to respecting ecological limits in the planning, design, and operation of our communities. Planning for sustainable communities is not simply a matter of avoiding a few wetlands, or saving a few acres of open space, or putting in place a few nonpoint best-management practices. Rather, it requires considering ecological limits and environmental impacts at every step of community development and in every aspect of community design, from the energy efficiency of buildings to the regional transportation system to how the industrial and commercial sectors in the community go about business. Planning for sustainability means reorganizing the social, physical, and political-economic landscape in very fundamental ways.

What will guide communities in determining how far to go in reducing their environmental impacts? How will we know when ecological sustainability is reached? A good place to start, perhaps, is with local and regional indicators, and with a concerted effort not to exceed the natural carrying capacity of regional-level ecosystems or bioregions (for a discussion of bioregion delineation, see Sale 1991). The notion offered by the National Commission on the Environment that we should be living off our ecological interest (as opposed to depleting natural capital) does have clear, although not uncomplicated, applicability to such actions as groundwater extraction, air and water contamination, use of agricultural and forest lands, and maintenance of biodiversity and habitat. Sustainable communities seek to live, develop, and operate within these natural "limits."

A sustainable community is a place that seeks to contain the extent of the urban "footprint" and strives to keep to a minimum the conversion of natural and open lands to urban and developed uses. The evils of urban sprawl are many and well documented (e.g., Kunstler 1993; Roseland 1992; Downs 1994). From an environmental or conservation point of view, loss of habitat and many other serious forms of environmental degradation find their roots in wasteful and destructive development patterns and in the economic and social system that encourages them. Increasingly, to have an effective environmental policy (whether the concern is with biodiversity loss, air quality, or coastal management) first requires an effective urban policy.

Sustainable communities, then, are places that exhibit a compact urban form. This is quite a challenge in the United States, where the trend has been in the other direction (Downs 1994). How we may bring about this compact form is discussed extensively in Chapter 3.

The 1994 "Full House" study, for example, renewed significant concerns about preserving remaining farmlands while "satisfying the demand for residential building, industrial sites, parking lots, shopping centers, schools, and recreation areas" necessary to accommodate further population increases (Brown and Kane 1994, p. 166). In sustainable places, the conservation and

protection of natural and undeveloped land is a primary goal that is not easily overruled by proposals for housing or other uses that could be accommodated within existing urban areas. A different physical form accompanies
such a vision and includes compact development patterns, higher densities,
and more land-efficient development projects; a more sensible and sustainable transportation system, with less reliance on automobiles, more availability of public transit, and more opportunities for walking and bicycling;
greater emphasis on infill, adaptive reuse of buildings, and reurbanization;
protection and avoidance of ecologically sensitive lands; and avoidance and
conservation of natural hazard areas, including flood plains, high-erosion
zones, and areas subject to wildfires and landslides. Curtailing the consumption of land at the urban periphery becomes a critical part of preserving
biodiversity, important ecological functions, and productive lands essential
for sustaining current and future populations. Serious urban-growth containment, then, becomes a central part of preserving these essential natural
and biological resources.

Sustainable places seek more broadly to minimize the extent of their
"ecological footprint," to use William Rees's important concept. To provide
food, housing, and energy for a community's population requires a tremendous drain on collective ecological capital—the equivalent of five hectares
per year per North American resident. These consumption levels can be
supported only by drawing upon the resources and carrying capacities of
other regions and nations. Sustainable places seek to better understand these
extra-local resource demands and to minimize the extent to which the carrying capacities and resources of other bioregions are "appropriated." A
sustainable place, therefore, thinks beyond its own local and regional ecological limits and capacities. It seeks every possibility to reduce these demands whether through energy-efficient buildings and transportation, other
sustainable building practices, use of renewable energy sources such as solar,
or pricing policies that discourage waste.

This necessarily raises the question of whether sustainable places should
aspire to being self-sufficient in terms of the resources they require and the
environmental impacts they generate. This is not an easy question to answer, and there is no hard and firm standard. Much of the current sustainability literature identifies self-sufficiency as a desirable goal (e.g., Sale
1991). The problems arise when cities (and nations) exploit and degrade the
environments of other regions and nations to satisfy wasteful and opulent
patterns of development and consumption at home. Trade among cities, regions, and nations, however, is not itself a bad thing and is, in fact, central to
the functioning of our global economy. Reducing the unnecessary import
of resources and goods from other regions, as well as the export of wastes

and pollutants, should be an important goal. Local food production is preferable, for example, because it results in lower energy consumption, less pollution, and healthier food. It may not be possible, for climatic or other reasons, to produce certain foods locally, however. Becoming self-sufficient in the sense of reducing unnecessary imports—things that are or could be produced locally—and minimizing or ceasing the export of wastes and pollutants, is a desirable goal.

## Sustainable Places Are Restorative and Regenerative

Some definitions of sustainability imply preservation of the status quo—simply protecting or ensuring that the conditions of the present are not diminished in the future. But the ethical imperative of sustainability calls for more: it calls for energetic efforts to reverse the degradation already brought about and for passing along to our children and their children a planet where both the natural and built environments are of a higher quality and condition.

There are, unfortunately, reasons to be skeptical about our ability to meet these challenges, given current global trends of population growth, consumption, and environmental degradation. Yet at local and regional levels, the higher standards implied by sustainability are not only more conceivable, but necessary from a practical as well as an ethical standpoint. Indeed, there are encouraging examples of efforts to restore the environment, or at least important pieces of the environment. These range from recreating prairies in the Chicago area to reintroducing the red wolf in North Carolina to the reforestation efforts under way in a number of places (see Baldwin, DeLuce, and Pletsch, eds. 1993; for a good discussion of ecological restoration as a new perspective on the relationship between humans and nature, see Jordan 1993).

## Sustainable Places Strive for a High Quality of Life

To be a viable paradigm, sustainability must incorporate a strong social component. Along with ecological issues, then, sustainable communities are equally concerned with social and human sustainability—creating and supporting humane living environments, livable places, and communities that offer a high quality of life. Characterizing the social dimension becomes much vaguer and more subjective than defining the environmental or ecological dimension; we cannot rely as readily on such measures as natural carrying capacity. Terms such as livability and quality of life, in turn, beg for definition and description and, ultimately, may be up to the community itself to clarify.

It seems fairly clear, however, that current patterns of urban development in the United States are becoming more socially and psychologically stifling. We have created, or allowed to be created, urban and suburban places that will not stand the test of time. Increasingly, downtown urban areas are devoid of activity after 5:00 P.M.; meanwhile, suburban and edge cities lack charm and a sense of place and depend heavily on the automobile. The zealous separation of land uses promoted by conventional zoning and the scattered, sprawling development patterns that characterize much of our contemporary landscape require an increasingly dysfunctional transportation system that is plagued with traffic congestion and long work commutes (Fig. 2.1). People are increasingly isolated from one another and from a connection to the larger community.

The creation of vibrant and active urban spaces is surely an important part of making places more livable. Europe abounds with urban places that bubble with aliveness—streets such as Las Ramblas in Barcelona or Stroget in Copenhagen, for example (Jacobs 1993). The characteristics of these timeless communities are neither mysterious nor surprising: walkability,

Figure 2.1 Automobile traffic is one of the most obvious manifestations of sprawling development patterns.

mixed land uses and activities, a density of people and commerce sufficient to create vital, active places of activity, and pedestrian and public spaces that encourage this activity. The successful renaissance of several U.S. cities— Baltimore is a good example—has recreated this kind of energy while at the same time increasing the efficiency of land use and encouraging greater use of public transportation.

Concern with the social dimensions of sustainability suggests that a sustainable community is one that addresses a host of related goals, including adequate and affordable shelter, health care, and other essential services to residents; a safe and crime-free environment; and humane and stimulating work environments. Marrying social and environmental concerns, then, is a major characteristic of a sustainable community.

## "Place" Matters in Sustainable Places

"Sense of place" is also an important dimension of sustainability. Many Americans have little attachment to place largely because many of the places we build are not deserving of attachment, or because we have been quick to demolish those community features that have traditionally provided meaning in our everyday lives. Absent this feeling of attachment, it is little wonder that we are so quick to uproot ourselves when a new employment opportunity arises, the local school system fails to deliver, or a new exurban development promises "country living with all the amenities." Ultimately, this pattern of mobility feeds a vicious circle: the more we move around in search of the elusive "better" place to live, the less we invest in our communities, such that those few features that do provide a sense of attachment are being abandoned.

To foster a sense of place, communities must nurture built environment and settlement patterns that are uplifting, inspirational, and memorable, and that engender a special feeling of attachment and belonging. A sustainable community also nurtures a sense of place by understanding and respecting its bioregional context—its topography and natural setting, its rivers, hilltops, open lands, native flora and fauna, and the many other unique elements of its natural context. A sustainable community respects the history and character of those existing features that nurture a sense of attachment to, and familiarity with, place. Such "community landmarks" may be natural—a meadow or an ancient tree, an urban creek—or built—a civic monument, a local diner, an historic courthouse or clock tower. Finally, in a sustainable place, special effort is made to create and preserve places, rituals, and events that foster greater attachment to the social fabric of the community.

The presence of one local gathering spot, whether it is the town square or a downtown coffee shop, can serve as a powerful focal point for community attachment. This concept—what Ray Oldenburg (1989) has termed "the third place"—is discussed further in Chapter 6.

## Sustainable Places Are Integrative and Holistic

Sustainable communities employ strategies and solutions that are integrative and holistic. They seek ways of combining policies, programs, and design solutions to bring about multiple objectives. No longer can we make, for example, transportation decisions isolated from land use considerations. Instead of endlessly constructing more roads and highways in response to traffic congestion, a sustainable community begins to examine ways that land use and development decisions can reduce such demand in the first place, and that transportation investments and land use can be integrated and coordinated to accomplish a variety of community goals, including air quality enhancement, open space preservation, and affordable housing.

A sustainable community is one that looks beyond narrow, conventional solutions to social and environmental problems and addresses them instead from a broad, holistic viewpoint. The issue of affordable housing, for instance, is typically viewed from a narrow housing perspective—the need to keep down the cost of new construction. But affordable housing and an affordable life are not synonymous. Affordability may be enhanced more dramatically through the development of an urban environment that does not require car ownership and all of its attendant expenses. Furthermore, affordable housing by itself may be counterproductive or even irrelevant without ready access to employment, services, open space, and other elements of a high quality of life. Promoting such activities as urban infill, adaptive reuse, and construction of secondary housing units could simultaneously provide more affordable living units and also reduce development pressures on environmentally sensitive lands.

The fragmented nature of planning policy has tended to discourage such integrated and holistic approaches (e.g., zoning decisions made separately from transportation, taxation, and other public investment decisions). A frequently cited example of a city in the developing world that has sought to implement more integrative policies is Curitiba, Brazil. Each sustainability initiative there addresses several concerns simultaneously. For instance, the city buys trash from the urban poor, providing not money but food or bus tickets in exchange. The city thus deals with solid waste and sanitation cheaply, while serving the food and transportation needs of the poor (Rabinovitch 1992). Curitiba illustrates how important integration, holism, and creativity are in moving toward sustainability.

## Sustainable Place Implies a New Ethical Posture

Sustainability is fundamentally about adopting a new ethic of living on the planet. This ethic expands substantially the "moral community" to which respect and duties are owed. Almost every definition of sustainability and sustainable development implies a substantial extension of the moral community to include future generations—perhaps many future generations— in the decision making of the present. Sustainability significantly focuses our moral attention away from the present, and from short-term time frames, to much longer time horizons. It is an ethical posture much more respectful of the natural world. Aldo Leopold (1949) foreshadowed much of this thinking some sixty years ago when he talked of the need for a new land ethic, one that would change *Homo sapiens* from conqueror of the land community to "plain citizen" thereof.

A sustainable community ideally embodies and implements an ethical framework in which physical and social form, consumption of land and resources, and basic operating principles are severely moderated with the interests of the future in mind. This framework also imagines other ways of expanding the moral community: geographically and spatially, for instance. A sustainable community considers the impacts of its actions and policies on neighboring jurisdictions and the region in which it is situated, as well as its continental and global impacts. Such morally inclusive visions are illustrated in the actions of the Chesapeake Bay communities that consider the impacts their developments will have on the Bay's water quality, or the efforts of cities such as Toronto and Portland, Oregon, to address their role in global climate change by curtailing carbon dioxide emissions. (For a more extensive discussion of expanding the moral community and ethical land use more generally, see Beatley 1989, 1994b.)

In many ways, then, the idea of a sustainable community represents a deeper and more modern vision of Leopold's land ethic. The policy implications of such a new ethical posture are many. Calls for five-hundred-year planning (Tonn 1986) no longer seem ludicrous, but perhaps even conservative. Such a moral time frame is clearly different from traditional comprehensive local planning, which considers the relatively short time intervals of fifteen, twenty, or twenty-five years. Looking so far into the future may also call for new planning techniques and visioning methods. Such a new ethical perspective emphasizes creating urban environments of enduring value, protecting the basic environmental and ecosystem functions essential for existence, and avoiding irreversible actions such as destruction of natural landscapes, species extinction, and the loss of cultural and historic resources. Such a perspective implies caring for soils, forests, oceans, and other life-giving renewable resources; reducing waste at all levels; and restraining ourselves from passing along an increasingly toxic environment to those who follow us.

The ethical underpinnings of sustainability go beyond obligations to the environment. The ethic also emphasizes equity in the distribution of social goods and resources, an effort to improve the lot of the least advantaged in society and eliminate environmental and other forms of racism.

How the new ethic will take hold is uncertain. Further thoughts about this are given in Chapter 7, but education, public discourse, and advocacy by the planning field are some of the likely avenues. As fanciful as they sometimes seem, we should consider mechanisms that will include explicit representation of the interests of future generations—a sort of future-generations ombudsperson, something like the Seventh Generation rule of the Iroquois tribe (see Beatley 1994a). Also critical is an ethic of place building and nurturing a responsibility to place and to community. The principles of bioregionalism—which emphasize the importance of identifying with, understanding, and committing to one's bioregional "home"—are helpful in this regard (e.g., Sale 1991).

## Sustainable Places Strive to Be Equitable and Just

Sustainability must also be about creating a more equitable and just society. We must always ask, Sustainable for whom? and be cautious that any vision of a sustainable community be an accessible one: one that is open to all racial, cultural, age, and income groups and that encourages social and cultural diversity. It is a place that strives to be gender neutral and to ensure physical access and social opportunity to all its members. A sustainable community, therefore, is a just and equitable community.

On the whole, contemporary patterns of urban development in the United States raise questions about social justice and fairness. With the march of sprawl and suburbanization has also come sharp separation and isolation of the poor and minorities (e.g., Downs 1994; Goldsmith and Blakely 1992). And there is growing recognition that, while the causes of these trends are complex, many features of traditional planning policy discussed earlier—auto and highway dependency and the separation of land uses, for example—have played important roles.

A sustainable community, then, is one in which diversity is tolerated and encouraged, where there is no sharp spatial separation or isolation of income and racial groups, where all individuals and groups have access to basic and essential services and facilities, and where residents have equality of opportunity (Beatley 1993).

Issues of equity also arise when considering the current patterns of use and exploitation of the world's resources, and these are not irrelevant in discussions about U.S. growth and development patterns. It has been frequently observed that, while the developed world accounts for only a small percentage of the world's population, its use of natural resources and its generation of waste and pollution is disproportionately high. Industrialized nations use more resources and pollute more than less developed countries in almost all categories. Per capita fossil fuel consumption for industrialized countries is almost ten times what it is for developing nations; use of nonrenewable resources such as cooper and aluminum is some seventeen and twenty times greater, respectively; and consumption of roundwood (wood from trees) is two-and-a-half times greater—although consumption rates for many of these resources are on the rise in the developing world (WRI 1994). Per capita emissions of carbon dioxide are also much higher; the U.S. rate is some nine times that of China and eighteen times that of India (WRI 1994). An oft-cited statistic is that about one-fifth of the earth's population is currently living in "absolute poverty," or with an annual income less than U.S. $370 per year (Carley and Christie 1993). Responsible local and regional efforts at promoting sustainability have the potential to reduce inequities that exist at both global and local levels.

Many believe that we have gone well beyond consuming our fair share, and that movements toward greater sustainability (and the promotion of sustainable communities) are called for on these grounds of equity. At an urban or local level, it is clear that many communities are able to maintain their lifestyles and consumption levels only by "appropriating" the carrying capacities of regions and communities beyond their borders, again raising basic questions of fairness (Roseland 1992; Rees 1992, 1995).

## Sustainable Places Stress the Importance of Community

The concept of community is central to the vision of sustainable communities. Contemporary development patterns do not create communities, although they may create developments. Typical patterns of suburban growth are viewed by many as antithetical to the creation of places where people can share a true connectedness with others and develop feelings of responsibility and closeness. Development and consumption patterns of the last fifty years reflect the long-standing American celebration of individualism. A paradigm of sustainability renews the commitment to community and rises above narrow individualism.

Amitai Etzioni has emerged as a leading spokesperson for the communitarian movement, articulating its key principles and beliefs most clearly in *The Spirit of Community* (1993). A major communitarian premise is that society has moved too far in the direction of individual rights and away from notions of personal responsibility and commitment to a larger "we-ness." As Etzioni asserts, "Americans are all too eager to spell out what they are entitled to but are all too slow to give something back to others and to the community" (1993, p. 15). The time has come, the communitarians believe, "to attend to our responsibilities to the conditions and elements we all share, to the community" (Etzioni 1993, p. 15; see also Galston 1991 and Etzioni 1988). Moving toward greater community does not, however, mean quashing individualism—only restoring a sensible balance between the desires of the individual and the needs of the community.

The implications of the communitarian ideal are considerable, and Etzioni and others have offered a number of specific changes and initiatives to advance the agenda. At the heart of it would be places where people are committed, invested, and involved, and places where people know and care about one another, participate in community activities, and take responsibility for the condition and health of the community and the environment. The agenda has both personal and public policy dimensions, both of which are explored in later chapters.

Obviously, a community's physical form and design influences the opportunities for true community. Low-density, scattered, cul-de-sac development patterns and a dearth of public spaces encourage isolation and discourage interaction. Sitting in bumper-to-bumper highway traffic may induce a sense of mutual empathy among commuters but does not create a community among them. The physical characteristics of a sustainable community help to create a sense of community—a sense of ownership, commitment, and a feeling of belonging to a larger whole. Walking spaces, civic buildings, plazas and parks, and other public places have the potential to nurture commitment and attachment to the larger collective.

The centrality of community suggests the need to look for a new politics—a politics more consistent with the communitarian spirit. DeWitt John (1994) calls for "civic environmentalism" as a response to both the command-and-control, top-down federal approaches pursued in programs such as the federal Clean Air and Water Acts and the highly personalized and localized politics of NIMBYism ("not in my backyard"). Sustainable communities—as both a vision and a movement—appear to hold considerable promise as an alternative form of politics concerned with the full range of issues that affect quality of life community-wide and a politics that has the potential to involve and be relevant to all or most individuals and groups. Community sustainability may offer a useful unifying framework that embodies a more integrative and holistic viewpoint, in which the health of the larger community is what becomes most important.

Community sustainability as a political movement is still very much in its infancy, but the concept has stimulated a great deal of local activism. Throughout the country, local organizations are emerging that have the ability to formulate a comprehensive and integrated vision, to transcend NIMBYism, and to be inclusive of a wide range of local groups and interests—from environmental groups to neighborhood groups to housing advocates to civil rights organizations. The number and strength of these groups will likely grow—a positive trend toward a new politics that is inclusive and more reflective of the true values of community.

## Sustainable Places Reflect and Promote a Full-Cost Accounting of the Social and Environmental Costs of Public and Private Decisions

What are the true environmental and social costs of air pollution, water pollution, and destruction of wetlands and wildlife habitat? And, similarly, what are the true social costs of racism, and of separation and isolation of income and social groups, and of a sterile and uninspiring urban landscape? A sustainable community seeks to assess and understand these full costs and to adjust its planning and other decisions accordingly. It attempts, wherever possible, to promote full-cost accounting in its decisions and policies, using the power of economic signals and mechanisms in promoting greater sustainability.

While modifying the economic and market signals to better account for the true costs of public and private decisions is not the entire answer to promoting sustainability, it will certainly facilitate a movement in that direction. Understanding how the many current subsidies and pricing policies for auto transport influence the choice of this mode over mass transit, for example, may lead to adjustments that support greater sustainability. There is a substantial advocacy for full-cost environmental accounting, and the tools and techniques for doing so have consistently improved (see Daly and

Townsend 1993; Kopp and Smith 1993; Cairncross 1992; Pearce, Mark-andya, and Barbier 1989). Examples include the use of "green fees" to account for the disposal of garbage and household wastes, local development impact fees to shift development in the direction of more sustainable sites and designs, and regional tax base sharing to encourage coordinated land use planning. The following chapters explore these techniques in greater detail.

## Conclusions

The concept of sustainable places means different things to different people. While the reader may not agree with every element presented in this chapter, there is a range of qualities and factors that should be addressed in planning for sustainable communities. Without some clarity and social consensus about the characteristics of such places, it will be difficult to achieve a more positive result. The principles articulated here suggest a better model for planning and managing in the future, and vast improvement over our current way of thinking about communities. The paradigm expressed here is both social and environmental, seeking a union of goals. The paradigm is also necessarily normative—that is, it explicitly expresses certain values and ethical responsibilities, including duties to live within ecological limits, to consider generations yet to come, to value the equity of our current relationships, and to rise to the demands of community.

## Three

# Principles of Urban Form

Low-density, sprawling growth patterns have characterized development in the United States since the post–World War II period, and it has become increasingly clear that many of the problems of American cities and regions stem from these spatial development patterns. Current patterns of growth in the United States are land-consumptive, environmentally damaging, and fail to create places that are livable and of enduring value. To paraphrase the Bank of America study *Beyond Sprawl,* our nation cannot succeed unless we find a way to move beyond the present development paradigm.

## Causes of Sprawl

The exact origins of sprawling development patterns are the source of some speculation and debate. No single cause can be identified; rather, current development patterns result from a number of interrelated economic and market forces, policy decisions, and cultural factors.

Government policy figures heavily into this equation. A host of government programs and subsidies have facilitated, and even actively encouraged, auto dependence and population decentralization, including the funding of the interstate highway system and federal housing subsidies. Provisions of the U.S. tax code that allow deductions for mortgage interest and property taxes—for second homes as well as primary residences—are one such subsidy. And the uniquely voluntary nature of federal public housing policy has allowed communities to choose not to apply for public housing, further exacerbating disparities between central cities—which house an increasing proportion of the poor—and the suburbs, which tend to shun public housing (Jackson 1996).

Much of the engine driving sprawl is economic in nature. Economic forces have included efforts by major corporate entities to reap profits from auto-oriented business activities, oil, and automobile production. Harvey talks of suburbanization as a "total restructuring of space to mobilize demand so as to make the consumption of the products of the car, oil, rubber and construction industries a necessity rather than a luxury" (Harvey as quoted in White 1994, p. 153). Redlining of urban areas by banks and lending institutions is another driving factor. And as Joel Garreau describes in great detail in his book *Edge City,* proximity to a major transportation center is, as it has always been, a critical factor in a company's decision of where to locate. As we approach the twenty-first century, that transportation center is no longer the shipping port or rail center, but the highway interchange (Garreau 1991).

The low price of gasoline in the United States has unquestionably played a major role in facilitating sprawl. Americans have enjoyed an unusually low price, substantially undertaxed compared with most other countries, especially European nations; France, the Netherlands, and Italy, for instance, impose per-gallon taxes of $3.54, $3.32, and $3.17, respectively (*Washington Post* 1996). Even less wealthy countries such as Mexico and Brazil have imposed higher gasoline taxes than the United States.

The structure of government itself is implicated, as the Bank of America study suggests. Most land use and growth decisions occur at the local level, and the fractured and fragmented nature of this system means that localities often compete against one another for tax base and economic activity. (For instance, there are some 700 localities in the New York City region, 263 in Chicago, and 245 in Philadelphia, as cited in Young 1995.) Sprawl is partially the result of many discrete localities attempting to make a host of what seem to be individually rational decisions (and that often end up not to be so), but that collectively lead to a devastatingly irrational regional outcome.

Cultural factors contributing to sprawl begin with the anti-urban attitudes of much of the American populace dating back to Jefferson, the founding fathers, and the "agrarian ideal." Such attitudes stem from fears about the relationship between urban areas and density, crime, and health, as well as an embracing of the popular cultural image of the "American dream" of a detached home on a spacious lot in a suburb or exurb. As the Bank of America report suggests, many of the causes of sprawl have to do with perceptions and beliefs—the belief that the suburbs or exurbs are safer than urban areas, that schools are better there, and that housing and cost of living are less expensive. Outright racism is undoubtedly also a significant cause of urban flight.

A strong belief in private property rights is also important in explaining sprawl. Land in this country has always been abundant, and, until recently, the natural landscape has been viewed as an obstacle to overcome rather than a scarce resource to nurture and protect. As a consequence, those who do consider urban sprawl and land development to be problematic tend to be concerned primarily with the economic costs they impose, rather than with the consumption and loss of irreplaceable land.

Finally, many planners and others involved in managing development and growth are understandably concerned about the legal and constitutional constraints on controlling and regulating land use. The "takings" clause of the U.S. Constitution has been a particularly potent consideration in cautioning local governments against actions to protect and conserve land. Overall, then, there have been few public or private obstacles to the development juggernaut as it slowly creeps outward from urban and town centers.

## An Alternative to Sprawl: The Compact Community

The taming of sprawl and the creation of more sustainable places require a concerted effort at promoting compact communities—human settlement patterns that consume significantly less natural and open land and that achieve higher average densities than current development patterns. In fact, the compact form of cities and towns has historically manifested itself in ways that facilitate human interaction and commerce. The enduring success of a number of European cities and older American communities illustrates that this is neither a new nor an outmoded concept. From Boston's Beacon Hill to Washington, D.C.'s Georgetown to the older districts of Charleston, South Carolina, and Savannah, Georgia, compact, dense cities and neighborhoods continue to thrive.

By the same token, it is useful to explore what the vision of a compact urban form does not mean. It does not mean, for instance, that all people would live in very high-density, Manhattan-style cities. Indeed, compact communities can occur at a number of urban scales, from Manhattan's Greenwich Village to Burlington, Vermont, to a densely populated village in rural Loudoun County, Virginia. Whatever its scale, the vision of a compact urban form does not imply "no growth," but rather its reconfiguration.

The neo-traditional, or New Urbanism, movement has helped popularize the merits of more compact places by returning to many of the design principles of the small American town: gridded streets, extensive public spaces, a mixing of uses, and so on. Unfortunately, however, few of the more prominent examples of New Urbanist development have actually contributed to a more sustainable pattern of urban form. Many New Urbanist developments are located in exurban and rural areas, outside the committed urban fabric, thereby promoting, rather than curtailing, land consumption. Places such as Seaside, Florida, and Haymount, Virginia, while admirable for many of their design features, are, at best, examples of how to minimize the negative social and environmental impacts of new development projects, but do not represent a comprehensive strategy or vision for how to bring about more sustainable urban form.

The pursuit of compact and sustainable urban form also does not take as its goal the sharp separation of the natural from the human-made, nor does it assume that the places where people live and work should be lifeless and devoid of nature. Quite the contrary; the compact city envisioned is a richly natural place. Cities and towns are by definition embedded within a complex natural system—a natural landscape that includes topographic relief, air and water resources, floodplains and creekbeds, trees, vegetation, and open space, among other qualities. The compact city can be a green city.

There are indeed many examples of communities that have sought to protect their unique and important natural features—places where residents have easy exposure to nature and whose features serve as important ingredients in nurturing a sense of place. Portland, Oregon, for example, has set aside large amounts of land for urban parks while at the same time containing regional growth and development. These goals, then, are not incompatible.

## The Elements of a Strategy for Sustainable Urban Form

There are a number of key elements and strategies that are necessary to achieving or advancing a more sustainable urban form. There is no one silver bullet, but rather a series of interlocking and reinforcing actions and policies that will help to bring about more compact places.

### Effective Growth Containment

To prevent sprawl, cities and towns must have an effective way of regulating the location of future growth and ensuring that it occurs both within desired spatial parameters and at densities that are high enough to support transit, walkability, and other positive characteristics of a compact community. The urban growth boundary (UGB) has been implemented with considerable success in a number of communities around the country, especially in the state of Oregon. Under Senate Bill 100, Oregon's statewide planning and growth management legislation, cities and towns are required by law to delineate a UGB. The boundary is to include enough land to accommodate growth within a twenty-year period, and it sharply delimits urban and potentially urbanized land from rural and resource lands. Urban development beyond the growth boundary is not allowed.

Oregon's system of UGBs has achieved some impressive results. In the Portland region, it is estimated that approximately 95 percent of new development occurs within the UGB (Nelson and Moore 1996). Administered by the Metropolitan Service District ("Metro" or MSD for short), the UGB has succeeded in combination with investments in public transit and the central city and a metropolitan housing rule that requires localities in the region to accommodate certain minimum development densities in their plans. The UGB is popular with citizens; in their recent "Region 2040" growth deliberation, residents of the Portland region chose to hold the boundary at its current location and to accommodate most new development within it. (Citizens also recently decided to tax themselves to purchase thousands of additional acres of open space in the region.)

In addition to containing growth, evidence suggests that these strategies have enhanced housing affordability in the Portland region. A study undertaken in the early 1990s, jointly sponsored by 1000 Friends of Oregon and the Home Builders Association of Metropolitan Portland, assessed development trends during a five-year period following the adoption of the Metropolitan Portland Housing Rule, which requires that each local government provide for a housing mix that is at least 50 percent multifamily or attached single family (duplexes and townhouses). The study concluded that there had been a "dramatic" increase in both the volume and proportion of multifamily and attached single-family housing and of single-family homes on smaller lots. They also found relatively little public opposition to higher-density development. In addition to augmenting the availability of a range of affordable housing types, zoning measures further enhanced home ownership opportunities by extending single-family options to include smaller lots. The study also calculated that had this development occurred at the lower densities that were common before the enactment of the housing rule, some 1,500 additional acres of land would have been consumed within the Portland UGB (1000 Friends of Oregon 1991).

The Oregon system is not without its limitations, however. A troublesome amount of growth still occurs outside the Portland boundary, primarily on lands already subdivided or otherwise committed to development and through non-farm-use development on farms and farmsteads. And UGBs have been less effective at containing growth in other cities in Oregon. In a study of four urban areas in the state, Nelson and Moore found considerable development occurring outside the UGBs in three of these cities, with Portland the exception (Nelson and Moore 1996). Most of this development was the result of already platted subdivisions (called "exception areas") and standards for development in farm and forest areas that contained loopholes or were otherwise too loose and permissive. Moreover, they found that land within the UGBs is being developed at lower than desired densities—for example, single-family units are occurring in multifamily zones—thereby undermining the ability to provide efficient urban services and perhaps causing the premature expansion of the growth boundaries. (This latter finding was consistent with the findings of the study conducted by 1000 Friends of Oregon.)

The occurrence of low-density development just outside UGBs is particularly troubling in that it threatens to undermine the efficient expansion of these boundaries over time. One interesting possible solution is to require that any development occurring in potential expansion areas be made to be consistent with the location of future urban facilities and development patterns through the advance approval of a redevelopment plan. More fundamentally, Nelson and Moore believe that the current twenty-year time frame of UGBs in Oregon is too short, and advocate a fifty-year horizon— perhaps protecting future areas of expansion as "urban reserves" as Portland is now doing, and as the Oregon Land Conservation and Development Commission is now beginning to mandate for certain cities.

In sum, the Oregon system of growth boundaries has done much to contain growth in that state—especially within metro Portland—but could, as these recommendations suggest, be made substantially stronger and more effective. Additional policy recommendations for strengthening UGBs include tighter controls on development outside UGBs, for example, by preventing nonfarm dwellings in farming areas; and the stipulation of minimum as well as maximum development densities (or at least an acceptable density range).

There are a few, but not many, additional examples of such clear and effective use of UGBs within the United States. The city of San Jose, California, has successfully restricted its growth to areas within its Urban Service Area Boundary, established in the early 1970s (Previtti 1995). Other cities that have adopted UGBs include Minneapolis–St. Paul, Minnesota; metro Dade County, Florida; and Sarasota, Florida (see Easley 1992; Nelson and Moore 1996).

Boulder, Colorado, has effectively implemented a growth containment policy for many years, dating back to 1959, when it adopted its limit line for the extension of water service. It has achieved a compact pattern and has limited sprawl through the use of a variety of tools, including an annual cap of 2 percent on development permits, a "point system" that encourages development closer to its center, and a phased-growth zoning system based on the availability of urban services within a certain time frame. The city made a concerted effort to keep government offices centralized and downtown and was able to convince Boulder County to agree not to provide public services outside the city. An extensive greenbelt acquisition program has served to further contain growth. Boulder's efforts are unique by American standards, resulting in a sharp and distinct separation between urban and rural/open space. The redirection of development energies toward the center of the city has not only fostered a vibrant and attractive downtown environment, but has also helped preserve Boulder's spectacular natural setting.

Boulder's growth containment strategy has not been without its critics, however. The annual 2 percent cap on development has been faulted as resulting in an increase in housing prices and a more socially exclusive community. The cap applies only to residential development and not to commercial growth, forcing many people to live outside Boulder and to commute into the city each day to work.

Other regions have experimented with a range of techniques to significantly contain growth, with varying degrees of success. Montgomery County, Maryland, one of the two Maryland counties in the Washington, D.C., area, has made largely successful strides in containing growth and protecting its farmland and rural open space. The county's key underlying planning document, the so-called Wedges and Corridors Plan, was adopted more than thirty years ago; although it has been updated several times, it remains in force today. The plan provides an overall framework for growth in the county, directing future development into designated corridors that correspond to transit routes. The county's growth policy and development regulations further reinforce these patterns, and growth-inducing investments such as public sewer and water services are not permitted outside designated growth areas. Within the open space wedges, development is severely restricted, although owners of farmland can transfer their unused development rights to designated zones under one of the oldest transferable development rights (TDR) programs in the country.

It is important to note that UGBs and other mechanisms for containing growth can have the positive feature of reducing uncertainty about where development can and cannot occur. Such uncertainty is a common concern expressed by landowners and developers, and its alleviation can often help to minimize conflict and facilitate consensus in land use negotiations.

## Protecting Open Space and Natural Lands

As evidenced by the proliferation of low-density development outside Oregon UGBs, the permeability of growth boundaries stems partly from our collective vision of how to treat agricultural and undeveloped lands. Typically, there is a presumption that rural landscapes are merely transitional areas on their way to more "productive" (and developed) economic uses. The fluidity of the current development regulatory system creates uncertainty about what will be allowed to be built where, leaving many with the impression that almost any site is "developable" given the right circumstances and the favorable disposition of a city council or county board of commissioners. Indeed, the flurry of zoning changes and plan amendments that tends to characterize planning in many jurisdictions certainly helps to reinforce this impression.

In addition, current zoning and land use regulations are typically structured to allow residential development as the "use of last resort," or as an underlying permitted use in farm, open space, and natural area use designations. While farms may be subject to certain minimum lot requirements, under conventional zoning they will almost certainly be allowed to accommodate some residential development.

It is no wonder, then, that landowners and developers have expectations of being able to build and develop on farm and natural resource lands, even outside UGBs. The sustainable urban form seeks to protect rural and resource lands outside UGBs much more effectively and stringently. Farmland and open lands should not be viewed or treated as transitional areas, but as areas valued for their nonurban functions, to be cherished and guarded for those important values. Achieving compact communities will therefore require strategies both to contain or limit growth and to protect those areas outside growth boundaries where development is inappropriate.

This is not to suggest that there are not legitimate concerns about the impacts of such a planning philosophy on private land values and development expectations. Although owners of farmland or rural land should not be entitled to compensation when they are unable to maximize its market use or value, fairness and political considerations suggest that localities should seek ways to creatively and efficiently minimize potential inequities.

There are several approaches that communities may consider to more effectively restrict development of lands that lie outside growth boundaries. One strategy is for localities to purchase such lands directly, either outright (fee-simple acquisition) or by acquiring the development rights (less than fee-simple acquisition), leaving farming and other resource conservation activities as permissible uses. In the past, U.S. localities have often been hesitant to involve themselves aggressively in land acquisition, recognizing the considerable expense involved in such efforts and viewing the appropriate role of government as a regulator of land uses rather than a direct landowner or participant.

Today, communities around the country are realizing the benefits of land acquisition and its role in helping to contain growth. In Boulder, Colorado, an aggressive open space program represents a particularly exemplary effort to complement growth containment efforts. Since the 1960s, the city has been acquiring land in a greenbelt around the city. Some 25,000 acres have been purchased to date, resulting in an extensive and relatively contiguous open space network. The success of the program is due to several factors, including a dedicated source of revenue (0.77 percent of the sales tax goes directly into an open space acquisition fund; Larmer 1994), thorough advance planning of acquisition sites (including the preparation of a long-range open space plan), and administration of the program by a separate open space division within the local government. Anyone who has been to Boulder understands the importance of open lands to the quality of life there, and some spectacular landscapes have been preserved as a result.

The commitment of reliable and steady sources of funding is extremely critical to land acquisition strategies. Several jurisdictions around the country, including Nantucket, Massachusetts, and Hilton Head, South Carolina, have successfully used land transfer taxes to fund open space acquisition. This approach has had the advantage of being relatively painless politically, as local officials are not required to raise tax rates. It is also viewed as directly connected with and justified by local growth pressures; the more land transfers, the greater are development pressures, hence the greater the need for acquisition. Some form of dedicated ad valorem tax might also be considered. The Midpeninsula Regional Open Space District, in the San Francisco Bay Area, has exacted a small annual assessment to preserve an impressive network of open lands along the spine of the Midpeninsula, many of which already represent dangerous development sites given their slope, geology, and exposure to earthquake hazards.

When local governments involve themselves in land acquisition, it is frequently with the goal of purchasing a school site, park, or other parcel of land needed to provide for a traditional public service or facility. Working in combination with regional and state initiatives, local governments should increasingly consider land-banking strategies in which relatively large amounts of land are purchased, kept in reserve, and released gradually at the periphery as contained-growth pressures dictate. In turn, additional land acquisition farther out can be financed by the sale of developable land closer in to existing development. In this way, government may reap, at least partially, any resulting increase in land values. (Of course, to be effective, such an acquisition approach may require the active involvement of a regional entity or state government, as a single local government may be faced with having to acquire land in other jurisdictions.) One very limited though creative example of the land bank concept is a program developed by The Nature Conservancy (TNC) on the Eastern Shore of Virginia. There TNC has been purchasing sensitive coastal lands (many of them "seaside farms"), preparing development plans for very limited development, and then placing them back on the market with covenants restricting future development.

Transferable development rights (TDR) represent another planning tool that is employed increasingly to protect lands outside growth boundaries. Once considered a radical and overly complex tool, the TDR has been successfully used in many jurisdictions in recent years. Two examples of places where it has been employed with particular success include the New Jersey Pinelands and Montgomery County, Maryland.

The New Jersey Pinelands is an area of about a million acres, encompassing a rich and unique habitat as well as a mixture of towns, rural development, and natural lands. Its Comprehensive Management Plan, prepared by the Pinelands Commission, classified the area according to a series of land capability types; development in the region and local plans must be consistent with the comprehensive plan. Varying development restrictions and performance standards apply in the different capability zones, with a general orientation toward directing growth into existing villages, towns, and certain designated growth centers. One provision of the plan designates "preservation areas," or "sending zones," comprising a total of about 337,00 acres in which only resource-related activities such as farming and forestry are permitted (Yaro and Hiss 1996). Residential development is generally not permitted in these areas, but landowners are given the option of transferring development credits to existing towns and growth centers. Under the Pinelands Development Credit Program, landowners are assigned development credits they can sell to developers, who can use the credits to increase density in towns and growth centers—the "receiving zones." Once a transfer is made, deed restrictions are placed on the preservation land, thereby preventing future development. A Pinelands Development Credit Bank has also been created to track and facilitate transfers and to buy and sell directly when necessary. Thus far the plan has been very effective at preventing development in preservation areas, with a small number of homes (80 of 25,000) built in these areas since the early 1980s (Ingerson 1995). More than 13,000 acres have been permanently protected through the development credit transfer program (Roy 1996; fee simple land acquisition has also been used in the Pinelands; see also Collins and Russell 1988).

The TDR program in Montgomery County, Maryland, centers around a "preferential agriculture zone" of some 89,000 acres; beginning in 1980, the maximum density of this zone was reduced from one unit per five acres to one unit per twenty-five acres. Developers can purchase one development

right per five acres for use in other areas of the county. The market for development rights is ensured through a publicly funded TDR bank, which
buys and sells rights in the absence of private demand. More than 4,000
credit transactions have occurred since 1983, protecting a total of more
than 20,000 acres of active farmland (Diamond and Noonan 1996; Tustian
1984, as cited in Platt 1996).

More recently, the TDR concept has been incorporated into an innovative plan to protect the Long Island Pine Barrens, in New York. Under a
new protection plan, some 52,500 acres in the core area will be off-limits to
development, but landowners will be allowed to transfer development
rights, as in the New Jersey case, to designated receiving zones (PCSD
1996).

### Increasing Average Densities

Almost by definition, the compact city is densely developed. An important
element of the strategy for more compact places is therefore to require
higher average densities for new development. Higher density will have
many benefits, including enhancing the feasibility and profitability of public transit, allowing greater opportunities for walking and bicycling, and reducing energy consumption and pollution.

But average densities in the United States have been declining rather than
rising. Table 3.1 shows the average densities of U.S. cities as compared with
other cities around the world. This table was adapted from one in a study
undertaken by Newman and Kenworthy that specifically examined the relationships of density, gas consumption, and "modal splits" (the percentage
of trips taken by public transit, by automobile, by bicycle, or on foot). As
the table indicates, population and employment densities are dramatically
lower in the United States. Phoenix, for example, has a density of only
about nine persons per hectare, while Amsterdam and Stockholm have
densities of more than fifty persons per hectare. Average "outer area" densities are even lower in U.S. cities, but are still thirty to fifty or more persons
per hectare in European cities (see Table 4 in Newman and Kenworthy
1991).

One point the Newman and Kenworthy study demonstrates is that it is
possible to achieve a very high quality of life with much higher densities
than we have in the United States; for example, consider the reputations and
living environments of places such as Paris, Amsterdam, and Vienna.

It is difficult to define sustainable places according to a specific density
threshold. There are a variety of ways to arrive at minimum threshold standards, however. One is to look at a community's historic growth patterns
and to establish, at minimum, required densities of no lower than historic

## Table 3.1.
### *Intensity of Land Use in Global Cities*

| City | Whole–city Density | | Central–city Density | | Inner–area Density | | Outer–area Density | |
|---|---|---|---|---|---|---|---|---|
| | Pop. (per hectare) | Jobs | Pop. (per hectare) | Jobs | Pop. (per hectare) | Jobs | Pop. (per hectare) | Jobs |
| *U.S. Cities:* | | | | | | | | |
| Houston | 9 | 6 | 6 | 443 | 21 | 26 | 8 | 4 |
| Phoenix | 9 | 4 | 17 | 67 | 19 | 24 | 8 | 4 |
| Detroit | 14 | 6 | 11 | 306 | 48 | 20 | 11 | 5 |
| Los Angeles | 20 | 11 | 29 | 472 | 30 | 14 | 18 | 9 |
| New York | 20 | 9 | 217 | 828 | 107 | 53 | 13 | 6 |
| *European Cities:* | | | | | | | | |
| Brussels | 67 | 42 | 74 | 592 | 101 | 85 | 50 | 16 |
| Paris | 48 | 22 | 235 | 400 | 106 | 60 | 26 | 8 |
| Amsterdam | 51 | 23 | 108 | 153 | 83 | 46 | 32 | 20 |

Adapted from Newman and Kenworthy 1989.

trends. Another is to ensure that the consumption of land in a community or region does not exceed its rate of population growth. In general, communities should be considered unsustainable, and moving in the wrong direction, if their average densities are declining.

Such density standards, however, are simply starting points, and higher average densities will be necessary in many places to bring about the desired conditions—including walkability and availability of public transit—of a compact place. To a large degree, it will be up to the community and region to consciously consider, and to choose, the density levels it desires.

Newman and Kenworthy recommend increasing density in U.S. cities in stages, with the ultimate goal of reaching an average overall density of between 30 and 40 persons per hectare and job densities of about 20 persons per hectare (Newman and Kenworthy 1991). Inner- and central-city density targets should be even higher, they assert: 300 persons per hectare for central cities, for instance, and 50 to 60 jobs per hectare. Their suggested outer densities are 20 to 30 persons per hectare and 15 jobs per hectare. More modest U.S. goals seem in order—for example, 20 to 30 persons per hectare overall density and 10 to 20 jobs per hectare, with much higher densities in central city and inner city/suburb areas.

For growth containment measures such as UGBs to be effective and to result in compact, higher-density places, additional complementary planning measures must be implemented. As implied in the case of Oregon, cities must find ways of modifying their zoning provisions to mandate minimum densities, rather than maximum allowable densities, as under traditional zoning. Even though the desired density of a potentially compact city may be eight, ten, or twelve units per acre, zoning usually does not prevent a developer from building a project at, for example, half that density. The Metropolitan Portland Housing Rule, which requires that local governments allow for 50 percent multifamily or attached single-family housing, is one unique example of an effort to address this problem. Even more significantly, these local plans (which in Oregon carry the weight of law) must meet certain density targets (e.g., ten units per buildable acre in the city of Portland and six to eight units in more suburban localities).

It is important to recognize that there are many different ways in which density can be increased and many different urban forms that could be advanced. Some metropolitan areas may wish to develop in a kind of star-shaped pattern, for instance, where density is concentrated at peripheral nodes (as well as in central city and inner suburban locations) and connected along public transit lines (a pattern that has been successfully promoted in a number of European cities, including Stockholm and Copenhagen). High-density new towns may also be an element in the strategy (used successfully in the Netherlands, for example).

Density increases can also be achieved in more rural environments by encouraging compact and infill development within existing towns and villages. Even modest increases in average development density can have remarkable results in reducing land consumption. The study of urbanization trends in California's Central Valley, for example, found that land consumption could be cut in half over a twenty-year period simply by raising average densities from four units to seven units per acre (Arax 1995).

## Infrastructure and Public Investments to Support Density

The accommodation of higher desired densities also usually requires that necessary public investments in services and facilities be made in advance in order to support and encourage such development. The experience of Austin, Texas, is telling in this regard. In the late 1970s, the city prepared an extremely progressive and ambitious growth management plan called AustinTomorrow. After thorough environmental analysis and an extensive process of public participation, the plan delimited a north-south corridor as the least environmentally damaging area in which to direct new growth. In the end, however, the city's residents failed to pass the bond measures needed to fund the necessary facilities to accommodate growth there, and several rezonings were permitted to allow development in other locations. Further undermining the approach was the ability of developers to create the Municipal Utility Districts necessary for the provision of sewer, water, and other public services outside city boundaries.

In sum, simply drawing a UGB on a map is by itself insufficient to ensure that compact cities and communities will occur. Rather, a host of additional complementary growth containment strategies and actions must be undertaken, including minimum zoning standards, key public investments in urban services and facilities (especially transportation), and measures to protect rural and resource lands and to prevent development outside boundaries.

In the same vein, local governments may need to become more active participants in the land development process than typically is now the case. This involvement could take many forms, but might include securing and improving development sites in locations where growth or redevelopment is to be encouraged.

## Infill, Reurbanization, and Brownfields

In the sustainable community, greater attention is directed toward using those lands already committed to the urban fabric more efficiently. The goals of sustainable communities are complementary and supportive of downtown and urban renewal efforts in that the focus is on reusing already committed lands before consuming, destroying, or otherwise wasting important natural and open lands on the periphery.

In addition to reducing the need to convert open and natural lands on the urban periphery, the reuse of existing urban land can help improve and reinvigorate urban areas. The goal of using and reusing urban lands more efficiently goes by many names. *Urban infill* focuses on the need to accommodate development, much of it incremental and small-scale, on undeveloped building lots or in areas that have been abandoned or are currently underutilized. Urban infill holds the promise of enabling cities and communities to grow and evolve organically, through many incremental and small additions and changes over time. Among other benefits, the emphasis on creating places of enduring value, and on restoring and reusing buildings and other existing elements of the built environment, creates positive common ground between sustainability and historic preservation efforts. The result is often places with a rich architectural, historical, and neighborhood texture to them.

Evidence suggests that there is great potential for accommodating new growth and development through infill as an alternative to developing new "greenfield" sites. In fact, most, if not all, of a region's or community's future population and housing growth can be accommodated through a combination of modest increases in density, renewal and reurbanization of abandoned or underused areas, and renovation and adaptive reuse of existing older structures (People for Open Space 1983). A recent national survey undertaken by the University of California's Institute of Urban and Regional Development attempted to calculate the amount of undeveloped land in the country currently zoned for high-density development (defined as fifteen units per gross acre or higher). Some 1,200 localities responded to the national survey, and its results confirm that enough infill land is available to accommodate some 6 million new households (based on actual development at these high densities). The survey demonstrates, then, that at least some of the most important conditions of infill development—availability of land and higher-density zoning—are already present (Pendall 1994).

Encouraging infill and increasing the density of existing areas is rarely an easy task, of course. Many potential infill sites are "brownfields," former industrial and commercial locations that are often environmentally contaminated. The recovery and redevelopment of brownfields present contamination and cleanup issues as well as the potential for legal and financial liability. But policy initiatives at local, state, and federal levels can help to facilitate cleanup and redevelopment, address many of these concerns, and represent an important part of any infill strategy. Under the EPA's Brownfields Initiative, more than 27,000 sites have been taken off the list of potential Superfund sites, and legislative reforms to Superfund would address other obstacles. (Not all brownfield sites are contaminated, of course, or are subject to Superfund restrictions.) Approximately two dozen states have adopted voluntary brownfield cleanup programs of their own, usually including a combination of regulatory provisions (e.g., streamlining permitting, relaxing cleanup standards) and financial incentives (e.g., loans, grants, and liability-limiting assurances such as covenants not to sue; see Dinsmore 1996 for a review of these programs). Localities have taken similar actions, such as allowing the use of tax increment financing districts to fund cleanup (Iannone 1996).

These programs, particularly those relaxing cleanup standards and removing properties from the list of potential Superfund sites, are controversial and should be considered with caution. However, where minimum environmental safety can be assured (and cleanup provided to levels consistent with their planned use), brownfield sites represent important resources for future development and should be tapped as part of a broader urban containment strategy.

Infill often will not be viewed in a positive light by existing neighborhoods, especially by nearby residents who fear the impacts of additional traffic, potential crime, and aesthetic blight. In general, the word *density* is often viewed pejoratively and tends to be interpreted as a kind of code word for these ill effects. Overcoming these perceptions and fears, while not insurmountable, is a significant challenge. The experience of Montgomery County, Maryland, is instructive. There, residents of neighborhoods designated as receiving zones have objected to additional density; efforts at increasing density around transit stops have encountered similar resistance. Richard Hawthorne, the head of the transportation planning division for Montgomery County, believes that we must start to do a better job at selling the benefits of density. For residents in existing neighborhoods, he recommends, "We have to convince them that there's something in it for them" (Hawthorne 1995). Indeed, there are clear benefits that can be highlighted, including increased mobility through transit and improvements in shopping, entertainment, and certain public services.

Development conditions and regulatory requirements may also create impediments to infill. Parking requirements for an infill development—often mandating one space per unit—may be overly expensive to provide and even unnecessary given a project's location and potential for utilizing other modes of transportation. Other requirements, such as those mandating a minimum amount of open space, have also been criticized. One developer of infill housing recently lamented that under one local ordinance, the amount of open space mandated for the four-story infill project he was considering undertaking exceeded the actual size of the building lot (Kennedy 1995). The provision of parks and open space is certainly important in cities, but there may be many ways—for example, through special transit-oriented development ordinances—that local zoning provisions can be modified or adapted to facilitate infill development.

There are many potential opportunities to reintensify and reurbanize areas, and successful examples abound. One interesting example is a development designed by Peter Calthorpe in Mountain View, California, called The Crossings (see Center for Livable Communities 1995a). The redevelopment site was originally a traditional suburban shopping mall surrounded by a vast parking lot; when the mall failed financially, the city promoted the idea of converting the site to denser, residential uses. The resulting project is a relatively dense, mixed-use development oriented around a transit stop. A population of more than 1,000 is accommodated on a site of about eighteen acres, with an average density of thirty units per net acre. The project also includes three parks, a daycare facility, and pedestrian access to a full-service grocery store (which already existed but was made more pedestrian accessible), as well as a mixture of residential units, including apartments, single-family homes, and townhouses, some 15 percent classified as "afford-able." The pedestrian-accessible nature of the project is impressive. Streets are narrow (twenty-eight feet), and it is only a few minutes' walk to the parks or grocery store. This project is a good example of a compact, transit-oriented, mixed-use, and pedestrian-friendly redevelopment, one that recy-cles land and at the same time creates a high-quality neighborhood. Com-munities need more of this kind of creative retrofitting of dysfunctional, underutilized spaces.

San Jose, California, has been making great strides in increasing develop-ment and densities around new transit stops along its Guadalupe light rail line. A new Corridor High-Density Housing designation has been incor-porated into its general plan, which will allow densities from twelve to forty-five units per acre around transit stations (Urban Ecologist 1995).

Seattle's new comprehensive plan has as its centerpiece the concept of "urban villages," which attempts to promote this kind of intensification on a larger scale. Spurred by the requirements of Washington State's 1990 Growth Management Act, the urban villages idea has become Seattle's so-lution to accommodating and managing future growth, which is projected at a 14 percent increase in the city's population over the next twenty years. The plan designates some thirty-nine urban villages, from very dense "urban centers" (e.g., downtown) to less dense "residential urban centers." Generally these areas are intended to be higher intensity, mixed use, and transit accessible. Zoning will be modified to allow greater density in urban villages, and areas outside the villages are to be downzoned (see Seattle, City of, 1994).

Toronto has similarly been promoting what it calls "reurbanization." In recent years, Toronto has been able to increase significantly the amount of new housing in the Central Area, with the added benefit (unexpected to some) of lowering the amount of commuter traffic entering the city each day compared with what it would otherwise have been, given increases in office employment (Nowlan and Stewart 1991).

## The Importance of Central Cities

Any sustainability strategy that is truly comprehensive requires concern about the condition and status of cities—whether older cities, inner cities, or inner-ring suburbs. While the concept may not yet have firmly taken root within the environmental community, the environmental agenda of sustainability must go hand and hand with a strong cities or urban agenda. In large part, the demographic pressure feeding unsustainable land use pat-terns today, and over the last thirty years, is a function of central-city population outmigration. Between 1970 and 1994, many larger cities experienced substantial loss of population: Philadelphia, 22 percent; Chicago, 19 percent; Detroit, 34 percent; Washington, D.C., 25 percent; Pittsburgh, 31 percent; and St. Louis an incredible 41 percent (Cohn 1996). The reasons for outmigration frequently cited are both "push" factors such as crime, reduced public services, and the perception of lower quality of life in these areas, and "pull" factors of lower taxes, larger and more affordable homes, and better schools.

Outmigration is a double-edged sword in that it results in socially unsustainable inner cities as well as environmentally destructive and land-consumptive outer suburbs and exurbs. Achieving sustainable places, then, requires concerted policies to turn the population tide and to enhance the conditions and perceived attractiveness of urban areas. It is ironic, in fact, that the urban areas of many older cities possess precisely the same qualities that are being touted but not realized by New Urbanist architects and developers. Compare the walkability, mixed-use, transit- and mobility-friendly qualities of Dupont Circle in Washington, D.C., or Cambridge, Massachusetts, with any of the New Urbanist developments.

Several recent studies have shown that the fate of central cities and their suburbs are inextricably connected, and there is considerable evidence demonstrating that it is in the long-term interests of all cities and jurisdictions in a region to have a central city core that is healthy and thriving. For example, an analysis for the National League of Cities of eighty-five metropolitan areas found that those regions with high income disparities between cities and suburbs also experienced diminished overall income growth (Ledebur and Barnes 1993).

An important ingredient, then, in any strategy of promoting sustainable, compact development is to improve inner and central city areas, to make them more attractive to businesses and citizens, and to move beyond simply neutralizing push factors (e.g., perceptions of crime) by transforming cities into more desirable places to live. Across the country, there are promising examples of how cities have been able to restore or enhance the economic and social viability of their urban areas. Notable examples include Baltimore, Maryland, which transformed itself into a popular tourist destination beginning with the revitalization of its Inner Harbor in the early 1980s; Cleveland, Ohio, now known not only for its Rock and Roll Hall of Fame, but also for its recent downtown revitalization successes; Pittsburgh, Pennsylvania; St. Louis, Missouri; and Oakland, California (Kelley 1996). On a smaller scale, Suisun City, California, once known as the worst place to live in the San Francisco Bay Area, has made extraordinary strides in reviving its inner core through the use of tax increment financing, the revival of its historic railroad station, and a plan to make commercial spaces affordable to local businesses and entrepreneurs (Peirce 1995).

In Kansas City, Missouri, the FOCUS (Forging Our Comprehensive Strategy) initiative represents a uniquely comprehensive, inclusive, and integrative approach to planning for the future of an entire region. It involves the private as well as public sectors, and places a strong emphasis on community and citizen input. The process began in 1992 with the appointment of a twenty-four-member steering committee of civic leaders. Phase One involved the preparation of a policy plan that was adopted by the city council in 1994. The plan—prepared through a unique process in which twelve appointed "perspective groups" were asked to respond to a series of sixty-two key questions about the future of the city—presents a vision for the future of the city and fourteen guiding "principles for policy" that provide the basis for the development of more detailed action plans.

In Phase Two, seven "work teams" prepared a series of interconnected plans for three areas: the physical environment, governance, and human investment. The physical environment area was further divided into five subareas: (1) a city-wide physical framework, (2) historic preservation, (3) the urban core, (4) the northland, and (5) neighborhood prototypes. In January 1997, after a year of collaboration involving more than 400 citizens, these plans were summarized in the working draft of a Unified Direction Statement that specifies twelve "building blocks" for specific future actions:

- Focus Centers
- Connecting Corridors
- Community Anchors
- Moving About the City
- Quality Places to Live and Work
- Neighborhood Livability
- Citizen Access and Communication
- Investing in Critical Resources
- Culture and Amenities
- Healthy Community
- Competitive Economy
- Life-long Learning

While the report is still considered very much a "work in progress," the FOCUS timetable calls for the transformation of the Unified Direction Statement into a Strategic and Comprehensive Plan to be approved by the city council, city plan commission, and FOCUS steering committee in the summer of 1997 (FOCUS 1997).

The FOCUS approach is exemplary in its recognition of the importance of financial strategies and governance structure to bringing about a more desirable and sustainable future. It also recognizes the importance of simultaneously working to improve the urban core and preserve existing areas of the city while seeking to improve the quality of suburban development.

These efforts illustrate the importance of taking a holistic approach to urban revitalization that relies on joint public and private participation, and that simultaneously addresses issues of economics, governance, design, and housing, among others. A bold vision and the celebration of existing, high-quality aspects of cities can also be an important but often overlooked strategy for sustainability. The National Capital Planning Commission's new framework plan for the monumental core of Washington, D.C., is an inspirational example of a program to further reinforce the beauty, specialness, and significance of the city. It is a bold set of proposals for shaping how the core will look in fifty to a hundred years. Among the more ambitious elements of the plan are proposals to remove and relocate major sections of freeways and railroad tracks, in the process restoring and extending key boulevards in the city. The plan also calls for reconnecting the city to its waterfront through the creation of a continuous, walkable, waterfront park along the Potomac linking parks, plazas, hiking and biking trails, and marinas. It would also substantially "green" the city and expand and reinvigorate the city's public transit system (including a system of water shuttles) (National Capital Planning Commission 1995). Whether this plan will be translated into reality is uncertain, but it presents a bold vision for improving and celebrating the nation's capital. The success of this effort may have symbolic importance for whether we ultimately decide to cherish, preserve, and strengthen these precious urban spaces, or whether we allow the outward flow of energy from central cities to continue.

### Tempering the No-growth, Slow-growth Impulse

Many communities, especially in California, have responded to the pressures of urban growth by attempting to close the door on it or to slow its pace substantially. Often accomplished through public referenda, this political backlash to growth is understandable, generated by concerns about traffic, noise, school overcrowding, and general degradation in quality of life. The result of no-growth or slow-growth restrictions, however, has been to deflect development and growth onto other communities, often exacerbating scattered land-use patterns by pushing development even farther out.

While there may be circumstances in which ecological conditions and limited ecological carrying capacities require severe growth limits, very often there are ways and places in which to accommodate additional growth where its impact is negligible and, in fact, may be seen to have positive benefits. As discussed in preceding sections, there are often opportunities for infill and redevelopment and ways to accommodate additional growth in more efficient, compact forms. In this way, the agenda of sustainable places is not antidevelopment. As Peter Calthorpe and Henry Richmond assert, "Development is not the problem. Rather, development in the right place, time, and form is the key to sustainable communities" (Calthorpe and Richmond 1993, p. 701).

## A Comprehensive View of Affordability

The promotion of a more sustainable and compact urban form can minimize a variety of significant short- and long-term social and environmental costs. In addition to the many expenses associated with sprawl outlined in Chapter 1, these include the costs of air and water pollution, loss of habitat and biodiversity, and loss of open space and areas of great recreational and spiritual value. Recognition of the price effects or other potential exclusionary impacts of urban growth boundaries does not imply that communities should refrain from attempting to contain growth. Rather, it simply means that communities, regions, and states must support containment measures with programs, policies, and funds that enhance opportunities for affordable housing, job training, and community development. Even a community like Boulder, Colorado, recognizes that it must redouble its efforts to make itself as affordable, inclusive, and diverse as possible.

It is also inappropriate to view housing affordability apart from other costs, both private and public, that result from low-density sprawl. The high cost of automobile ownership alone suggests that when considering these types of price effects, it is important to take into account a more comprehensive measure of affordability and to seek to promote the goal of an "affordable" life or lifestyle, not simply affordable housing.

## New, Creative Housing Solutions

Compact cities create both the opportunity and necessity for more creative solutions to housing problems. While a compact growth paradigm does not envision (or necessarily advocate) the abandonment of conventional single-family, detached housing, it does argue for the need to expand the range of housing options available.

Within the sustainable community, there are a variety of different housing options to be considered and accommodated. One is the notion of housing in downtown areas. Encouraging a greater mix of housing along with office and commercial uses is a challenge, but such an approach can make for more dynamic, vibrant places while reducing the number of cars and people commuting into downtown areas each day. By all indications, it appears that a significant number of traditional commuters would love to find ways to live closer to their jobs, if the perceived negative aspects of downtown living could be addressed.

In this regard, there is considerable potential in the notion of urban villages, in which relatively dense, multifamily or single-family attached housing is designed around high-quality pedestrian environments, near public transit, and with access to shops, cafés, theaters, and a variety of other attractive amenities. Many examples of urban villages already exist in the United States, including Dupont Circle in Washington, D.C., Virginia Highlands in Atlanta, and many of the older neighborhoods of Boston, New York, and San Francisco. Urban villages exist in older downtown areas, but can also emerge in suburban areas, as in suburban Virginia around the Clarendon and Ballston Metro stops. (For a good discussion of the concept of urban villages, see Newman and Kenworthy 1992.)

Another related housing option is the traditional model of housing above shops and offices. States and localities can promote this model by providing access to creative funding opportunities. New Jersey's Upstairs Downtown program, for example, a pilot program of the state Mortgage Housing and Finance Agency, provides renovation loans to owners of multistory buildings who agree to provide apartments along with commercial space (Garbarine 1996). In addition to providing affordable housing, such programs serve as an effective tool for stimulating downtown economic activity.

One fairly simple way to increase housing density while providing an attractive form of affordable housing is to allow or promote the use of secondary housing units. Sometimes called "granny flats," these are accessory residential units that are usually developed as part of an existing home—for instance, in or over a garage. Secondary housing units are also known as "elder cottage housing opportunities" (ECHO) because they represent an important housing option for the elderly. They provide an alternative to the placement of aging parents in nursing homes, while at the same time offering a degree of privacy and independence. With the number of people over the age of sixty-five predicted to rise from 31 million in 1990 to more than 52 million by the year 2020 (Hamilton 1995), the ECHO concept represents an important element in housing strategy.

Cohousing is another potentially effective housing option. This innovation began in Scandinavia (Denmark, in particular) in the late 1960s. The basic concept involves a clustered (usually attached) housing project in which certain common areas are shared. The projects typically include about twenty families, who are frequently involved in democratically designing the project. (For the classic work on cohousing, see McCamant and Durrett 1989.) Most cohousing projects have at minimum one common house where meals can be shared, but also typically include daycare, laundry, and other facilities. There are usually common open areas where residents can meet and interact and where children can play and be watched over by the community.

While the idea is a new one in the United States, cohousing is beginning to catch on around the country. In the early 1990s, it was reported that some seventy-five cohousing projects were under way (Sit 1992). The cohousing model has several features that recommend it as a housing option in support of sustainable places. Such projects use space more efficiently than the traditional housing model, and the homes are frequently somewhat smaller and have the advantage of shared walkways, open space, and other features. Often these projects incorporate important environmental features such as solar energy and energy conservation measures. The clustering of housing units and the sharing of common space provide a built-in feeling of community. In addition, the sharing of amenities and maintenance equipment reduces the tendency for overconsumptive lifestyles and facilitates the sharing of belongings such as bicycles and automobiles. (Imagine the advantages of having access to a car for occasional trips without the full expense of ownership, not to mention the resulting reduction in traffic and required parking.) Muir Commons in Davis, California, the first cohousing project to be completed in the United States, illustrates the potential (see Norwood and Smith 1995 for a discussion of this and other similar communities). Of course, the biggest fear for many is the potential loss of privacy that comes with such close proximity to one's neighbors. Cohousing projects attempt to weave a delicate balance between protecting the privacy of one's home while providing the opportunity for collective interaction.

Again, perhaps the greatest obstacle to facilitating these various development options is the negative image of higher-density housing that people tend to hold in their heads. High-density developments tend to be seen as sterile, gray, and unattractive living environments. As described, however, there are many working models of higher-density housing that provide extensive amenities and a higher quality of living.

## The Importance of "Unsorted" Places

More than thirty-five years ago, Jane Jacobs argued passionately in her groundbreaking book *The Death and Life of Great American Cities* for the importance of diversity in urban environments—diversity of buildings, housing types, uses, people, and neighborhoods. Mixed-use developments have become a key tenet of the New Urbanism, and we tend to take these ideas for granted today. Yet maintaining the vibrancy and livability of cities depends on concerted efforts to promote such mixing, efforts that in turn are facilitated by containing growth or refocusing density inward. Jacobs was highly critical of the approach to cities and to city planning that emerged during the 1960s and the era of urban renewal: the razing of older neighborhoods and buildings; the construction of large, high-rise housing set far back from streets; and the proliferation of highways that displaced older neighborhoods and businesses, further separating and isolating uses.

There are many forces working toward the "sorting" of uses that Jacobs so vehemently opposed, forces that pose significant challenges to planning communities in ways that mix uses and activities. The traditional "Euclidean" form of zoning employed in the United States, which separates different uses (residential, commercial, industrial), is still largely in use. This approach is generally a throwback to the days when keeping the tanning factory away from residential areas was essential to public health and safety. While some industrial facilities will still need to be separated from residential areas, many are now able to meet strict performance standards and have the potential to become compatible neighbors. But Euclidean zoning is still often supported out of a fear that these will diminish residential property values. While mixed-use zoning has many advantages, its adoption will require addressing homeowners' concerns and general "fear of the unknown," particularly when it involves adding new types of uses to a preexisting residential district.

Reform of the zoning system has become a common recommendation in recent years. Low-density, single-function zoning clearly serves to spread out development and growth, consuming more land, exacerbating air quality problems, and generally costing more in public expense to serve. Instead of separating uses, we should be actively encouraging, if not mandating, the mixing of uses. Hence, the new zoning regime required to promote and facilitate compact communities will have several fundamental characteristics. It will allow the mixing and interspersal of residential and commercial uses, encourage the mixing of different housing densities, provide greater flexibility in allowing secondary housing units in residential zones, and utilize performance-based measures wherever possible to determine whether commercial industrial uses are incompatible with residential areas.

## A Balanced Transportation System

The creation of more compact urban forms and the reduction of the urban footprint also call for new, more sustainable modes of urban transportation.

Considerable literature has focused on the environmental impacts of the automobile, and a consensus has emerged that a sustainable community is predicated on a more balanced transportation network (e.g., Freund and Martin 1993; Hart and Spivak 1993; Nadis and Mackenzie 1993; Zuckerman 1992; Lowe 1990).

In most other parts of the world, the percentage of trips taken by public transit, by bike, or on foot—is much higher than in the United States. Walking and biking to work in most U.S. cities consists of only about 5 percent of the trips made, and public transit 12 percent, compared with 20 percent and 35 percent, respectively, in European cities. For the United States, Newman and Kenworthy (1991) recommend targets of 20 to 30 percent for public transit and 20 percent for walking and biking. These are ambitious goals, but they are desirable and would indeed be possible with the development of a much different urban form.

Rather than reducing our dependence on the automobile, however, we are actually increasing our auto use. In the United States, the number of cars in use, the vehicle miles traveled, and the average length of commute time have all continued to rise. These trends are symptoms of our scattered, decentralized land use patterns, which, in turn, serve to reinforce these trends. Marcia Lowe notes the "vicious cycle in which auto dependence leads to inefficient land use, which results in increased driving" (Lowe 1994, p. 83).

One of the clear reasons for the vicious cycle of auto dependence is that auto users are not confronted with the full costs of this choice; in fact, auto usage appears to many to be the least expensive transportation option. In addition to the low price of gasoline, the provision of free parking by employers is a significant element of this factor in encouraging auto dependence. Some three-quarters of those who commute by car to work in the United States do not pay anything for parking, with employers providing parking benefits that average nearly $700 per employee. By some estimates, parking subsidies amount to $85 billion a year in the United States; employers also receive tax breaks from those subsidies (Chesapeake Bay Foundation 1993). In fact, large companies have been known to relocate to areas with more open space for the sole benefit of more available parking space. Anyone who has ever been involved in moving an office is familiar with the disruption that relocation can cause—a testament to the lengths that employers are willing to go in order to provide free parking.

Consumers should be given a choice as to whether or not they want to receive free parking by their employers, or whether they would like to receive those benefits in some other form. A recent California proposal would have required employers in that state to give their employees the option of receiving this parking subsidy as a cash benefit if they wished. An analysis of the effects of this policy if it were applied nationally suggested a savings of 1.1 billion gallons of fuel and a reduction in carbon dioxide of 15 million tons per year (CBF 1993).

## Planning and Design to Deemphasize the Auto

Any practical vision of more compact places, therefore, will require a substantial deemphasizing of the role and importance of the automobile. From a planning and design perspective, there are a number of ways that auto usage can be discouraged and other forms of mobility enhanced. It should be acknowledged that movement away from the automobile is difficult given current settlement patterns, low gas prices, and other subsidies described earlier. Even in relatively dense, walkable European cities, the auto remains an important, often necessary part of the transportation mix.

In many communities, traffic presents a major impediment to greater pedestrian or bicycle activity. Increasingly, it seems, roadways are designed with the primary purpose of moving cars efficiently, which generally requires greater width, multiple lanes, and high speeds. The safety and mobility needs of the pedestrian or bicyclist are rarely part of the equation. To provide a safer and more accessible environment for walking and biking, many American cities are recognizing the virtues of "traffic calming" measures that slow traffic down, restrict the areas in which cars are allowed, and otherwise manage the flow of traffic and its negative impact on communities (Portland, Oregon, City of, undated). The technical options for calming and slowing auto traffic are many, and in countries such as the Netherlands there seem to be as many variations as can be imagined. These include raised center pavements, barriers of all sorts, narrowing of streets, and use of traffic circles. Within the United States, speed bumps are a popular mitigation measure. One community recently planned by Peter Calthorpe (see Chapter 4) employs the creative idea of placing tree wells a few feet into the streets and along major boulevards.

We must begin to reemphasize the importance of streets as more than just a medium to move cars and start to restore vibrancy to them. A number of European cities, from Copenhagen to Barcelona, have designated walking streets where cars are prohibited or strictly limited to certain times of the day. For all the obvious reasons, the concept of the pedestrian or walking mall has been less successful in the United States. A few good examples do exist, however, in places such as Boulder, Colorado (Fig. 3.1); Charlottesville, Virginia; and Burlington, Vermont—cities that have been able to redirect energies downtown, promote a critical mix of housing and

**Figure 3.1** A pedestrian mall in Boulder, Colorado.

commercial uses, and creative vibrant and attractive urban spaces that people want to visit.

To reduce dependence on the automobile, more accommodation must certainly be given to walking. The New Urbanism movement has done much to popularize the need for pedestrian-friendly places. The standard of the five-minute walk is a good one; that is, the idea that basic services, shops, and civic spaces should be located within a quarter-mile radius of residential development. It is useful to keep in mind the many additional benefits of creating more walkable places. According to a recent report of the Centers for Disease Control, one in three adults in this country is overweight, a record high (McKenna 1997). More active lifestyles—in which walking and biking are part of the normal daily routine, not something one has to go to the gym to experience—would certainly help address the health implications of our national sedentary lifestyle. And there is some polling data to suggest that many more people would like to have these mobility options available (Williamson 1995).

Transforming our cities and communities into pedestrian-oriented places means making them visually enjoyable, and a number of cities have undertaken public art programs that attempt to do that. Portland, Oregon, for example, has a public arts program that requires that at least 1 percent of the budget of public buildings and projects be dedicated to public art. There is much to look at and enjoy as a pedestrian in downtown Portland, including some impressive architecture (such as Michael Graves's Portland Building) and a great deal of public art.

Short blocks on a grid layout can also enhance downtown street life, as Portland illustrates well. Largely as a result of the way the city was originally platted in 200-foot blocks, the downtown is very open and walkable—one is never more than 100 feet from an intersection.

Limits on building height in the downtown diminish the feeling of a "canyon effect," common in many cities with skyscrapers that block out light and a view of the sky. Washington, D.C., employs strict building height limits (nothing is to be higher than the Capitol building), a practice that allows for limitless vistas from various locations around the city.

Restrictions on downtown parking are also an important part of the solution. In most American cities the number of parking spaces per capita is very high, and in some cases there are more spaces than residents (Newman and Kenworthy 1991). Here, again, Portland provides an instructive case study. Under the city's innovative Central City Plan, downtown parking is severely curtailed. For many years, Portland placed an absolute cap on the number of parking spaces permitted, and the city strictly limits the number of spaces—to no more than 0.7 spaces per 1,000 square feet of office space—that each new development is allowed to provide. (Newman and Kenworthy recommend limiting spaces to no more than 200 per 1,000 workers.)

Portland has also made a concerted effort to shift the emphasis downtown away from cars and parking and toward walking and public transit. Perhaps the most symbolic expressions of this commitment in the downtown have been the conversion of a large downtown parking lot to a pedestrian square called Pioneer Courthouse Square and the ripping out of a freeway along the Willamette River to create the delightful Tom McCall Riverfront Park. Public transit is extremely easy to use: there is a twelve-block transit mall in which bus fares are free, as well as a light-rail system—known as MAX, for Metropolitan Area Express—that connects all major downtown points (Fig. 3.2).

Congestion pricing, or peak-period pricing, has proven useful in some cities. Oslo, Norway, has raised some $74 million per year to finance public transit by charging a fee for cars driving into the downtown area (Urban Ecologist 1994). Another creative idea for reducing auto use in cities is the development of car co-ops. These are increasingly popular in Europe (especially the Netherlands and Germany) and usually involve members paying a monthly fee that entitles access to an auto when needed, at daily and

**Figure 3.2** The MAX light-rail system in Portland, Oregon, has helped strengthen its downtown and channel growth into the central city.

hourly rates lower than those of commercial rental car companies. A similar program has also been started in Quebec City, Canada.

### Sustainable Forms of Mobility

A sustainable community facilitates and encourages such nonpolluting forms of transportation as bicycling, as well as an urban form that supports it. Bicycling holds tremendous promise as a major element in creating more sustainable places. Amsterdam and Copenhagen serve as excellent models for bicycle-friendly design, yet only a few U.S. cities—Davis, California; Boulder, Colorado (Fig. 3.3); and Eugene, Oregon, for example—have given serious attention to the bicycle. In many ways, this is a chicken-and-egg dilemma. Do we wait to design our streets and infrastructure until more people begin using bicycles as transportation, or do we install the infrastructure, make it possible for people to use them, and encourage residents to explore this mobility option? In either case, there is no question that bicycles will not be well received without the many urban design and transportation accommodations that would make them easy and enjoyable as a transportation option. The Netherlands, for example, provides protected bike lanes, bike signaling, abundant bike racks at destination points, provisions for taking bikes onto trains and streetcars, and even seemingly small

Figure 3.3 A bicycle path in Boulder, Colorado.

features such as bus mirrors configured to seem less threatening to bicyclists. And, of course, effective traffic calming does much to create a more hospitable environment for bicycles.

There are a number of creative ideas for promoting greater use of bicycles that are beginning to take hold within the United States. Several cities—including Portland, Oregon; Austin, Texas; Madison, Wisconsin; Charleston, South Carolina; Missoula, Montana; Orlando, Florida; and Denver and Boulder, Colorado—are experimenting with providing public bicycles; that is, bicycles that are painted a distinguishing color and that are available (at a public transit stop, for example) to anyone wishing to use them. Another creative idea is to require or encourage developers to provide bicycles as part of the package of amenities offered to new homeowners. John Clark, developer of Haymount (see Chapter 4), is proposing to offer each resident who joins this community a new bicycle.

Compact urban form requires greater emphasis on a balanced and integrated public transportation system, which might include intercity rail, trolleys and trams, and bicycles as well as autos. Many communities have rediscovered the benefits of mass transit and the power of such investments in shaping land use and growth patterns. "Transit-oriented development" (TOD), strongly advocated by Peter Calthorpe and others, recognizes the importance of coordinating land use and transportation decisions, and the need to cluster housing, commercial activities, and overall density along transit routes. According to Calthorpe and Henry Richmond, "The TOD concept is simple: moderate and high-density housing, along with complementing public uses, jobs, retail stores, and services, is concentrated in mixed-use developments at strategic points along an expanding regional transit system. The TOD provides an alternative to standard development by emphasizing a pedestrian-oriented environment and reinforcing the use of public transportation" (Calthorpe and Richmond 1993, p. 706).

Robert Cervero refers to TOD communities as "transit villages," and while successful examples abound in Europe, only a few examples exist in the United States (Cervero 1994). Some local governments in California have begun to encourage transit villages by creating redevelopment districts around transit stops and allowing increased density (through density bonuses) and the mixing of uses. Land assembly costs for these developments are often funded through the use of tax increment financing. Among other incentives, the city of Sacramento has reduced the parking requirements for transit village developments in an effort to encourage them along its light-rail system. Such incentives may also help to reduce the costs of rail-based housing; Cervero reports that reducing parking requirements (from two spaces per unit to only one) would serve to decrease per-unit cost by some $12,000 (Cervero 1994, p. 10).

A number of U.S. cities have discovered the power of light rail, with notable systems initiated in Portland, Oregon, as well as in San Jose, Sacramento, San Diego, and Los Angeles, California. These programs have generally been successful, and these cities are beginning to experience firsthand the critical role that public transit can play in shaping land use patterns and facilitating private investment. Evidence shows that citizens prefer light-rail systems over bus systems because of the comparative simplicity of their routes and the perception of their permanence (Newman and Kenworthy 1992).

Portland presents a good example of how public transit investments can help to shape land use. Its MAX light-rail system has so far been tremendously successful in inducing development or redevelopment along its route. Since its inception, some $1.2 billion worth of development occurred immediately adjacent to the MAX line. Almost all major new attractions and civic venues—including Pioneer Place, the $180 million Rouse project; the Oregon Convention Center; and the new Trailblazers arena—have located along its route and are accessible to rail stops. According to G. B. Arrington, director of the MAX system, "In downtown MAX has accelerated historic renovations, influenced the design of office buildings, and helped make new retail development feasible. Virtually every parcel of vacant land adjacent to MAX downtown has changed hands, been developed, or had development plans announced" (Arrington 1994). Portland has been somewhat less successful in shaping land use around its suburban stations, but there is every likelihood that the MAX lines will constitute the region's major growth corridors in the future. Portland area voters recently passed a $475 million bond measure to finance expansion of the system (its north–south route); this bodes well for further shaping of growth along transit lines, consistent with the TOD idea.

Among North American cities, Toronto represents another success story in the use of public transit. The city made a conscious decision in the 1950s to invest in a regional metro system and has expanded this system no less than six times since. This has occurred partly because of the lack of an aggressive federal highways program in Canada like that which exists in the United States, and partly due to the vocal opposition to highway construction by residents—including Jane Jacobs—who battled fiercely to stop construction of the Spadina expressway, which would have run from the northern suburbs to the downtown (the group won their fight, and a new metro line was built down the right-of-way instead). As a result, Toronto has maintained a relatively compact urban form, with development strongly organized around transit stops. As Newman and Kenworthy note, the subway system has had a tremendously positive influence in that city:

> Not only did the central business district prosper, but new sub-centres sprang up around the stations on the subway network. Falling public transport patronage was reversed. Land around the subway stations became valuable, and developers took advantage of it to build high-density apartments, and commercial development.
>
> Several decades down the track, the vision of Toronto's city fathers has been vindicated and Toronto has avoided the surrender to the car that characterizes many of its southern neighbours. As a result it has become one of North America's most attractive and livable cities (Newman and Kenworthy 1992, p. 11).

Light rail is slowing catching on, and generating important development benefits, in cities throughout the United States. In Dallas, Texas, the recent advent of light rail is already fostering high-investment, high-density development downtown (Surface Transportation Policy Project 1997). And Washington, D.C.'s Metrorail system has generated investments of $970 million along its routes (Center for Livable Communities 1996).

Efforts to strengthen the nonauto components of a transportation system may not always require tremendous financial investments (as is usually the case with light rail), and there are numerous examples of small actions with sizable results. The Regional Plan Association's 1996 Regional Plan for New York has quite creatively recommended a series of modest investments in the region's rail system, including the consolidation of seven different systems into one coordinated system, and a variety of linkage improvements that together will substantially reduce travel times (Yaro and Hiss 1996).

Greater support for public transit between cities and regions also makes considerable sense. Intercity, high-speed rail in particular could help facilitate the model of compact urban form in many regions, thereby reducing dependence on the interstate highways that serve as conduits for scattered growth throughout the country. Compared with conventional highway construction, high-speed rail is also likely to be more economically viable. As just one example, it has been estimated that the cost of adding a new lane in each direction on Interstate 5 between Seattle and Portland would cost about $2.4 billion, or about $6.5 million per mile. The cost of high-speed rail, with roughly the same benefits in terms of moving people, would be only about $500 million, or $2.3 million per mile (MacDonald 1996).

## A Regional Perspective

There is considerable consensus among the planning community that effective strategies for creating more sustainable growth and land use patterns will require regional perspectives and strategies. There are, however, many current obstacles working against a regional perspective. Local governments have significant economic and political incentives to act parochially. When local economic activity, homeowner tax rates, and the quality of public services are all seen to depend primarily on the continuing expansion of the local tax base, a divisive and competitive framework emerges. Local officials have every reason to think locally, and politicians who fail to attend to these local needs are often turned out. A proliferation of tax breaks, moreover, is frequently offered to large industrial and commercial operations (another hidden cost of sprawl development) to entice them to locate in a particular community. This can create circumstances in which each locality is trying to outbid the others. Even commerce willing to remain in the urban core is able, in a context of competition between local governments, to reap substantial tax benefits.

The creation of more compact and sustainable forms of development will require that these underlying disincentives to a regional perspective be addressed. Competition for tax base can be defused through some form of tax base sharing. Unfortunately, while this idea has considerable academic and theoretical appeal, few places have actually tried it. The most notable case is Minneapolis–St. Paul, Minnesota, which dedicates 60 percent of each community's tax base to a regional transportation and planning pool. The program has succeeded in pooling 40 percent of the regional increase in industrial and commercial tax base (Diamond and Noonan 1996). This program has had considerable success—particularly in reducing inequities between cities, older suburbs, and newly developing suburbs—but the politics of adopting such programs are difficult (Youngman 1996).

Local governments act parochially in defensive ways as well—for instance, to guard against the location of too much (or any) low- or moderate-income housing. Some framework for ensuring a fair and equitable distribution of low- and moderate-income housing is therefore an essential ingredient in any regional planning perspective. Several important examples can be cited. In Oregon, Goal 10—also known as the "housing goal"—essentially prohibits localities from zoning out multifamily or more affordable forms of housing. Specifically, each community is required to take into account regional housing needs and to accommodate a mix of housing types. The Metropolitan Portland Housing Rule, as discussed earlier, takes these requirements even further by setting minimum density targets and minimum mixtures of multifamily and attached single-family housing.

From an environmental perspective, real progress toward community sustainability may require the creation of new social institutions. The boundaries of political jurisdictions, for instance, rarely match the boundaries of important natural systems or functions; thus entities such as cities and counties are often ill-equipped to deal with environmental problems. Communities, or alliances of communities, organized along watershed, topographical, or other relevant bioregional units can be very effective in working toward sustainability (Sale 1991; Andruss, Plant, Plant, and Wright, eds. 1990; Dodge 1990).

The achievement of more sustainable land use patterns also will likely require some form of regional governance or framework. The relative success of Portland's Metropolitan Service District and regional growth boundary suggests the potential here (Downs 1994; Nelson 1994), as does the Regional Plan Association, which covers the New York–New Jersey–Connecticut area. California has taken the promising step of dividing the state into thirteen bioregions and establishing a bioregional council for each (Jensen, Torn, and Harte 1993). New Zealand, which has perhaps made the furthest strides to incorporate sustainability into its planning, has completely restructured its government by creating a series of regional councils with boundaries drawn to correspond to water catchments or watersheds (Furuseth and Cocklin, 1995). Admittedly, the U.S. experience with voluntary regional governance (e.g., council of governments, or COGs) has not been very successful; still, the examples noted here suggest that models of effective regional governance do exist.

State governments can also play an extremely important role in creating regional planning policies and requirements. Again, the Oregon system is perhaps the best example. There, Senate Bill 100 and the statewide planning system have done much to drive Portland's success. As discussed earlier, localities in Oregon are required to draw urban growth boundaries, contain development, and address a number of statewide planning requirements. Another example is the statewide transportation planning rule, which requires localities to begin to move (slowly and incrementally over time) away from auto reliance. Specifically, under this rule (adopted in 1991), jurisdictions must reduce parking spaces and vehicle miles traveled by 10 percent within twenty years, and within two years they must have adopted land use and subdivision provisions that allow transit-oriented development.

A number of observers have commented on the importance of politics in promoting sprawl and low-density development patterns, suggesting that at least part of the solution lies in instituting political reforms. Urban growth and sprawl are indeed lucrative businesses, and the interests of real estate development (e.g., developers, builders, and landowners) certainly exert themselves in support of the extension of public services, rezonings, and other facilitating measures. In Washington State, for example, some 5 percent of contributions to state legislative races comes from the real estate industry— twice the amount contributed by the timber industry (Durning 1996, p. 29). Local government boards also frequently enjoy a high degree of representation by real estate, commercial, and other interests with a direct stake in promoting sprawl. Helpful political reforms might include strengthening conflict-of-interest provisions and tightening restrictions on campaign contributions.

### Reforming Tax Policy

If compact development is to be encouraged, the existing system of local property taxes must be reformed in several important ways. One possible reform involves finding a way to share tax base on a regional level and to overcome, or at least significantly reduce, the pressures to compete for tax base among jurisdictions. As mentioned, Minneapolis–St. Paul is the only notable region with experience with this method.

A second area of reform involves a powerful idea that was promoted by Henry George in the 1800s. It is based on the recognition that today's local property tax is really a dual-tax system—it represents a tax on the land as well as on the structures and buildings that occupy the land. Low tax rates on land create an incentive for owners to hold on to, but not develop, speculative urban land; meanwhile, the relatively high price of urban land sends developers to the suburbs and exurbs, where land is comparatively inexpensive. Development leapfrogs over speculative land closer to the city center in its search for low-priced land. At the same time, the property tax on housing and improvements represents a disincentive to landowners to undertake renovations of existing urban buildings. In the end, the least expensive option is to build anew in suburban or exurban areas, leaving land in the central city undeveloped.

One solution to this conundrum is to tax land at a higher rate than improvements. Seventeen Pennsylvania communities, including the city of Pittsburgh, have adopted a split-rate property tax system. In Pittsburgh, the largest jurisdiction using this tax approach, the land tax is five to six times the tax on buildings and improvements. The practical experience in this city, despite the devastating decline of the steel industry, has been a significant increase in the amount of development and construction occurring in its downtown—more than is occurring in its suburbs. In fact, following the adoption of the new tax rate, development within these communities has exceeded that of many similar neighboring cities ("Tax Reform Fights Sprawl," undated).

Another powerful local taxation reform would be the modification of certain tax advantages intended to encourage open space preservation, but which are frequently exploited by land speculators. Use-value taxation provides preferential tax assessment to owners of farmland and forest land by assessing the land at its farm value rather than its market (i.e., development) value. This form of taxation should be restricted to those areas outside designated growth areas and applied to legitimate (and relatively permanent) agricultural and silvicultural operations.

## Adjusting Financial Incentives

As has been shown, the cost of sprawl manifests itself in many different ways. Compact development patterns are not actively encouraged—and, in fact, are discouraged—by our existing systems of financial incentives. One potentially powerful sprawl-reduction strategy is to find ways for new development and growth to internalize these costs, thereby creating financial incentives to build and grow in more compact patterns. The concept of impact fees, introduced earlier in this chapter, represents an important element of the mix. The secondary mortgage market represents an important area in which financial obstacles to compact development arise. Mixed-used developments, for instance, are harder to underwrite. Overcoming these institutionalized obstacles is a necessary but highly challenging part of the equation for compact places.

Impact fees and other forms of development exactions are one way to pay for the costs associated with community growth. There has been an explosion of late in the use of such measures to fund new streets and roads, parks and open space, and a variety of other growth-related public services. Within a UGB, impact fees may serve an extremely useful function in providing the funding necessary to pay for urban services (i.e., associated with urban villages) in a timely fashion. Impact fees are also considered equitable in the sense that the costs associated with new development are passed along to those who generate it. As long as there is a clear nexus between the fee and impacts generated by the development being charged, impact fees are legally defensible.

Impact fees can also be structured in ways that serve to reinforce growth containment objectives. They should create positive incentives for the location of infill and new development in places where existing services and facilities (e.g., schools, roads) already exist, or disincentives to locating where public operating (and infrastructure) costs are higher. One notable example is the city of Lancaster, north of Los Angeles. Its unique Urban Structure Program assesses development fees based in part on distance from its urban core. The Lancaster program does not prevent growth outside the urban core, but rather seeks to charge the full costs for that growth by imposing a distance surcharge on new development to account for the extra costs of servicing development and population farther away from existing municipal services (Lancaster, California, City of, undated).

There is a concern, however, that very high impact fees will result in higher housing prices, further undermining affordability. The imposition of a flat impact fee of several thousand dollars can render the purchase of a home prohibitive to lower-income buyers. The pricing of impact fees should therefore be structured with an eye toward equity.

## Visualizing Alternative Paths

Very often, individuals have a negative preconception that increased densities will be out of scale or aesthetically unacceptable. Therefore, an important element of any approach to selling higher density and intensification in existing areas is to show citizens and public officials what it can look like. Technological advancements have enabled the computer to play an important role in this arena. For example, the Regional Plan Association in New York has successfully employed computer simulation to show that increased density around rail stations would not be unacceptable—and, in fact, would be preferable to single-story, lower-density forms of development. Robert Yaro, executive director of the Regional Plan Association, tells the story of how officials reacted in response to computer simulations of various development scenarios around one rail station. Through the simulation it became evident that the single-story development that officials thought they wanted was clearly not, when visually displayed, very exciting or desirable. In the end, once officials saw what three-story development looked like—when they could get a visual hook on the density—this became the preferred alternative (Yaro lecture 1996).

The simulations need not be very complex, either. Yaro, Randall Arendt, and others at the Center for Rural Massachusetts demonstrated the power of simple simulation techniques through their pioneering *Connecticut River Valley Study*, published as a design manual in 1989. In putting forth their recommendations for conservation and development in the Connecticut River Valley, the authors presented a series of drawings, each depicting three scenarios: (1) the existing rural landscape, (2) the proposed development as built according to typical zoning regulations, and (3) the proposed development under their recommended new rules (Kunstler 1993).

On the Eastern Shore of Virginia, similar techniques have been employed at the community level. As part of an ongoing planning effort toward sustainable economic development in the region, citizens of the Willis Wharf community created and published colorful maps illustrating their vision of a "small, thriving seaside village" (Center for Compatible Economic Development, undated, p. 5.4). Graphically depicting images of a more sustainable Willis Wharf helped participants visualize, refine, reinforce, and ultimately communicate their vision to others in the community (Herd and Gavrilovic 1995).

Simulation exercises can be extremely useful at larger scales of analysis as well. If local officials and citizens can be shown how the future projected growth and development in a jurisdiction—or indeed, the entire region—can be accommodated through infill, redevelopment of center-city areas, and other techniques, arguments for the need for exurban or greenfields development become defused. One of the early illustrations of this strategy was a study prepared by an environmental group in the San Francisco Bay Area called People for Open Space, now called the Greenbelt Alliance. The study, entitled *Room Enough,* demonstrated convincingly how future expected growth in the San Francisco Bay Area would be fully accommodated within existing urban areas without the need to consume or develop greenfields. Five specific strategies were advocated: using vacant land more efficiently (at higher densities); accommodating more housing along existing major streets; directing future growth into the area's downtowns, where large amounts of abandoned or underutilized land can be found; allowing secondary or accessory units in residential areas; and recycling industrial lands (People for Open Space 1983).

More recently, more sophisticated regional growth models have been developed that provide similar analytic and simulation capabilities. One of the most interesting and powerful examples is the Urban Futures Model, developed by planning researchers at the University of California, Berkeley. In essence, this computer model enables public officials and citizens to understand the development implications of different policy assumptions about growth. For example, how much land in the community will be consumed in the future under a "business as usual" scenario (i.e., at the current rate and pattern of development)? How much would be consumed, on the other hand, if certain environmentally sensitive lands (such as wetlands and flood plains) are declared off-limits and a more compact growth pattern (i.e., higher density) were stipulated? Such a model can help highlight the ramifications of doing nothing, as well as test the results of a variety of "what if" scenarios.

Another useful visualization model is one recently prepared by the U.S. Geological Survey (USGS) to depict growth trends in the San Francisco Bay Area. The USGS has created a video that depicts, in a thirty-second time frame, some 140 years of urban growth in the region, in which urbanized areas of the region are shown in red over a relief map. Such a video can be useful in showing citizens just how much growth and consumption of land has happened over a modest time period, as well as what current rates and patterns of growth will result in the future if left unchecked.

## Making the Case for Compact Cities

There is little doubt that achieving a more sustainable and compact urban form is highly dependent on political support, and educating and gaining the support of key stakeholder groups is essential to any strategy for doing things differently. The business community is potentially both a formidable foe and powerful ally. There is considerable evidence that cities and regions that protect the local and regional environment, ecological capital, and quality of life have a better chance of faring well and prospering economically. This is true both anecdotally and empirically and is discussed in greater detail in Chapter 5.

More fundamentally, it is important to address what it is that people seem to want when they buy homes in exurban and outlying areas, and what developers and banks think they are responding to in the way of demand. Much of the reason for market demand for exurban and sprawl development is simply a matter of affordability. For many, finding an affordable housing unit necessitates looking in outlying areas. In *Edge City,* Joel Garreau describes the case of Gilbert and Caron Merrill, an educated couple in their early thirties who, to purchase their first home, were forced to look forty miles outside Boston, where they finally located a $139,000 town-house: "There they sat, waited for son Wyatt to arrive, living like that, out there in their late-twentieth-century version of tenement housing for yup-pies—Lordvale" (Garreau 1991, p. 87).

What else is motivating such locational demand? Some of the factors are based on perceptions that simply do not correspond to reality. The ten-dency to view central-city or inner-ring communities as crime-ridden and dangerous can be one such inaccurate perception. University of Virginia re-searcher William Lucy has done some interesting recent work on the rela-tive safety of suburbs and exurbs compared with central cities. After re-viewing statistics for forty-nine cities and counties in seven metropolitan areas in Virginia, Lucy concludes that if fatalities from traffic accidents are taken into account, along with homicides, it is actually safer to live in cen-tral cities (Lucy 1995). While the homicide rate is higher in central cities, the rate of homicide perpetuated by strangers, which appears to be what people fear most, is quite low. Lucy concludes, "the irony is that some peo-ple in choosing exurban rural residential locations, partly to avoid what they envision as more dangerous, dense cities and inner suburbs, have traded one type of vulnerability for a greater danger" (Lucy 1995, p. 8).

Alan Durning makes a similar point about the fear of "stranger danger" in the Seattle area. While the per capita crime rate for neighborhoods closer to downtown is much higher than for more distant suburbs, the rate is still relatively low, and the risks much lower, when compared with the risks as-sociated with driving a car. According to Durning, the residents of these more distant suburbs "commonly drive three times as much, and twice as fast, as urban dwellers. All told, city dwellers are much safer" (Durning 1996, p. 24).

Good schools are often another motivating factor underlying housing decisions. And while there is no question that part of the agenda of com-pact communities must be to improve the quality of schools in older, urban areas (indeed everywhere), it is ironic that parents in search of good schools sometimes fail to understand the important educational functions afforded by vibrant streets and neighborhoods. Suburban and exurban development patterns can isolate and detach youth from any kind of community life and from experiencing community in a genuine way. In his book *A Better Place to Live,* Philip Langdon questions the desire of parents to "ensconce" their children in suburban subdivisions "at the cost of impeding children's edu-cation, maturity, and independence" (Langdon 1994, p. 25). As Langdon ar-gues, much of our youth's education occurs outside the traditional school classroom: "For a full connection to one's society and surroundings, there is no substitute for direct experience. Yet this is sharply limited by the layout of the recent suburbs. A modern subdivision is an instrument for making people stupid" (p. 49). Jane Jacobs, in *The Death and Life of Great American Cities,* makes a similar argument about the importance of active streets and neighborhoods in the raising of a child. She includes a most insightful and convincing chapter on the role of neighborhoods in assimilating children into society. According to Jacobs, "In real life, only from the ordinary adults of the city sidewalks do children learn—if they learn it at all—the first fundamental of successful city life: people must take a modicum of public responsibility for each other even if they have no ties to each other" (Jacobs 1961, p. 93).

Another motivating factor is the pervasive desire for a rural or small-town atmosphere and the perceived importance of open space and a bucolic setting. To many prospective home buyers, the single-family, detached unit on a one- or two- or five-acre lot in the exurbs holds the promise of providing "space" and a "closeness to nature." Ironically, traditional suburban development patterns do not actually afford much real open space and are anything but "natural" environments.

Overall, these perceptual influences give us clues about what people seem to want, indicating that if one plans to entice prospective home buyers to reconsider urban and existing communities, these qualities must be created and/or expanded, and their existence emphasized, within the urban form.

Cities can and should be much greener, for example. Through sustainable community planning, citizens are more likely to end up with access, visual and otherwise, to open spaces or greenspace and to many of the other natural qualities they seek in an exurban subdivision. Promoting the urban alternative requires a concerted effort to provide important collective open space and natural areas—areas and experiences that are perceived as being at least equal, if not superior, to the natural and open space opportunities available in outlying areas and through less sustainable development patterns. Many of these strategies are explored in Chapter 4.

## Overcoming Other Obstacles

Achieving more compact development patterns will not be easy. There are important forces working against this goal, as well as clear legal, political, social, and other obstacles to the effective use of tools such as UGBs.

As noted earlier, one of the most important obstacles seems to be an almost knee-jerk fear of any increases in density. Indeed, the very word *density* seems to conjure up tremendous fear for many members of the public. Opponents of multifamily and higher-density development projects have effectively been able to paint a picture of higher density as one of increased traffic, crime, lowered property values, and the presence of more "undesirable" types of people.

There are some who fear that the compact city will not be able to compete economically with other cities in the global economy. Kenworthy et al., in a recent study for the World Bank, effectively debunked this notion. They reviewed economic and other data for thirty-seven cities worldwide. Comparing gross regional product (i.e., the gross domestic product of metropolitan regions) and such indicators as population density and car use, they concluded that there are "no obvious gains in economic efficiency" from lower-density, car-dependent patterns (Kenworthy, Lauber, Newman, and Barter 1996, p. 21). Indeed, their evidence highlights the high economic productivity of some very dense cities in other parts of the world (e.g., Brussels and Zurich).

Density by itself means little, however. Certainly an ill-conceived multifamily housing project, or a badly designed infill project, could have some of the feared effects—as could many low-density development schemes. The real questions are what quality of environment will be created or brought about, and how to find better ways of communicating the benefits and vision of a more compact urban form. Gary Lawrence, former planning director for Seattle and a main architect of the urban villages concept there, argues that much depends on how density increases are pitched to the public:

> One of the ways that cities have really failed in doing comprehensive planning is that the development community in their advertising is selling emotion and dreams, and we're talking about parts per billion of $NO_2$ emissions . . . One of the things we tried to do with the urban village concept is fight a fairer fight—to start talking about the positive attributes of urbanity, about what can we do to make this a competitive advantage for those people willing to make the choice to live more compactly (as quoted in Gurwitt 1994, pp. 51–52).

This means accentuating the many positive features of compactness, but not just compactness itself. These positives include more walkable environments, less reliance on the automobile, and easy access to shopping and other amenities, among other benefits.

Market studies conducted in the Seattle area suggest that the positive qualities of neighborhoods may be more important than the desire for single-family, detached units, and that other, denser forms of housing may be acceptable if accompanied by additional positive neighborhood features. As Durning reports:

... while three-fourths of people prefer detached houses to higher-density options, most people care more about the quality of the neighborhood and owning their own home than they care about housing type. In the right circumstances, more than 90 percent would trade low-density living for high-density neighborhoods—some would move into high-rises, others into low rises, townhouses, or detached houses on small lots. Where in-city town house and condominium development make home ownership more affordable, for example, buyers are already abundant. Other powerful magnets include good neighborhood schools, a sense of community, local parks and a feeling of openness, good transit service, neighborhood shops, and most important by far—low crime rates. Indeed, fully one-third of low-density dwellers in greater Seattle would enthusiastically move into a medium- or high-density neighborhood if they felt safe there (Durning 1996, p. 18).

A visual preference survey (VPS) conducted for the Portland region in 1993 by Nelessen Associates further illustrates the importance of careful planning and design in high-density development. The VPS methodology involves showing an audience a number of slides of different development and community images (in this case, some 240 images presented to 4,500 citizens) and asking them to write down a numeric score (positive and negative) reflecting their "gut" reaction to the image. This particular study focused on design issues surrounding transit stations, main streets, and neighborhoods (A. Nelessen Associates Inc. 1993). The results are telling and effectively illustrate the difference that certain design and community features can make in the perceived acceptability of particular types and density of housing. High-density housing around train stations (i.e., twenty-five to forty units per acre) was deemed very acceptable if it incorporated the following features: "inviting landscaped sidewalks, with shade trees and a combination of low trellis, fencing or walls to define the semi-public realm (front yard)" (p. 5). High-density housing was perceived negatively in the VPS when it presented monotonous building and housing façades, when high fences were used, where little vegetation was provided, and where buildings were not oriented toward the street. Density itself, then, may be less meaningful than the design components of the project or neighborhood. Respondents appear to value "the quality of development design and its relationship to the public street and the surrounding neighborhood, over the perceived overall unit density shown in the image" (p. 5).

The need to create positive streetscapes and street features is an important conclusion of the Portland VPS. Among the important elements are pedestrian-oriented streets and the creation of inviting pedestrian environments, adequate sidewalks, continuous shade trees, narrow roads with parallel parking, and housing with short, defined front yards and prominent entry porches. Among the positive main-street images were colorful awnings, brick-accented sidewalks, shade trees, large storefront windows, decorative benches, and street lighting. Such community features as flowerbeds, tree-lined boulevards, and pocket parks were also rated positively by respondents (A. Nelessen Associates, Inc. 1993).

Robert Cervero and his colleagues at the the National Transit Access Center at Berkeley have attempted to gauge the potential attractiveness of transit villages through similar visual means, using computer-generated images of several different transit neighborhoods with various mixtures of densities and amenities. Some 170 residents of the Bay Area, as well as representatives of major developers there, were shown these computer "walkthroughs" of transit villages with some similarly encouraging results. Higher-density villages with lots of amenities fared relatively well:

> Far more respondents were willing to reside in a transit village setting with densities of 36 du [dwelling units] per acre and nicer amenities than in a similar setting with 24 du per acre but fewer community services or amenities. Notably, people preferred tightly spaced two-and-a-half-story row houses located near a public park and retail shops, to one- or two-story row houses with larger yards but no nearby park and fewer local services (Cervero 1994, p. 10).

The experience of communities that have sought to promote infill and reurbanization suggests that special sensitivity toward the needs and concerns of existing residents is necessary. Particularly important is a process of involving residents in the design and formulation of such plans (Previtti 1995). This is certainly one of the lessons from Seattle, where there has been substantial opposition to increasing densities, especially from existing neighborhoods. While there was extensive public involvement in the early stages of the Seattle plan's development, little involvement occurred in the year and a half during which many of the details of the plan were being fleshed out. As a result, the plan had a top-down feeling to many, and the neighborhoods were being asked to accept significant change (a mix of new housing types in neighborhoods primarily made up of single-family houses) without much direct participation (Gurwitt 1994). While the plan was adopted, some of the specifics of the villages (e.g., their precise boundaries and density targets) were handed over to a neighborhood planning process, giving residents much more say in how the concept would be implemented. Neighborhood "buy-in" appears essential, as are clear design standards that provide residents with some confidence about what can and cannot be expected on an infill or redevelopment site.

Any planning scheme that significantly regulates private property will encounter legal and political obstacles. Many forms of land use regulations have been undermined as a result of unfounded fears by public officials that these measures will be struck down by the courts as unconstitutional "takings" under the Fifth and Fourteenth Amendments of the U.S. Constitution (and many state constitutions as well). A careful analysis of judicial opinions leads to a different conclusion, however. Most local actions to limit development or contain growth would not amount to a taking—such a conclusion usually applies only to those land use circumstances in which a landowner essentially has no remaining economic use. (And even these circumstances would be sustained if a nuisance were being prevented.) These circumstances are, in reality, quite infrequent. Where such circumstances do occur, and where no development should be allowed at all in a particular area or on a particular parcel (e.g., in sensitive habitat area or on a dangerous floodplain or perhaps a UGB "urban reserve"), density transfer or acquisition may be appropriate actions.

There is no doubt that the public pursuit of more compact and sustainable urban forms will create some winners and losers and will readjust economic benefits and values among some individuals. In their study of Oregon UGBs, for instance, Knapp and Nelson do conclude that there will likely be a land price impact from this mechanism: land values will be higher within the UGB and lower outside (Knapp and Nelson 1992). Those who will be losers are likely to oppose such restrictions. Defusing this opposition may require programs that provide some form of compensation to the losers (e.g., through land acquisition or TDR) or an effort to energize politically those who will likely be winners (e.g., suburban homeowners and businesses within the UGB). It may be important to emphasize that through mechanisms such as UGBs all parties tend to be winners in the long run, in the sense that they are given greater certainty about what can and cannot be done with their land. Indeed, the land value changes that result from UGBs are a sign that the mechanism is working. It is a sign that land development expectations have adjusted, and that people and businesses are making investments and other decisions with the belief that this boundary will shape and guide growth in the future.

# Conclusions

A compact urban form is essential for promoting more sustainable places. There is no single magic trick for achieving a more compact form; rather a number of interconnected actions and policies should be explored and pursued. Among the more important of these are:

- effective growth containment, especially use of techniques like urban growth boundaries;
- stringent limits on development of open space and natural lands beyond growth boundaries;
- actions to increase average densities through such measures as minimum density zoning;
- placement of critical infrastructure and public investments to encourage development in desired locations;
- encouragement of infill and re-urbanization wherever possible;
- efforts to revitalize central cities and to make them more attractive places to live and work;
- tempering of no growth, slow-growth tendencies;
- promotion of a comprehensive view of affordability and the exploration of creative housing solutions;
- promotion of a mixing of uses and activities in growth areas;
- a more balanced transportation system, deemphasis of the role of the automobile, and greater emphasis on walking, bicycling, and public transit options; and the encouragement of development that accommodates these alternatives (e.g., TOD); and
- the need for a regional perspective.

## Four

# The Ecology of Place

Regions, cities, and other human settlements are inextricably and profoundly embedded in an ever-present and ever-changing environmental and ecological context. The paradigm of sustainable places holds that we must increasingly understand regions and cities as organic entities—entities that require environmental goods and inputs that interact with one another, modify and influence the natural environment, and transform resources from one form to another.

The planning and design fields have devoted much greater attention to environmental conservation issues in the last thirty to forty years. Ian McHarg's *Design with Nature* was particularly influential in changing the way we approach planning and development. And there is no question that, beginning in earnest with the environmental movement of the 1960s, communities, states, and the federal government have given serious and unprecedented attention to environmental protection and preservation issues.

## Natural Cycles and Ecological Footprints

The emergence of geographic information systems (GIS) technology, moreover, has enabled McHargian-style environmental analysis to become a commonplace methodological step in undertaking almost any form of local planning. But while these analyses, and their resulting policies, are extremely important, a more comprehensive and holistic approach is required. In addition, for example, to steering development away from an environmentally sensitive site—say, an area of high scenic value or productive farmland—planners must concern themselves with the impact of the materials and design of the resulting structure itself, as well as the source and impacts of the energy used to construct and operate the structure. They must consider the ways in which people earn their livelihoods and the impacts of the economic base and sector on the environment. To paraphrase Paul Hawken, we need an "ecology of commerce" as much as an ecology of place (Hawken 1993). In the same way, while the operation and management of cities create environmental stresses, they also hold a significant piece of the solution to environmental and ecological sustainability.

A second, related notion has to do with how we view nature. The ecological view of cities and towns rejects the tendency to view nature as "somewhere else"—as outside and separate from where people live and work. Nature is all around us, and with this appreciation may emerge a sense of the ecological significance and aesthetic importance of many different types of lands and landscapes, whether it be the corner woodlot, the suburban creekbed, or the urban waterfront. In other words, nature does not reside exclusively in national parks and other protected areas.

The concept of sustainability also implies that our cities, towns, and communities should strive to function as ecosystems do. Architect William Mc-Donough talks about the fundamental laws of nature that can inform design. The first of these is that there is no such thing in nature as waste: "All materials given to us by nature are constantly returned to the earth without even the concept of waste as we understand it. Everything is cycled constantly with all waste equalling food for other living systems." (McDonough 1993, p. 7). Second, these natural cycles rely upon and are powered by the energy of the sun; in this way, nature operates on "current solar income." Finally, nature functions the way it does, and is able to sustain itself, because of the diversity of life. According to McDonough, "What prevents living systems from running down and veering into chaos is a miraculously intricate and symbiotic relationship between millions of organisms, no two of which are alike" (p. 8).

Viewed from this perspective, sustainable communities strive to replicate the basic processes and principles of nature: they strive to generate only substances or by-products that are "food for nature"; minimize the production of things that can only truly be considered waste (e.g., toxics); live off current income (e.g., solar and renewable sources of energy); and, finally, respect and preserve diversity.

Another basic idea is that communities should strive to "fit" within and nurture their ecological home, or, that is, the environmental, biological, topographical, and geohydrological conditions within which cities and communities are inherently situated. A community should attempt to live within these conditions and to forge a sustainable relationship with its ecological home, recognizing natural carrying capacities and limits, and planning and functioning within them.

Urban populations have considerable resource needs and generate tremendous amounts of waste. Resource needs often strain regional ecosystems (for example, through the overdrawing of aquifers), and waste generation often exceeds the natural assimilative capacities of the local and regional environment (e.g., degradation of estuaries such as the Chesapeake Bay as a result of nonpoint source pollutants). Often, resources such as water and food are imported while their wastes are exported, whether to outlying landfills or as carbon dioxide pumped into the atmosphere.

William Rees's concept of the "ecological footprint" has done much to educate about the resource needs and ecological impacts of an average individual. The "footprint" of the average North American is quite large, and the resource requirements of North American population centers extend well beyond their limited jurisdictional boundaries. Rees's analysis of the lower Fraser Valley in British Columbia is particularly telling. He finds that the land requirements of the 1.7 million inhabitants of the region—requirements for such needs as food production and forest uptake of carbon dioxide—total 8.3 million hectares. The region, however, comprises only 400,000 hectares. Thus, the resident population of the lower Fraser Valley requires something like twenty times its total amount of land to meet its own needs. The result is the need to "appropriate" the carrying capacities of other regions to supply these needs. Rees therefore concludes that:

> . . . land "consumed" by urban regions is typically at least an order of magnitude greater than that contained within the usual political boundaries of the associated built-up area. However brilliant its economic star, every city is an ecological black hole drawing on the material resources and productivity of a vast and scattered hinterland many times the size of the city itself . . . (Rees 1992, p. 125).

This analysis suggests that sustainable communities should be conscious of their resource needs and waste streams, ensure that they do not destroy and exhaust the bioregion in which they are situated, and seek to minimize the environmental pressures placed on other regions and countries. Moreover, they should attempt to estimate, analyze, and track these demands and take a long view in planning for future resource needs.

Of course, the development of a more compact urban form will go a long way toward reducing wastes and the unnecessary consumption of resources. Reducing the role of the automobile and providing more energy-efficient, less-polluting forms of mobility are also clearly important to ecological sustainability.

## Rethinking Waste

Sustainable places, then, attempt to reduce waste streams and particularly the waste that ends up in landfills or in municipal incinerators. A number of innovative local waste reduction and recycling programs exist in communities around the country. Cities like Seattle and San Jose, for example, give residents an incentive to reduce their household waste by charging for collection according to the volume generated. (Public Technology Inc. 1993). Such variable-rate programs are even more popular in rural areas as an alternative to greenboxes and other public dumping receptacles. In North Carolina, surveys indicate that residents would prefer a unit-price program rather than feel that they are financing the disposal of other people's waste. (North Carolina Recycling Association 1995). These programs are perhaps more popular in rural areas, where residents are more accustomed to disposing of their own waste, than in cities, where many citizens take garbage collection for granted. Thus, the institution of any variable-rate pricing program must involve extensive public education.

Identifying ways to treat wastes as benign and productive inputs to other activities and processes is also important. The city of Sarasota, Florida, in collaboration with several other governmental units, has been developing a regional wastewater reuse program that eventually will allow the return of some 50 million gallons of wastewater per day to other uses, such as agricultural irrigation (Perciasepe 1996). This program will simultaneously reduce pumping pressures on the Florida aquifer—which is currently being overdrafted, causing a saltwater intrusion problem—and reduce the input of damaging nitrogen pollutants into the Sarasota Bay Estuary.

John Todd and other industrial ecologists have successfully demonstrated the importance of treating wastes as inputs to other natural processes. Todd's idea of "living machines" suggests that cities and communities can harness natural processes to perform many important public functions while adhering to natural principles. Urban wastewater can be cleansed through ecological processes, and many localities are beginning to experiment with the use of constructed wetlands systems to perform this process. Michael Hough reports that some 150 communities in the United States are already using wetland treatment systems for their wastewater. Particularly promising are solar aquatic systems, an advanced form of wetlands treatment system that utilizes a complex regime of plants and animals (e.g., zooplankton, snails, fish), in combination with sunlight, to break down and purify wastewater naturally. In a sense, these are small ecosystems in which the waste becomes food as the zooplankton eat the algae and the fish eat the zooplankton. The result is clean water, with operating costs less than for conventional wastewater treatment plants. Hough identifies several U.S. cities that have been using this technology, including Providence, Rhode Island; Harwich, Massachusetts; and Muncie, Indiana (Hough 1995).

Land treatment of wastewater, which utilizes the natural treatment capabilities of fields and forests, is another option. There has been considerable success in using wastewater to irrigate forests, which again turns wastewater into a resource to be used productively—an input to another natural process that represents a benefit rather than a liability. Perhaps regional urban forest systems can be established to convert wastewater into resource water at the same time that carbon dioxide sequestration occurs and other ecological benefits of the forests are realized (Hough 1995).

The ecological view also values taking responsibility for the export of waste and attempting to minimize, if not eliminate, extra-local harms. Largely in recognition of the impact that local pollution and consumption can have on global warming, several North American cities have developed carbon dioxide reduction strategies. Toronto's strategy, for instance, set a target of 20 percent reduction in carbon dioxide by the year 2005. Elements of the plan have included planting more trees in the city, encouraging greater use of mass transit and bicycles, and exploring the possibility of a district heating system for the downtown, among others (White 1994). Other cities, including Minneapolis–St. Paul, Minnesota, and Portland, Oregon, have developed similar strategies under the UN-sponsored Cities for Climate Change Program (Public Technology Inc. 1993; Portland, Oregon, City of, 1993).

## Minimizing Urban Resource Needs

Urban populations create tremendous resource needs—basic needs for energy, food, and water. How these resources are provided to urban populations will, of course, influence the environmental impacts generated. There are several primary strategies that cities can adopt to manage resource needs. One strategy is to search for ways to reduce the absolute quantity demanded or used by residents and businesses in the first place.

One way to reduce resource demand is to create positive incentives for the adoption of energy-efficient technologies or practices. The city of Austin, Texas, provides financial incentives to customers of the Austin Electric Utility for energy-efficient appliances. The Appliance Energy Program provides customers with a rebate when they choose to purchase high-efficiency air conditioners and heat pumps, as well as solar water heaters, with the amount of the rebate depending on the specific appliances and their efficiency rating (Austin, Texas, City of, undated [a]).

Many communities, especially in arid climates, have undertaken impressive water conservation programs to reduce resource demand. Natural landscaping can reduce substantially the amount of water required (see, for example, the Florida Yards and Neighborhoods program, Perciasepe 1996). In urban areas, the combination of warm weather and extensive paved, glass, and concrete surfaces can cause a "heat island" effect in which temperatures exceed those of surrounding countryside. This effect—and hence air-conditioning demands—can be reduced through the use of lighter forms of pavement and strategic placement of trees and vegetation (Gangloff 1995).

Another strategy is to develop and pursue only those technologies and methods of meeting resource demand that cause the least environmental damage or impact. An example of this approach is seen in the admirable efforts of some cities to develop and utilize more sustainable sources of energy, to begin to adhere to the principle of living off current solar income. Austin, Texas, is a leader in this area. It recently signed an agreement with the Lower Colorado River Authority to purchase a 10-megawatt share in the Texas Wind Power Project—a project, developed through state, local, and private interests, to harvest the abundant wind energy of west Texas. Austin's share will be sufficient to provide power to 4,000 homes in the city. The project is expandable, and in the future the city may use this renewable energy source to provide power for an even larger number of homes (Austin, Texas, City of, 1995).

In recent years, the incorporation of solar energy into the public power mix has shown promising results. In California, the Sacramento Municipal Utility District (SMUD) has developed a renewable energy program that relies on a combination of solar thermal, solar photovoltaics (PVs), fuel cells, biomass, wind, and hydrogen. The electricity generated from this program, the utility claims, will power 375,000 homes by the year 2000. Indeed, SMUD's solar PV power plant is the largest such utility-owned plant in the country, producing some 3.5 megawatts of PV-generated power. Part of SMUD's strategy to increase solar use has involved the installation of hundreds of PV generators on the rooftops of customers' homes. Other utilities are collaborating with SMUD to increase the demand for and use of PVs, which ultimately would serve to lower their costs (Smeloff and Asmus 1996).

Solar energy can be encouraged in other ways as well. A number of jurisdictions in the United States have adopted solar-access ordinances, which protect the ability of future homes and businesses to take advantage of passive and active solar energy potential. Development projects, furthermore, can be required to be designed on east-west axes to maximize solar orientation, and communities can provide density bonuses and other incentives for incorporation of solar features, as well as more general renewable energy and energy efficiency features. Communities may choose to issue solar design guidelines—advice to developers and builders about how to maximize solar benefits—as San Jose, California, has done (Public Technology, Inc. 1993).

Support for local and regional food production is another example of a strategy to reduce overall energy consumption, particularly the energy used in transporting food products from hundreds of miles away. Food production considerations can and should play a much more central role in the ecology of sustainable places. Support for local agricultural activity—provided that activity is environmentally sustainable—can serve the dual purpose of preserving farmlands at the urban periphery and supporting a local economy that provides for the food needs of the regional population (or at least a significant portion thereof). Local agriculture also holds greater potential for providing citizens with fresher, more healthful food.

In many cases, supporting local agriculture requires a concerted effort to enhance and strengthen the economic viability of farming activities. One approach seeks to develop and communicate clearer and stronger connections between urban populations and their food sources. "Community-supported agriculture" (CSA) is one promising idea. Also called subscription farming, the concept originated in Japan. Simply put, consumers sign up and pay in advance to receive fresh (and often organic) vegetables, helping to share the economic risk of farming with, and providing an important source of income to, financially strapped local farmers. Among other benefits, it helps to reconnect people with their food supply, providing a strong educational feature, particularly for urban children who may have the opportunity to visit a farm or even help with farming activities (Fig. 4.1). In some areas, shareholders with children enjoy the convenience of picking up their produce at local schools; in other areas, counties provide yard waste to fuel CSA composting. Local governments can and should work to support these CSA programs and to serve as liaisons between producers and consumers.

Many communities also sponsor weekly or biweekly farmers' markets, which create an additional economic outlet for local farm products and provide a pleasant opportunity for community residents to gather together. Opportunities may also exist to help modify local farming practices and to help agricultural producers move in the direction of more sustainable modes of production.

Community gardens represent another local food source option. In many cities around the world, vacant spaces (e.g., land adjacent to rail right-of-ways) have been converted to community gardens (sometimes called allotment gardens), and systems have developed for allocating these areas for citizens and neighborhoods to use. In lower-income areas, community gardens can serve as a significant and much-needed food source, as well as a form of recreation and community building. As just one example, the San Francisco League of Urban Gardeners (SLUG) is working in low-income communities to provide jobs for hundreds of area youth, a steady supply of produce

Figure 4.1 In addition to providing fresh produce,
community-supported agriculture offers educational
and recreational opportunities for children.

for local families, and greener neighborhoods (SLUG 1996). Local governments can help by making potential garden spaces available and encouraging their active use. Even rooftops are potentially important areas for community gardens, an idea that is being encouraged in Toronto (Hough 1995).

In all of the above ways, urban populations can begin to take greater responsibility for understanding their resource needs and for minimizing the
ecological footprint associated with satisfying these demands.

## The Greening of Cities and Towns

A compact, sustainable city need not be a sterile one. Indeed, sustainable
communities seek the greening of urban life and emphasize such design
features as extensive trees and landscaping, urban parks and community gardens, and connected systems of regional open space (Platt, Roundtree, and
Muick 1994; Gordon 1990). There are a variety of ways in which existing
cities and towns can be made "greener," many requiring only modest cost

and effort. One of the most straightforward strategies is to look for ways to increase the amount of vegetation and green areas within the urban landscape.

There is increasing evidence that trees and vegetation provide benefits that are even more profound than those considerable aesthetic and environmental benefits usually cited. Dwyer et al. argue convincingly, for instance, that humans have very deep emotional, symbolic, and spiritual ties to trees (Dwyer, Schroeder, and Gobster 1994). There is, moreover, considerable evidence of the positive health benefits of trees and, more generally, vegetation. Positive physiological reactions—lowered heartbeats and blood pressure—and calming effects have been recorded among humans in response to urban scenes that contain trees, forests, and vegetation (Ulrich 1981). Trees can induce feelings of serenity that can be measured physiologically. The greening of the urban environment, then, is clearly critical to our psychological and emotional well-being, as well as to our general health.

Urban parks represent an important element in creating green places, serving as areas of both reflection and more active recreation. Many cities have made important strides in providing parks and green space and in promoting the significance of these areas to the quality of life of residents. Impressive examples include Golden Gate Park in San Francisco, Fairmount Park in Philadelphia, Central Park in Manhattan, and Prospect Park in Brooklyn. For the residents of these large cities, these parks (all of which, perhaps not coincidentally, were designed by Frederick Law Olmsted a century ago) add tremendous value to city life. In addition to their greenery, they provide excellent recreational facilities, such as ball fields, boathouses, and even skating rinks; in warmer months, they offer cultural activities such as outdoor concerts and plays.

To some critics, the provision of extensive parks and open space within urban boundaries conflicts with the goals of compact development and growth advocated in Chapter 3. But this does not necessarily have to be the case. Growth and development patterns can occur in very compact ways, protecting natural lands, farmlands, and open areas outside UGBs while at the same time providing significant exposure to nature within these growth areas. Portland, Oregon, is a case in point. Despite a compact growth pattern and containment of growth within a UGB, the city has implemented an impressive network of parks and open spaces. Within Portland alone, there are some 280 parks; in fact, the city has one of the highest acreages of parks per capita of any major city. They include 4,800-acre Forest Park (a wilderness area virtually a stone's throw from downtown) and Mt. Tabor Park, an extinct volcano. Portland's network of local parks and open space is closely linked to its regional open space and greenway systems, forming a broad-based, multifaceted approach to greening the city.

To protect these sensitive areas, Portland has implemented an interesting system of environmental zoning overlays. About 17 percent of Portland's land area is included within the overlays, which consist of wetlands, wildlife habitat, flood plains, buttes, and other sensitive areas. Two classifications are provided: environmental protection zones and environmental conservation zones. Building in conservation zones is allowed, but only if unavoidable, and then only as subject to mitigation requirements. Development in protection zones involves much more stringent approval criteria and is therefore virtually prohibited. In both cases, development decisions in these areas are guided by more detailed natural area and watershed protection plans. For landowners who are unable to build in the protection zones, there are provisions that allow the transfer of unused density to other sites in the city; in some cases, the city will purchase these lands.

Many European cities have developed parks based on the "city farm" concept. These are essentially farms that provide a host of different experiences and opportunities; they typically include community gardens and greenhouses, livestock and horse and pony stables, arts and crafts, and other activities that encourage hands-on involvement on the part of visitors. These "farms" can also serve an important educational function. While they are often located on the edges of cities, city farms have been suggested as a model for inner-city neighborhoods as well (Hough 1995).

Another important issue to consider is the ease with which residents of a city can reach surrounding forests, farms, and open space. In addition to consuming these areas, sprawling development patterns often serve to distance open and natural lands even farther away from urban residents. With a compact development pattern, these areas can exist only a short distance away (Newman and Kenworthy 1992); in most compact European cities it is a short ride, perhaps a half-hour, to reach these open areas).

Part of making cities greener requires making the natural systems and processes upon which they rely as visible to its citizens as possible. Hough is eloquent in making this point:

> Much of our daily existence is spent in surroundings designed to conceal the processes that sustain life and which contribute, possibly more than any other factor, to the acute sensory impoverishment of our living environment. The curb and catchbasin that make rainwater disappear without trace below ground, cut the visible links between the natural water cycles, the storm sewers that dispose of it into streams and the lakes and the rivers that ultimately receive it. We are unaware of the eco-

logical degradation that occurs to aquatic life and to the beaches that have to be closed after a heavy rain. Soft fruits grown in warmer climates and transported thousands of kilometers to cold ones are available in the supermarkets in winter . . . . The supply of electricity and water, the processing of waste, are not visible to urban people and they consequently do not feel responsible for them (Hough 1995, p. 30).

Communities can take many actions to make important ecological processes more visible or apparent to its residents. Many cities have begun to "daylight" streams and creeks—that is, to restore and bring back to the surface waterways and natural drainage patterns that had been piped and channeled underground. The result is often a more ecologically responsible drainage approach that allows natural percolation, restores flora and fauna, and keeps storm water out of the flow sent to sewage treatment plants. Equally important, these systems provide valuable green spaces while enhancing public appreciation of the hydrological system.

Trees play an extremely important role in virtually any ecological place. American Forests has estimated that urban trees provide $4 billion in energy savings each year (e.g., through shading and cooling) and that this savings could be doubled if a program were undertaken to plant trees in strategic vacant places (Moll 1995). In fact, a number of cities now have active urban foresting programs and on-staff arborists. Urban forestry programs involve actively promoting the planting of new trees as well as the reforestation of urban areas where die-out of trees has occurred in the past. A number of communities have enacted local ordinances that restrict the cutting of trees, usually of a certain diameter or size, as well as requirements to mitigate for tree losses that might occur during new development.

Adopted in 1983, Austin's tree protection ordinance is one of the oldest in the country and requires a permit for the removal of any tree measuring more than nineteen inches in diameter. The city has aggressively applied the ordinance, and many builders and developers have been asked to redesign projects to avoid the need for tree removal. (A developer must also submit a detailed inventory of all trees exceeding eight inches in diameter on a site.) The city has also prepared a comprehensive urban forest plan, which applies to trees on public property, and has appointed an Urban Forestry Board to oversee its implementation. Other communities have mandated that development must meet minimum tree "density factors"—for example, Fulton County, Georgia, mandates fifteen basal units per acre—or provide for the maintenance of a certain percentage of woodland cover (e.g., Prince George's County, Maryland, Woodland Preservation Ordinance; see Redwood 1994).

In 1989, under the leadership of then-Mayor Richard Daley, Chicago adopted an Urban Greening Initiative. Concerned that the city had been removing more trees than it had been replacing, the mayor initiated a moratorium on the removal of healthy trees along the city's parkways and boulevards (International Council for Local Environmental Initiatives, undated [a]). Two new ordinances were adopted: one that requires tree planting in all new developments in the city and one that creates an Accelerated Real Estate Sales (ACRES) program. The latter facilitates the acquisition by community groups of tax-delinquent land if they agree to convert these areas to community greenspace.

Other elements of the Chicago greening initiative have included community workshops on creating gardens; the city-wide distribution of free gardening and landscaping materials; and the creation of a Green Corps, which trains disadvantaged inner-city residents in gardening and landscaping and then employs them in helping to develop new green sites around the city (for a more detailed description, see ICLEI, undated [a]). The Chicago program further illustrates the multiplicity of benefits that can be provided by such programs. It emphasizes the importance of trees and greening as essential elements in making the city a more attractive place for citizens to live and for businesses to locate; at the same time, programs such as the Green Corps provide not only important greening functions but also needed employment.

There are a variety of additional, creative ways to make urban environments green and wild, and more ecologically sustainable ways in which to maintain natural urban landscapes. Some communities are making an effort to implement less environmentally destructive management practices—for example, by curtailing completely the use of pesticides and herbicides in parks and greenspaces. Others are planting trees wherever possible, utilizing vacant spaces throughout the city for greenspaces, and even converting rooftops to urban gardens and forests. Converting the spaces around and between buildings from turf and grass to trees, meadows, and more heavily (and diversely) vegetated areas will reduce the costs of mowing and the need to apply damaging chemicals, and will create important natural areas for children and adults to explore and enjoy. In the hills above Oakland, California, extensive sheep grazing is helping to control grass and vegetation growth to minimize the potential threat of wildfire.

One of the most dramatic examples of a U.S. city that has recast itself in terms of green principles is Chattanooga, Tennessee. This city of 152,000 residents has transformed from one of the country's most heavily polluted industrial cities to a community that is proud to declare itself the "Environmental City." While the greening of Chattanooga is definitely a work in progress, its transformation, and particularly the community-wide, collaborative effort that has driven that transformation, is striking. The result of more than sixteen years of active community participation and the infusion of millions of dollars of private capital, Chattanooga's successes include a plan for a twenty-two-mile-long river park greenway, six miles of which have already been completed, and a vision to expand it to regional greenway of seventy-five miles. Plans are under way for an "eco-industrial" park (see Chapter 5). Most important, Chattanooga's two-decade metamorphosis has infused its citizenry with pride and a greater awareness of nature and environmental principles.

## Ecological Infrastructure and Natural Capital

The ecology of sustainable places also assumes an understanding and appreciation of the topography, landscape, ecological conditions, and processes—the natural or ecological infrastructure—within which a city or community functions. Its wetlands, hillsides, shorelines, flood plains, riparian areas, forests, and habitats comprise its ecological wealth—natural capital that provides many local and regional benefits, and that should be understood and protected. These landscapes and ecological features provide many important benefits and functions.

One important way in which many communities and cities are understanding and protecting this ecological infrastructure and natural capital is through the development of systems of greenways and open space. Greenways may consist of many different types of land, from pristine wilderness to heavily used recreational land. Increasingly, communities are viewing the protection of greenways and open space as critical to ensuring the quality of life.

In many cities, rivers and waterfronts make up the core area of greenways. Atlanta has been working to establish a greenway along the Chattahoochee River. Washington, D.C.'s Rock Creek Park is an impressive greenway that winds throughout the city, providing easy access to areas and paths for biking and jogging. In Boston, the greenbelt along the Charles River provides a pleasant pedestrian path connecting Boston to Cambridge.

The protection of these lands can provide important natural services and benefits and, rather than being costly, can actually save community funds. Flood plains and other natural hazard areas are best left in an undeveloped state, and maintaining them in this way helps to keep people and property out of harm's way. Maintenance of natural wetland areas can provide important ecological benefits in the form of storm water management and flood water retention. Forested lands can help to improve air quality and moderate the urban heat island effect. And, as described earlier, preserving agricultural lands in and around a city can protect food production capabilities.

Evidence suggests, as well, that these features are valued highly by housing consumers, as property adjacent to parks and greenways is consistently more valuable than similar property elsewhere (Grove 1994) and may make developments more saleable (Beatley 1994a).

Recent reconsideration of the economic effects of restrictions on extractive uses in the American West (largely in response to fears about possible devastating effects of logging restrictions as a result of the spotted owl case) is instructive. Increasingly, it is being recognized that extractive industries such as timber, mining, and ranching do not account for as much economic activity and as many jobs as once thought, and that maintaining and protecting the natural environment may have a much greater positive economic effect (Power 1996b). Thus, preserving a region's ecological capital— its forests, mountains, rivers, and open lands—can be one of the most effective economic development strategies possible. This concept is explored further in Chapter 5.

## Natural Hazards and Community Resilience

One of the most important ways in which sustainable communities can achieve an ecological "fit" is by understanding the natural forces and hazards to which they are subject, and attempting to live and grow within them. Dramatic damage levels in recent years from hurricanes, floods, and other types of natural disasters suggest that some patterns of human settlement are not very sustainable. Our historic approach to natural hazards has been one of resisting and armoring against them. In the United States, this is especially evident in coastal areas, where the strategy is to construct seawalls, jetties, and other structures to resist the forces of nature rather than trying to understand them and live within their limits. An ecological view of sustainable place recognizes that events such as hurricanes, earthquakes, and floods are natural (though they may be exacerbated by human activities), and that only when we choose to build structures and place settlements in their paths do they become "hazards."

Sustainable communities seek first to avoid exposure of people and property to natural hazards. This means not building on floodplains, avoiding steep-slope and landslide-potential areas, and setting development back from high-erosion coastal zones.

The concept of sustainability also suggests that communities should look for opportunities to reduce exposure to hazards over time and to begin to retreat from high-risk locations. A number of cities and communities have succeeded in this effort. Tulsa, Oklahoma, is known for taking a more cautious path, one that to a large degree has involved the moving of people and property out of harm's way. Located along the Arkansas River, Tulsa has a history of vulnerability to floods. Especially in the 1970s and 1980s, the city experienced major flood events, with nine declared flood disasters in a fifteen-year period. Tulsa's general response to flooding extends back to the 1940s (the Army Corps of Engineers built levees in 1943), but it was not until the devastating floods of 1984 that the city began in earnest its effort to move people and homes out of the flood plain. In 1984, most of the flood damage occurred in east Tulsa, within the Mingo Creek watershed. During that year the city removed 284 homes; altogether, more than 900 homes have been moved out of the flood plain since the 1980s (Tulsa, Oklahoma, City of 1994; Patton 1993). These flood prone areas have now been converted to public open space (see Figure 4.2 for "before" and "after" views).

Tulsa has done more than simply relocate homes out of the floodplain, however. Its program of building community resilience is comprehensive and holistic, moving well beyond the employment of structural components to the general reduction of long-term flooding vulnerability. Among the other elements of its strategy are watershed-wide regulations on new development, a master drainage plan for the city, and a unique and stable funding source for storm water management in which each home and business in the watershed is assessed a monthly storm water fee as part of its utility bill. (Businesses are assessed based on the extent of their impervious surfaces.) This fee raises $8 million annually. The strategy also includes flood mitigation requirements that go beyond the minimum required under the National Flood Insurance Program, including "free boarding," the practice of requiring construction to be elevated, on fill or pilings, beyond what is mandated by the National Flood Insurance Program.

Most important, Tulsa's strategy involves a fundamentally different way of looking at floodplains and flood-prone areas. Under the new view, these areas are transformed from areas of danger and liability to resources that are part of the essential natural capital of the city and region. The cleared areas become locations for open space and recreation. Drainageways and maintenance roads along creekbeds have been opened up to the public as biking and hiking trails, and the city has been working on developing a city-wide trail system to which these would be connected (Patton 1993).

Another early pioneer in adopting a more sustainable strategy of enhancing community resilience is Soldiers Grove, Wisconsin, a community repeatedly devastated by flooding of the Kickapoo River. Eventually it chose

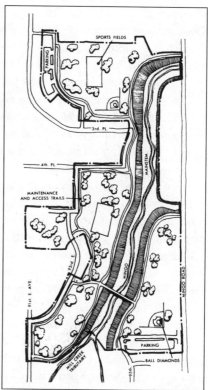

Figure 4.2 In 1984, the city of Tulsa, Oklahoma, moved 284 homes out of the Mingo Creek watershed. The aerial photograph at left was taken in 1974, ten years before the floods; the diagram at right shows the first phase of the buy-out area reuse plan. *Source:* City of Tulsa, Oklahoma.

to relocate its business district entirely out of the flood plain, while at the same time achieving a number of other sustainability objectives, including the use of solar energy (new businesses were required to obtain at least half of their energy from solar), life-cycle analysis of building materials, siting buildings and landscaping based on microsite analyses, and the mixing of housing into its downtown (Becker 1994).

The 1993 Midwest floods presented an unprecedented opportunity for redirecting development out of flood plains. The Clinton administration initiated perhaps the largest buyout-relocation program in modern history, directing a tremendous amount of federal resources toward the program and making relocation its mitigation priority. All told, some 9,000 structures will have been moved out of the flood plain.

At the same time, the Midwest floods provided opportunities to restore many of the natural functions of the Mississippi and Missouri Rivers. Though most levees were in fact rebuilt, several were not. The experience has also triggered a national debate about how best to address the flooding problem, with further calls for additional natural restoration and a further backing away from the structural philosophy of the past.

The need for resilience in the face of natural hazards and forces lends even greater support to arguments for protecting the natural environment. The protection of a robust, healthy ecosystem is often the most effective form of protection for people and property. In coastal environments, history has shown that preservation of the natural dune system acts as a natural form of seawall, and that people and development located behind a healthy dune and beach system will be much more resilient in the face of hurricanes and coastal storms. Similarly, wetlands serve as natural sponges, and preserving them represents an important hazard mitigation strategy.

The community of natural hazards professionals has begun to awaken to the potential of sustainability, and hazard mitigation and disaster redevelopment efforts are increasingly described under the rubric of sustainability. A number of recent examples can be cited that illustrate the increasing relevancy of sustainability to natural hazards and that show that these concepts are resonating positively with the natural hazards community. Following the disastrous Midwest floods, for instance, efforts to rethink redevelopment patterns were defined in terms of promoting more sustainable communities. A group calling itself the Midwest Working Group on Sustainable Redevelopment formed to encourage flood-damaged communities to think about more sustainable patterns of redevelopment and rebuilding. With U.S. Department of Energy funding, a conference was convened to explore possibilities, bringing together experts on various aspects of sustainability and community leaders from the region.

Several flooded communities took up the charge, in particular Valmeyer, Illinois, and Pattonsburg, Missouri. Valmeyer chose to relocate entirely out of the Mississippi flood plain and to create an essentially new town, designed and built, at least in part, based on sustainability principles and concepts. While there have been some positive results, including efforts to encourage energy conservation and solar and geothermal energy, in many respects the Valmeyer experience was a failure from a sustainability point of view. The resulting town looks very much like a conventional suburban development, heavily reliant on the auto, with few building or town design features that minimize resource consumption or otherwise reduce the ecological footprint of its residents. The town is clearly more sustainable from a flood exposure point of view (though it had never, before 1993, been flooded); in recreating itself, however, it chose to locate on an open site of forests and farmland that include possible habitat of the endangered Indiana bat and significant archeological ruins. While it is an understandable impulse to want to keep the community together as a whole, there is little question that the town's population could easily and more sustainably have been accommodated through infill in other existing towns in the region (and at a much lower cost to federal taxpayers.)

Pattonsburg, which also relocated completely outside the flood plain, represents a much more aggressive effort to incorporate sustainability concepts and technology into its redesign. The town even adopted a Charter of Sustainability (Fig. 4.3) to guide this redevelopment. The sustainable design features include new energy efficiency and resource conservation standards, a pedestrian-friendly and solar-oriented new street layout, the creation of a Sustainable Economic Development Council to encourage new sustainable local businesses, and development of a waste minimization policy for the town, among others. Pattonsburg also has an interesting plan to satisfy its electricity needs through conversion of hog manure to methane gas (the town is surrounded by hog farms and estimates that it needs the manure from only 16,000 hogs to satisfy the town's needs). A new town hall will be designed to incorporate passive and active solar energy and will be superinsulated. There is a plan to plant trees to serve as windbreaks from winter winds and to lesson noise from the highway.

Perhaps most interesting, though, and what the town itself describes as the centerpiece of its redevelopment plan, is a planned system of constructed wetlands and a natural storm water management system to treat urban runoff. Building on the existing riparian system, the town intends to create new wetlands adjacent to existing streams and convert several farm ponds to detention basins (Pattonsburg Sustainable Economic Development Council, undated). These green corridors will also be the basis for a network of recreational trails and wildlife habitat corridors. The system will take the place of a conventional storm water system and will result in lower downstream pollutant loads than for predevelopment agriculture. The natural storm water system is impressive in concept, and the town has received a sizable matching grant from the EPA to implement it. Through these types of measures, Pattonsburg has the possibility not only of moving its people and property out of harm's way, but of restoring and enhancing the environment, in effect reducing the ecological footprint from what it was in its previous site.

Yet even the case of Pattonsburg exhibits some troubling aspects. Like Valmeyer, Pattonsburg choose to relocate in an undeveloped area, a greenfield site, carving out a new town where before there had been only farm and forest land. Indeed, there were other existing towns in the region that

## Charter of Sustainability New Pattonsburg, Missouri

In accord with the decision to ensure our community's future by its relocation from the flood plain, we, the elected officials and contracted development professionals of Pattonsburg, Missouri, agree to uphold the following principles of sustainability. In doing so, we recognize our responsibility to plan for the needs of the present generation without compromising the ability of future generations to meet theirs. In good faith with the agencies and organizations supporting our relocation and redevelopment, we will strive to achieve these accepted objectives of sustainability in the areas of economics, ecology and community process.

### Objectives for a Sustainable Economy

To build a sustainable and sustaining economic system, providing equitably for our material needs and the needs of future generations, we agree to:

- Encourage local ownership by building skills and encouraging entrepreneurial innovation;
- In considering distant ownership, seek business people who have demonstrated good citizenship in their local communities;
- Build local capacity to support financing of sustainable economic activity;
- Consider the full environmental and social impacts of economic decisions;
- ecologically sensitive businesses;
- Encourage and give priority to businesses that add to the economic value of regional agricultural and other resources, instead of exporting unprocessed resources to be developed elsewhere;
- Capitalize on the economic opportunity presented by New Pattonsburg's proximity to an interstate highway, both as a connection to the transportation network and as a provider of access for new consumers to New Pattonsburg's marketplace.

### Objectives for a Sustainable Ecology

To build a sustainable and sustaining ecological system, providing equitably for a thriving human and natural community ourselves and for future generations, we agree to:

- Preserve the character and health of our natural environment, using and reusing the materials, energy and water we need as efficiently as possible and eliminating waste;
- Utilize clean, renewable resources extracted and processed within the community whenever possible;
- Preserve and expand the choices of present and future members of our community, providing information and design alternatives that encourage use of sustainable resources, technologies and methods suitable for our environment and culture.

### Objectives for a Sustainable Community Process

To build a sustainable and sustaining process that empowers all community members to participate in determining their present and future quality of life, we agree to:

- Provide full, accessible information and education on issues that affect the community to all members, including our children;
- Sponsor community gatherings, community based committees and other forums that solicit ideas and convictions of the people, encourage the exchange and development of new ideas and promote full and diverse participation in decision making;
- Seek consensus within the community to guide the work of leaders and professionals charged with the responsibility

Figure 4.3 The Charter of Sustainability for New Pattonsburg, Missouri.
*Source:* Pattonsburg Sustainable Economic Development Council.

could have accommodated the people and growth from old Pattonsburg (and one town whose mayor actually went so far as to inquire about the possibility). Nevertheless, Pattonsburg may well end up being a demonstration sustainable small town, showing what is possible to achieve in the process of seeking higher ground.

## Ecosystems and Bioregions

The ecological view of sustainable places recognizes that urban areas are embedded in larger ecosystems. In recent years considerable attention has been given to the concept of ecosystem management, as well as a growing consensus that this should be the organizing paradigm for resource management activities. Increasingly, cities and towns must understand and connect with the larger ecological context in which they are situated, assuming an ecosystem perspective when making decisions about land conservation, recreation, and placement of new development.

David Crockett, the city council member most often recognized as one of the key figures behind Chattanooga's renaissance, describes the importance of Chattanooga's sense of place as a special scenic area, one of the most biologically diverse temperate regions in the country, "where the mountains meet the cotton." "The key elements in talking about Chattanooga's history," he explains, "always start with what God made and with what was here (personal communication 1995)." Crockett's words define the very essence of the bioregional perspective—the ability to view one's community as inhabiting a larger ecological community organized around natural processes.

There are a number of examples of efforts to assume ecosystemic or bioregional perspectives. The Portland, Oregon, Metropolitan Greenspaces Program is one such example. Spearheaded by the Portland Metropolitan Service District ("Metro"), it has involved a comprehensive analysis and mapping of the region's natural areas and greenspaces through the use of aerial photography, on-site survey data, and classification of natural areas, all entered into a GIS database (Poracsky and Houck 1994). The analysis covers not only the Oregon portions of the region, but land in Washington state as well. The ultimate goal is to create a regional system of protected areas, and acquisition of lands has already begun as a result of the approval of a $135 million regional bond measure to fund open space acquisition. The regional system also yields a comprehensive picture of the existing natural systems and biodiversity of the region, which can be invaluable in regional and local planning. The Greenspaces Program experience also shows the advantages of regional, cooperative strategies—local communities have begun to work toward a common protection goal or vision for the region and have already begun to incorporate the data and maps from the program into their own local plans and planning decision making (Poracsky and Houck 1994).

Another important example is the development of a regional habitat conservation plan near Austin, Texas. The plan, known as the Balcones Canyonlands Conservation Plan (BCCP), addresses a sensitive area to the west and northwest of the city. This is an area of canyons, ridgetops, and plateaus that is home to a number of endangered species, including two species of migratory songbird, several species of salamanders, rare plants, and a number of unique, cave-adapted invertebrates that live in the subterranean limestone habitats of the Texas Hill Country. Beginning in the late 1980s, a collaborative community process, including development and conservation interests, worked on developing an acceptable plan for conserving the habitat and natural features while also allowing development to take place. Extensive regional-scale analysis of the habitat was conducted using remotely sensed data and GIS technology. The process of designing a system of protected areas also sought to build onto the existing system of parks and protected lands in the area (including, for instance, lands that could not be developed under Austin's comprehensive watersheds ordinance). The plan also took a watersheds, or ecosystem, approach, attempting to protect larger regional ecological functions and conditions.

The final plan, recently approved by the U.S. Fish & Wildlife Service, calls for the creation of a regional preserve system that will protect some 30,000 acres of land in six primary preserve units that range in size from 400 acres to more than 9,000 acres. The Balcones Canyonlands National Wildlife Reserve is also a direct result of this planning process and will itself be 35,000 acres in size. Ultimately, about 70,000 acres of natural lands will be set aside, making it one of the largest land acquisition programs in an urban area ever. The BCCP is an admirable effort in many respects. It takes a regional, ecosystem approach to habitat protection and considers the habitat needs of multiple species (including candidate species). It seeks to dovetail habitat conservation with other important local objectives, including water quality and open space preservation. It also involves a collaborative partnership between groups that are often adversarial. (See Fig. 4.4 for a map of Balcones Canyonlands Reserve.)

Nevertheless, the Balcones Canyonlands approach also illustrates the inherent difficulties in effectively undertaking such broad-scale efforts. The plan has been criticized by some in the environmental community, for instance, as not protecting enough land and resulting in a highly fragmented system of habitat (see Beatley 1994c). The plan also ended up not being as

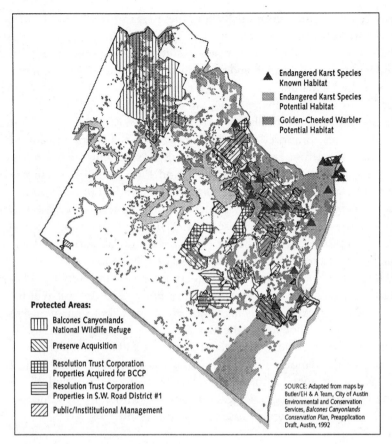

Endangered Karst Species
Known Habitat

Endangered Karst Species
Potential Habitat

Golden-Cheeked Warbler
Potential Habitat

**Protected Areas:**

Balcones Canyonlands
National Wildlife Refuge

Preserve Acquisition

Resolution Trust Corporation
Properties Acquired for BCCP

Resolution Trust Corporation
Properties in S.W. Road District #1

Public/Instititutional Management

SOURCE: Adapted from maps by
Butler/EH & A Team, City of Austin
Environmental and Conservation
Services, *Balcones Canyonlands
Conservation Plan*, Preapplication
Draft, Austin, 1992

**Figure 4.4** The Balcones Canyonlands Wildlife Reserve in Austin, Texas. *Source:* Lincoln Institute of Land Policy, 1995.

ecosystemic and regional in scale as hoped. (One reason was that an important county withdrew from the process.) Finally, the plan has been criticized for opening up some 200,000 acres of land for development characterized by low-density sprawl. This example also illustrates just how expensive such ecosystem conservation strategies can be, with the entire program ultimately costing about $170 million.

In some ways, an even bolder program—and one that covers a much larger area and many jurisdictions—is presented in the Third Regional Plan for the New York metropolitan region. The plan's "greensward" campaign presents an ambitious vision for a regional, multistate system of natural areas and greenspace. The goals of such a regional system are many, but key purposes are to protect the region's "environmental infrastructure" (and the many, resource and recreational values these areas provide) and to help induce a more sustainable pattern of development (i.e., to place limits on urban expansion). The system would result in, among other things, an extensive network of bicycle and walking trails that "directly reconnects the cities to the big natural systems at the water's edge or just beyond the urban core" (Yaro and Hiss 1996, p. 88).

The campaign specifically proposes the creation of a system of eleven regional reserves comprised of, and tying together, the region's major estuaries, rivers, waterfront areas, mountains (e.g., the Catskills), and forests (e.g., the New Jersey Pinelands, the Long Island Pine Barrens). These reserves range in size from 100,000 to 3 million acres. Building upon existing parks and protected areas, additional land acquisition appears to be the key implementation strategy, though use of other measures (regulation and TDR) is also envisioned, with a heavy emphasis on collaboration and alliance building to bring it about (Yaro and Hiss 1996).

The plan, however, is an advisory document—and the Regional Plan Association, which produced it, an advisory body. Ultimately, it will require strong advocacy and convincing a variety of agencies to pursue its vision. But as a visionary document, the plan accomplishes some important things: it explicitly acknowledges the reliance of cities and city populations on the ecology of the region and the vast ecological services provided by it (from drinking water supplies to food production to recreation) and, like Portland's Greenspaces Program, creates a template through which more coordinated regional, ecosystem-based action can occur.

## Green City Management and Environmentally Sustainable Development

The idea of sustainable place also implies major changes in how our existing communities are operated and managed, and in how public investment policies and decisions should be made in the future. Such changes might include creating more aggressive recycling and waste reduction programs, stepping up energy conservation and solar retrofit efforts, promoting water conservation and pricing policies that reflect actual environmental costs, developing procurement and purchasing policies aimed at reducing waste, and encouraging the use of more sustainable products.

Significant strides can also be made in influencing how a city or community builds, operates, and manages the buildings and lands it typically owns (from school buildings to public parks to the town hall). Green city management requires, for example, that all city buildings strive to reduce energy consumption. Toronto has established an Energy Efficiency Office that has been engaged in retrofitting some twenty buildings, including its city hall, to be more energy-efficient (White 1994). Improvements in the efficiency of the city's street-lighting system will also be undertaken, and energy audits of all city buildings are being prepared. Local parks and open spaces can also be maintained in more natural and sustainable ways. Some localities, for instance, have banned the use of pesticides in all public parks, grounds, and facilities.

Moreover, cities must be demanding clients when it comes to the design and construction of public facilities, insisting on sustainable designs and negotiating architectural and design fees based explicitly on the performance of the buildings and facilities over the long run. Each public building represents an important practical and symbolic example of what can and should be done to reduce the ecological footprint of the community.

Communities can seek creative ways of incorporating sustainable practices wherever and whenever they can—for instance, by looking at city rooftops as potential locations for photovoltaics and solar collectors. One interesting recent example of this can be seen in San Marino, California, just designated by California Edison as a "solar neighborhood." There, a portion of the grounds of the city's main library has been converted into a grid-connected solar farm, generating enough power to serve the energy needs of 1,000 households.

Adopting a policy of sustainable landscapes is another management practice that can provide opportunities to restore the landscape, reduce the stream of pollutants and chemicals entering the community, and also save money. Ahern and Boughton provide one of the best definitions of *sustainable landscapes* as

> . . . those that exist with a minimum of non-solar inputs of energy, materials and labor. They are productive landscapes in that they accumulate more organic matter than they consume. They provide forage and habitat for wildlife species. They are regionally appropriate, supportive of the native biodiversity of plants and animals in their locale. Finally, sustainable landscapes are responsive to human needs. They foster human understanding of the natural history and natural processes of a place. They also provide delight and address functional needs; if they do not, they enjoy limited support, especially in urban areas (Ahern and Boughton 1994, p. 173).

There are many places where conventional landscaping can be replaced with sustainable landscapes, from the grounds of libraries and other public buildings to parks and public picnic areas and even to public golf courses, among many others. Ahern and Boughton advocate the increased used of "wildflower meadows" as a clear form of sustainable landscape. One example of the potential here can be seen in the efforts to convert some corporate office parks in the Midwest (perhaps not a very sustainable land use in the first place) back to natural tall-grass prairies. In addition to aesthetic and ecological benefits, the cost savings are significant: maintenance costs are estimated to be about one-tenth the costs for a conventional lawn and installation about one-third the cost (Malin 1995).

The procurement policies of localities, particularly larger ones, have the potential for exerting tremendous positive influence in the direction of sustainable practices. A number of communities have now adopted such practices, governing a variety of types of purchases and acquisitions. Toronto, for instance, has adopted a procurement policy that sets a high fuel efficiency standard (of 5.2 liters per 100 km) for its fleet of city vehicles (White 1994).

A number of communities are now regularly asking suppliers and contractors about their environmental standards and practices and requiring adherence to some form of environmental management regulation (such as the ISO 14001). In many places, suppliers are now regularly required to fill out an extensive questionnaire or checklist that asks about these practices and standards. These standards should be considered minimum ones, and local governments should not be timid in stipulating stronger conditions. As is required in some cities, each major acquisition or purchase should be accompanied by an environmental impact analysis.

How a community manages its workforce is important as well. Localities can seek to minimize, for example, employees' transportation impacts (energy consumption, air pollution). Strategies can include initiating rideshare programs, and auto commuting can be discouraged by curtailing mileage and parking benefits and by providing free or discounted public transit passes. Some localities assist employees in finding housing closer to work, reducing both commuting time and the likely personal stresses that accompany that process.

Local utilities, especially those fully or partially owned by municipalities, can also be operated with greater priority placed on sustainability. Local electric companies can give greater attention to renewable energy sources. Green pricing programs are currently in use in several states and can take several forms. These programs provide utility customers with the option of selecting a package of green power sources—for example, power generated from renewable sources such as wind, solar, biomass, or geothermal. There is often an additional per-kilowatt-hour premium charged, but customers are protected from future (fossil fuel) rate increases (Swezey 1997). Customers may also be given the opportunity to contribute to the underwriting of a specific renewable energy project (e.g., the construction of a solar or wind park) or to a fund dedicated to expediting the development of renewable energy sources. Market research suggests that consumers are concerned and very much desire that their energy sources are renewable and sustainable (Shirley 1997).

Utility rate structures—for the provision of electricity, water, and other services—can be modified to promote conservation and more efficient use and reflect more accurately the full environmental and other costs associated with their supply. Some local power companies employ a form of linear time-variable electric charges. Such a system charges consumers by the time of day as well as the amount of usage, with higher prices for consumption during peak hours and lower prices for off-peak times. Such systems can serve to reduce overall demand and help consumers become more conscious of their overall energy consumption patterns. Similar pricing policies can be employed for water (e.g., San Jose, California, offers rebates and price reductions for water conservation measures) and wastewater.

At the very heart of the idea of green city management is the notion that cities and towns can and must begin to take more direct responsibility for the environmental implications of their many actions and policies. Important to assuming this responsibility is more explicitly understanding the nature and magnitude of these impacts, and there are a number of analytic tools and techniques that communities can utilize in doing this. Environmental auditing (something begun by businesses in the United States concerned with their legal liabilities under environmental laws) is increasingly employed by local governments and refers to a package of approaches directed toward understanding the environmental ramifications of a government's actions, programs, or policies. Such audits, sometimes called eco-audits, can be done for specific policy decisions (e.g., which type of office furniture to purchase), for specific sectors (e.g., for energy, land use, procurement), or more comprehensively for a city's entire operation.

A common initial step in the process (sometimes referred to as the external audit) is the preparation of a state-of-the-environment report for the city, which identifies environmental conditions and trends in the community. The second part of the audit typically includes a review of the internal practices of the locality (e.g., the impacts of its procurement practices, energy consumption of its buildings, the number of miles traveled by city employees, the amount of solid waste generated by city agencies and offices), a review of the impacts of the community's existing policy framework, and an assessment of the ability of the existing management system to take into account and address these impacts. Such audits, moreover, can be used as a way to identify measures for change—ways that a city or town can do things differently, or purchase a different product, to reduce or eliminate various impacts. (For a more detailed discussion of the components of an eco-audit and the process and methodology of environmental auditing generally, see Barton and Bruder, 1995.) Supporters of environmental auditing argue that the technique should not be seen as a one-time assessment, but as a continuous, ongoing process.

Life-cycle analysis (LCA) is one way in which the full environmental implications of a decision can be assessed and is typically an important element of an environmental audit. It "involves carrying out an inventory of the main impacts associated with the manufacture, use and disposal of a product, from the mining of the raw materials and energy used in its production and distribution, through to its use, possible re-use or recycling, and eventual disposal." (Stead 1995, p. 201). Any significant purchase made by a community should include an LCA, where possible, to determine the full environmental impacts of a purchased product or service over its entire lifetime. While an LCA can end up being complex, and the methodologies are still being developed, it provides a sensible technique for communities to evaluate the full, long-term ecological implications of their various policies and decisions.

One promising green city management practice is the concept of "environmental budgeting." The key idea here is that just as a city council must periodically prepare, adopt, and implement a financial budget, so also should it prepare a budget concerning its environmental spending. An environmental budget for a community would identify a range of environmental problem areas (e.g., air pollution), establish baseline indicators, and set targets for these areas. It would then project the "spending" (i.e., generation of new pollution) and the "revenue" (i.e., reductions in pollution from existing sources) necessary to reach the target. Politicians and elected officials can, through such a process, would be held accountable for ensuring that the budget is "balanced" and that ecological spending does not lead to unacceptable budget deficits (i.e., exceeding allowable limits).

Existing resource stocks in a community (e.g., forests, biodiversity) can also be accounted for in the budgeting process in the form of an assets summary (Erdmenger et al. 1997). Reductions in these assets (e.g., loss of habitat) can in turn be counted as environmental spending. While this methodology is currently in the experimental stage, it holds promise as a way to take into account in a comprehensive fashion a community's ecological assets and its annual (or semiannual) environmental spending, and to ensure that officials make clear commitments and are held accountable when those commitments fail to be met.

These are just a few ideas that may be useful in helping a community assess the environmental impacts of its actions and policies and set tangible goals and targets for the future. The topic of community benchmarks and indicators is discussed in Chapter 7.

## Sustainable Neighborhoods and Eco-Developments

Some of the most interesting and innovative green community building is occurring at the project or neighborhood level. While any single development or neighborhood-level initiative will not by itself substantially transform a larger city or landscape into a sustainable or green one, the cumulative implications of these designs are considerable. Again, the notion of creating sustainable places is one of nested scale—the concept that important and necessary work at creating more sustainable places can and must occur at a number of geographical levels.

One extremely impressive project that has existed long enough to exhibit its desirability and worth is Village Homes in Davis, California. It was conceived and built by town planner Michael Corbett and his wife Judy Corbett. Begun in the mid-1970s, this development consists of 220 individual homes and 20 apartments located on about 60 acres. The homes are oriented along a series of interlocking natural "fingers" of green, with homes grouped in clusters of eight, each cluster sharing a common open area (Fig. 4.5). Most homes are relatively small in size, from 800 to 1,800 square feet. The roads serving the development are narrow (twenty to twenty-four feet wide) and tree-lined. All homes are oriented to the south, to allow use of solar energy, and front on the greenspaces of the development. Solar energy is utilized in several ways: the structures are designed with overhangs, which allow winter sun to come in but provide shading in the summer (Fig. 4.6); the thermal mass of the buildings allows heat to be captured during the day and gradually dissipated in the evening; the homes are well-insulated and most utilize solar hot water heaters (Center for Livable Communities 1995b; Browning 1991).

The development contains a great deal of greenspace. In addition to the walking and biking paths, there are two "village greens," a community garden, orchards, and vineyards. "Edible landscaping" (fruit-producing trees and shrubs) is interspersed throughout. In the center of the open space "fingers" are natural swales (and several retention ponds) that make up the project's drainage system (Fig. 4.7). No traditional storm drains were installed, and lots are graded to drain away from the streets and into the swales (Browning 1991). There has been no flooding of streets or homes in the twenty years since the project was built. The project also includes a solar-heated

**Figure 4.5** Aerial photograph of a segment of Village Homes, Davis, California. *Source:* Michael N. Corbett.

**Figure 4.6** A solar home at Village Homes, Davis, California. *Source:* Michael N. Corbett.

community center and daycare, as well as a commercial building including offices, a dance studio, and a café.

The results of the Village Homes experiment are very impressive. Energy consumption is substantially lower in these homes (one-third to one half of a normal Davis home), drainage is handled through the ecological infrastructure of the development, residents can easily get around on bike and by foot, the environment is delightfully lush and green (almost junglelike in spots), and residents are more likely to know their neighbors here than in other developments. There is a definite sense of community and, as a result, the crime rate is lower. And the project has been successful from a market perspective, since the neighborhood is seen as a very desirable one. (Though this may have the negative effect of making these areas not very affordable: prices of the homes have risen to $11.00 per square foot more expensive than other homes in Davis, when originally they were no more expensive.)

Many of the recent New Urbanism development projects have green components in their designs. Their attempts to deemphasize the automobile, to allow walkability and the mixing and integration of uses, and to pro-

Figure 4.7 The drainage system at Village Homes relies on natural swales and retention ponds. *Source:* Michael N. Corbett.

vide access to parks and greenspaces certainly represent significant improvements over contemporary suburban-style development. Positive examples include Seaside, Florida (the first of these projects), and Kentlands, Maryland (both designed by Plater-Zyberk and Duany), Laguna West in Sacramento, California (designed by Calthorpe), and Playa Vista in Los Angeles (designed by Moule and Polysoides et al.), among others.

Many of these projects have received critical acclaim for their architecture and planning. Laguna West, which has received considerable attention in the planning and design communities, includes many of the key elements of neo-traditional design. Marketed as an "old-fashioned community," it will eventually accommodate 3,000 units on 1,000 acres, organized around a 100-acre town center, that includes a town green, town hall, library, daycare, and retail shops. The homes are to be built to a design code that requires front porches and garages behind or on the side of residential structures. Granny flat apartments are also to be permitted. The design is intended to be green, with some 15,000 trees to be planted and the innovative idea of placing tree wells interspersed along the main boulevards radiating out from the town center. The tree wells serve several functions in Calthorpe's design, including slowing traffic and eventually resulting in a fuller tree canopy to cover (and cool) the streets (Calthorpe 1993).

Laguna West, though, is emblematic in many ways of the limitations of the New Urbanist projects. While design features often include trees and greenery, environmental considerations typically are not prominent in these projects. The homes being built in Laguna West, for example, reflect little concern for green design: home lots were not platted to protect solar access, and the town hall, which was intended to incorporate passive solar, did not do so because it proved too expensive. And despite the New Urbanists' stated goal of creating less auto-dependent communities, very often these developments, many of which are located in exurban locations, are not accessible via public transit. Laguna West is touted as a transit-oriented development, yet there is not yet a train stop (though it is hoped there will be), and the current density and mix of uses there virtually require residents to depend on the automobile for almost all their needs, including getting to work each day (Fig. 4.8). Even internally, it is not clear that these projects succeed at creating pedestrian-friendly places. Laguna West elicits the feeling of being in a conventional suburban tract housing development. The highly touted design features, such as porches and side garages, seem almost "gimmicky" and do not offer an antidote to the prevailing auto orientation of the residents living there so far. (In fairness, the project has not been completed yet, and it should be noted that several developers have veered from Calthorpe's original design guidelines.)

**Figure 4.8** At Laguna West, the density of homes and mix of uses necessitate a heavy dependence on the automobile.

Several of the projects in the neo-traditional genre do, however, exhibit a significant green orientation and are worthy of highlighting. One of the more interesting is Prairie Crossing, north of Chicago in Grayslake, Illinois. This project will include 350 free-standing homes on about 700 acres (Fig. 4.9). Several important environmental design aspects can be noted. Indeed, of the project's stated "Guiding Principles," environmental protection and enhancement is the first listed (Fig. 4.10). One feature is the conservation of open space. The homes will be clustered, with some 60 percent of the site left in prairie and wetlands and others in cultivated agriculture. Some 150 acres will remain in active farming, with a small piece of this used as a "subscription organic farm" (also referred to as the "community-supported vegetable garden"). This is one of the more interesting features of the project and has already been in operation for four years. For an annual fee of $400, shareholders of the garden receive a weekly basket of fresh organic vegetables and fruit grown by the community's resident farmers and summer interns. This distribution lasts throughout the growing season, usually twenty weeks. Over a hundred families are shareholders, many not yet even living in the development.

In addition to the community-supported garden, Prairie Crossing offers

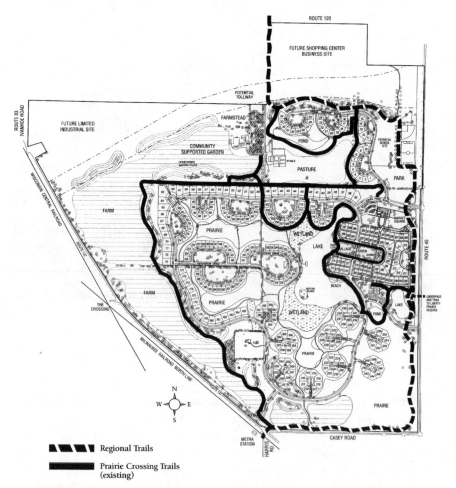

**Figure 4.9** Site plan for Prairie Crossing, Grayslake, Illinois. *Source:* Prairie Crossing.

two other models for agriculture on the metropolitan fringe. People who wish to grow their own agriculture can rent plots in the community garden, and Prairie Crossing also hosts a Friday evening organic farmers' market, the first in the Chicago area.

The homes are being designed and built to minimize energy consumption; as just one example, the need for air conditioning has been reduced by allowing cross-breezes and incorporating extra insulation. Prairie Crossing is the first community in the nation to adopt Building America, a unique partnership between the residential home-building industry and the U.S. Department of Energy designed to develop new technologies for energy conservation. Other features of Prairie Crossing include the development of

> **Guiding Principles For Prairie Crossing**
>
> Prairie Crossing is a new community dedicated to conservation of the environment. The following ten important principles guide this innovative "conservation community."
>
> 1. Environmental protection and enhancement.
> 2. A healthy lifestyle.
> 3. A sense of place.
> 4. A sense of community.
> 5. Economic and racial diversity.
> 6. Convenient and efficient transportation.
> 7. Energy conservation.
> 8. Lifelong learning and education.
> 9. Aesthetic design and high-quality construction.
> 10. Economic viability.

**Figure 4.10** Guiding Principles for Prairie Crossing.
*Source:* Prairie Crossing.

ten miles of walking trails (which will connect with the Liberty Prairie Reserve), a village green, a market square (to include several historic buildings that have been saved), a twenty-two–acre lake, and homes with porches and architectural designs that are similar to homes found in Midwest farming communities (Shaw Homes, Inc. 1995, undated; Kent 1994).

Following the devastating effects of Hurricane Andrew in Florida, there were a number of efforts to rethink development patterns there. The community conducted a series of design charrettes (a structured process for eliciting creative design ideas for a site or community), and one of the more important of these resulted in an impressive affordable housing project near Homestead that is being built by Habitat for Humanity. Called Jordan Commons, the project reflects a new sense among Habitat for Humanity officials that their efforts should be focused on creating viable and sustainable neighborhoods, rather than on building individual housing units. The project is based on four "community-building principles: physical design, services for families, environmental sustainability, and community self-sufficiency" (Habitat for Humanity, undated, p. 1). The project will incorporate a number of impressive environmental features, including: white reflective metal roofs (donated by the American Iron and Steel Institute), which will reduce air-conditioning costs, and other energy conservation features (resulting in a 38 to 48 percent overall reduction in energy use); low-volume toilets and low-flow showerheads; water reuse and recycling; use of landscaping to shade buildings; and use of concrete streets instead of asphalt to reduce ambient heat levels (part of a "cool communities" demonstration project). Along with these environmental measures, the project seeks to build community, address social needs, and foster a sense of self-governance. Buildings are also constructed with steel frames that should perform much better in the next hurricane. Clearly, Habitat sees Jordan Commons as a model effort: "A terrible tragedy may yet promise a brighter future. Hurricane Andrew's lasting legacy might indeed be a major and positive contribution to the debate about how best to help the poor help themselves" (Habitat for Humanity, undated).

One of the most impressive eco-developments planned in recent years is a project called Haymount, located outside Fredricksburg, Virginia. When the project, sited on more than 1,600 acres, is complete, it will approximate a small town of 4,000 housing units. The lead designers were Andres Duany and Elizabeth Plater-Zyberk, and the project design clearly has the marks of a neo-traditional community, making Haymount perhaps the most ecologically grounded New Urbanist development. The project's developer and inspiration, John Clark, has ensured that the design is holistic, taking into account an amazing number of environmental and social features. Environmentally, a number of impressive design elements are included. The developed uses in the town are clustered on 32 percent of the site, leaving the remainder in wetlands, forests, and other natural uses. An extensive natural inventory of the site was conducted, and the habitat needs of a number of sensitive species were identified; special efforts will be made to protect and enhance these habitats (e.g., a management plan was prepared for an American bald eagle found on the site). Other environmental features include: protection of wildlife corridors; the planting of 50,000 trees in the developed portion of the site; storm water management through the creation of new wetlands ("biotechnical storm water control measures"); restrictions on the use of pesticides and fertilizers; a variety of nonpoint source best-management practices (e.g., use of porous pavement); a special shallow vertical well design for groundwater intake; an integrated pest management program; and an advanced wastewater treatment system, which "combines sequence batch technology, advanced tertiary treatment and constructed wetlands to produce discharge water cleaner than that which is withdrawn from the river" (Clark, Payton, and Tice, undated, p. 3).

The plan also envisions an organic farm to provide residents of the county with sustainably grown products, as well as a farmers' market. Codes regulating development in the project will also stipulate energy performance, the use of healthy building materials, and landscaping. Construction debris is to be recycled. Buildings are to be designed so that they can be adapted to different uses at a later time.

The town is designed around a linked-grid system that incorporates mixed uses and walkable and bikable streets. A shuttle bus system that would connect to the Virginia Railway Express—a commuter train line serving Washington, D.C.—is also planned. (An estimated half of daily work trips will be accommodated in this way.) Commuting will also be reduced through the promotion of local jobs (with a goal of 1.2 jobs per household) and telecommuting.

One of the most interesting features reflecting the holistic design of this project is a plan to promote more sustainable businesses in the community. As Clark et al. describe it:

> Perhaps the most far-reaching environmental component of the project is the sustainability component being developed. Using sophisticated ecologic and economic modeling developed by the management team, the flow of resources and transactions among all of the major economics sectors and commodity groups will be evaluated. This will include not only direct effects (for example, the impact of healthy building materials), but indirect ones as well (including household expenditures). With the size of Haymount's economic contribution as a powerful leverage, the team will work with suppliers and other businesses to effect environmentally responsible voluntary agreements, and identify funding sources to assist businesses in the region to meet strict environmental standards (Clark, Payton, and Tice, undated, p. 8).

Haymount has also been designed with affordability in mind, accommodating a range of housing types, from small apartments (starting at just 440 square feet in size) to townhouses to single-family detached units, with a corresponding range in price. A community land trust established by the developer will also help to provide housing in other parts of the county.

Other elements of the design include parks and civic spaces (including a large riverfront park), schools, a college, and churches. In an interesting move (some believe, cynically, to win local support for the project), Clark offered free building sites for any churches interested in locating in Haymount, and a number have chosen to do so.

In theory, at least, Haymount is an admirable and impressive effort at planning a sustainable community—it goes well beyond the neo-traditional mold and represents a much more holistic approach to development design. It also provides an example of a development that explicitly looks beyond its borders and understands that broader environmental (and social) obligations exist.

The idea of "eco-villages" is also beginning to find an application in the United States. While currently only a handful of such projects have been developed, they represent another possible ecodevelopment model. The eco-village idea is quite similar in many respects to cohousing, discussed in Chapter 3. Unlike most conventional housing developments, eco-villages employ a collective decision-making process, in which a group of individuals and families come together to plan jointly what is essentially a new community or neighborhood. The common design features include clustered housing, a common house, and the setting aside of a large portion of the site in open or natural land. Environmental features usually include the use of solar energy, energy conservation, development of renewable energy sources (e.g., wind), the use of open lands for organic gardens, orchards, or wildlife habitat, and innovative wastewater treatment. Only a few eco-villages have been developed in the United States. One of the first is Ecovillage Ithaca. This project eventually calls for a six- to eight-neighborhood community, with each neighborhood containing fifteen to twenty homes (Baker 1996). Construction on the project began in 1995, and, as Baker describes it, the community has been able to keep costs down and incorporate many sustainability features:

> The first neighborhood, one of five, was planned to include fifteen duplex housing units. These range in price from $80,000 to $133,000, including the cost of the shared land and facilities. Each is superinsulated, incorporates environmentally sensitive systems and passive solar utilization, and has 14 foot south-facing windows. The cluster design has limited the impact of the units on the land, incorporating such strategies as shared parking lots instead of driveways, footpaths instead of streets, and shared orchards and gardens instead of individually owned lawns. Almost 150 acres have been devoted as open space to gardens, fish ponds and wetlands. Now two acres of organic farm are in place. The common house will include eight offices with already established businesses—a software company, a communications consultant, an agriculture business, an energy conservation consultant, and a therapist. The development seems to meet everyone's needs. (Baker 1996, pp. 31–32).

This project met with many obstacles along the way, especially bumping up against the upfront costs of some of the environmental technology (e.g., photovoltaics and ground source heat pumps) and health department and zoning regulations (the latter were overcome by designating the community as a special land use district, which allowed a number of deviations). Most of the eco-village projects have been sited in exurban or relatively nonurban environments, and one challenge in the future will be to conceive of how this model might work in more urban contexts.

Other important eco-developments are located in resort or recreation-oriented communities. In the U.S. Virgin Islands, developer Stanley Selengut has pioneered the concept of low-impact, sustainable tourist development. His 1974 development Maho Bay, on St. John Island, was his first experiment, consisting of small, canvas-tent cottages connected by a raised walkway system, with virtually no disturbance of the existing land and vegetation. His more recent project, Harmony, takes an even more holistic approach, with units (organized in clusters along a raised walkway system) constructed from recycled materials (e.g., carpet made from recycled plastic soda bottles and wallboard from recycled newspaper) and electricity for the units provided entirely through solar and wind power. The project is entirely "off the grid." Natural air conditioning is provided through a "wind scoop" in the roofs of the units. Water is provided from rainwater collected in a cistern, and wastewater is recycled and used to irrigate vegetation (Frank 1995). While staying in such accommodations may not be for everyone, these projects illustrate that many forms of resort development could be designed and built with significantly less impact on the natural environment. Selengut claims that the costs of building such units may actually be less than costs for conventional construction (e.g., the power tools used to build it were powered by solar energy).

Despite the admirable environmental features of many of these projects, they have fundamental flaws in their sustainability. The density of development in Prairie Crossing is quite low and consists entirely of single-family homes. Prairie Crossing is forty miles from Chicago, requiring auto commuting, although there are plans to construct train stations to allow rail commuting. Haymount raises similar commuting concerns; furthermore, it lies along the banks of one of the more pristine and environmentally significant rivers on the United States East Coast (prompting the Chesapeake Bay Foundation to oppose the project, calling it "the right development, in the wrong place"). There are also concerns about the social diversity and affordability of these projects. Despite the vision of making communities more affordable, the realities are often quite different. Seaside, for instance, is neither affordable nor particularly socially or economically diverse in terms of its residents. Haymount is admirable in its explicit concern for affordability, but it remains to be seen if this goal can be realized.

Despite their limitations—and it must be emphasized that there are few development projects that meet all of the criteria of sustainability—these projects are vast improvements over conventional development patterns. Each project has a number of innovative features worthy of emulation, and considerable progress toward sustainability would be made if even some of these ideas found their way into conventional development practices.

The limitations of many of these projects highlight the inherent difficulty of effectively bringing about many of the green and ecological sustainability qualities we wish to promote. These must ideally complement and occur within regional strategies for providing transportation and public transit investments, open space and habitat conservation, housing affordability, etc. It makes little sense to spend time and energy designing a development around transit accessibility if the necessary transit investments have not or will not occur—witness the example of Kentlands, where an otherwise walkable community is situated in a sea of conventional suburbia, with no direct access to public transit. It makes little sense to plan extensive bike paths within a project if they do not connect with a larger system of bike trails and bikeways that permit use of bikes as a practical mode of transportation.

To one degree or another, these green developments and eco-projects face substantial obstacles, and existing development codes and requirements typically do not encourage these types of designs, and in fact often make them quite difficult. Obtaining local approval for narrow streets, for example, is often a problem, frequently due to concerns about access by fire and emergency vehicles. In Village Homes the developer had to incorporate a three-foot easement on each side of the streets to protect emergency access (with no buildings or vegetation higher than six inches allowed in this area). In addition, the city was skeptical about the efficacy of the project's natural drainage system and required the developer to put up a special guarantee bond. (Peter Calthorpe tells the story of having to convince local officials that his plan for narrow streets and placement of tree wells in the streets in Laguna West would indeed allow for adequate emergency vehicle access. He set up a demonstration, hiring fire trucks to simulate an emergency response, and then videotaped the performance.) And the alleyways behind residential structures, a key characteristic of neo-traditional designs, often raise objections because of concerns about security and crime.

## Green Architecture and Sustainable Building

The ecological place is also one in which efforts are made at all levels to minimize the environmental and other impacts of buildings. There is no question that many of the ways in which we live unsustainably are directly tied to the design and construction of homes, businesses, and built structures of all types. As noted in Chapter 1, the construction and operation of buildings account for an astounding 40 percent of the materials entering the world's economy and one-third of the global energy consumption (Worldwatch Institute 1995). How we design and build our homes, offices, and public structures will have a substantial impact on the ultimate ecological footprint of the community. As Barnett and Browning note, "The biggest 'guzzlers' in America are not cars but homes":

> In 1990, for example, American households consumed $110 billion worth of energy. As houses consume lumber, energy and other resources, they excrete wastes. The average household now produces each year about 3500 pounds of garbage, 450,000 gallons of wastewater, and 25,000 pounds of $CO_2$ along with smaller amounts of $SO_2$, $NO_x$, and heavy metals (Barnett and Browning 1995, p. 4).

In addition to the energy used to heat and cool a home or building once it is constructed, it is also important to consider the "embodied energy," or the energy used to produce the building's materials and to assemble them. This energy can be substantial and can represent a number of years' worth of annual heating and cooling costs (the equivalent of almost eighteen years in the case of an energy-efficient Vancouver home; Malin 1993). Sustainable buildings seek to minimize embodied energy, either in the selection of materials or in the design of the structure (e.g., reducing the size of a structure through careful design). Designing buildings so that they can be reused or recycled later will also reduce embodied energy and other environmental impacts. For this reason, embodied energy is also a factor in making a case for the preservation of historic buildings.

There has been a considerable awakening within the architectural community to the need to design and build in more environmentally benign ways. The American Institute of Architects (AIA) has been a leader in addressing green architecture. Among other things, it has appointed a standing committee on the environment, convened national video conferences on the subject, and produced an extremely influential AIA Environmental Resource Guide (1996) to provide architects with information and ideas. There has been much reflection and debate over the last decade about the environmental responsibilities of the profession, due in large part to the leadership and advocacy of Susan Maxman, who was the AIA president during the early 1990s. Among the accomplishments on her watch was the joint signing by the AIA and the International Union of Architects (UIA) of a Declaration of Interdependence for a Sustainable Future (Fig. 4.11).

The potential to design and build structures that are less environmentally destructive is impressive. There have been a number of prominent examples of environmentally sustainable buildings that illustrate effectively that building design and construction need not be environmentally destructive—and indeed may be restorative in the end. Energy-efficient and environmentally restorative design, moreover, has been shown to be cost-efficient in rela-

**Declaration of Interdependence for a Sustainable Future.**

U.I.A.-A.I.A., Chicago,
18-21 June 1993

After the Assembly and Congress in Chicago, a Declaration on behalf of the architects of the world was adopted. We publish the text in extenso.

In recognition that:

- A sustainable society restores, preserves and enhances nature and culture for the benefit of all life, present and future; a diverse and healthy environment is intrinsically valuable and essential to a healthy society; today's society is seriously degrading the environment and is not sustainable;
- We are ecologically interdependent with the whole natural environment; we are socially, culturally and economically interdependent with all of humanity; sustainability, in the context of this interdependence requires partnership, equity and balance among all parties;
- Buildings and the build environment play a major role in the human impact on the natural environment and on the quality of life; sustainable design integrates consideration of resource and energy efficiency, healthy buildings and materials, ecologically and socially sensitive land-use and an aesthetic sensitivity that inspires, affirms and ennobles; sustainable design can significantly reduce adverse human impacts on the natural environmental while simultaneously improving quality of life and economic well-being;

As members of the world's architectural and building design professions, individually and through our professional organizations, we

Commit ourselves to:

- Place environmental and social sustainability at the core of our practices and professional responsibilities;
- Develop and continually improve practices, procedures, products, curricula, services and standards that will enable the implementation of sustainable design;
- Educate our fellow professionals, the building industry, clients, students and the general public about the critical importance and substantial opportunities of sustainable design;
- Establish policies, regulations and practices in government and business that ensure sustainable design becomes normal practice;
- Bring all existing and future elements of the built environment—in their design, production, use and eventual reuse—up to sustainable design standards.

Figure 4.11 The Declaration of Interdependence for a Sustainable Future, sponsored jointly by the American Institute of Architects and the International Union of Architects (AIA-UIA). *Source:* UIA Work Programme, 1996.

tively short time frames, and it can increase worker productivity and reduce absenteeism.

One impressive example is the Croxton Collaborative–designed renovation of the New York headquarters of the National Audubon Society. One of its first sustainable aspects was the simple decision to renovate a historic building:

> The Audubon building itself can be viewed as a gigantic recycling project. The client decided to renovate rather than construct anew, choosing a building which had been partially abandoned for ten years and was close to the subway. Much of the glass, concrete, wallboard, masonry, and carpeting removed during demolition of the interior was recycled, and many of the new materials used, such as steel, aluminum, and gypsum board, were selected for their ability to be recycled in the future. Croxton even helped establish guidelines for the client to purchase office supplies that are recycled or can be.
>
> The architects estimate that recycling the old building—a neo-Romanesque pile designed by noted New York architect George B. Post in the early 1890s—saved 300 tons of steel, 9000 tons of masonry, 560 tons of concrete, and the energy that would have been expended to create these new building materials (Crosbie 1993, p. 20).

Significant green design features of the building include high energy efficiency (R–30 insulation in the roof, for example), a heater/chiller system that eliminates the use of CFCs, use of materials with no toxic off-gassing, use of natural and low-energy lighting in the building, windows that can be opened, and a high degree of air circulation (an exchange rate of six times per hour, as described in Crosbie 1993). One of the most interesting features is how the building was designed to facilitate recycling. Specifically, four recycling chutes are provided on each floor, allowing sorted materials to be collected easily in the building's basement.

The construction of the ING Bank headquarters building in Amsterdam, the Netherlands, a 528,000-square-foot structure, is a frequently cited example of a large institutional building designed according to ecological principles. Finished in 1987, the building incorporates a number of interesting environmentally friendly design features, described by Romm and Browning (1994).

The energy savings from the ING building have been dramatic, reduced from 422,801 BTU per square foot per year to only 35,246 BTU per square foot in the new building. The economics of this project are also impressive, strongly supporting the rationality of more environmentally friendly design. The energy efficient design was reported to cost only $700,000, while the yearly energy savings are $2.6 million—obviously these energy efficient measures also make good economic sense. And, the resulting building is a more desirable and enjoyable place to work. Absenteeism has been reduced by some 15 percent, and the building has also substantially improved the bank's public image (Romm and Browning 1994).

Another example is the so-called "eco-mart" Wal-Mart built in Lawrence, Kansas. Constructed in 1993, the design includes such features as native plants used in landscaping, constructed wetlands to deal with runoff, a roof system built from sustainably harvested wood, and a building shell designed to be reused later for housing (although, as discussed in Chapter 5, there are many aspects of the Wal-Mart design that are inherently unsustainable). The building also incorporates extensive daylighting, light-monitoring skylights, and an HVAC using ice-storage technology and includes an environmental education center and a recycling center, among other features. These design features did add some 20 percent to the cost of the building. Interestingly, however, cash register data show that sales for those departments located in the skylighted portions of the store were significantly higher than for other departments and for similar departments in other Wal-Mart stores. In addition, employees seem to want to work in the daylight sections of the store (Romm and Browning 1994).

One way in which architects can design buildings more sustainably is to account directly for their environmental impacts and to mitigate or compensate for those impacts in some way. Architect William McDonough has designed several projects with this sense of compensatory obligation. One, a renovation of a New York clothing store, resulted in the planting of 1,000 oak trees to compensate for two English oaks that were used for paneling. Another example, on a grander scale, involved a design competition for a high-rise office building in Warsaw, Poland. Among other green features, McDonough's proposal involved a requirement for the planting of ten square miles of trees as compensation for the global warming impacts from the energy used to build and operate the structure (McDonough 1993).

There are increasingly many examples of successful sustainable architectural designs for commercial and office structures, with impressive savings and a host of other benefits, including increased worker productivity. Benefits have been realized on retrofits of buildings and in the design and construction of new buildings. A lighting retrofit for the main post office building in Reno, Nevada, for instance, resulted in a 6 percent increase in worker productivity and a six-year payback period. A lighting system upgrade for Pennsylvania Power and Light's drafting facility resulted in a 15 percent increase in productivity and a 25 percent reduction in absenteeism—this, in addition to a 69 percent reduction in energy costs. A recent Rocky Mountain Institute (RMI) study documents a number of cases in which companies have made such improvements essentially for energy savings, yet also experience valuable improvements in worker productivity and reduction in absenteeism. And, in most cases, the payback periods for these energy-efficient investments are relatively short.

The direct human benefits of greening buildings are considerable and illustrate how very often firms make decisions that are penny wise and pound foolish. Consider the relative amounts spent on energy, ventilation, and the direct costs of office space versus the amounts spent on the workers themselves. The RMI study shows that for most firms the cost of paying the worker (on a cost-per-square-foot basis) is some seventy-two times that of the cost associated with the energy needs of the space. If, through daylighting or the provision of fresh air and more pleasant and stimulating working conditions, productivity goes up even a small amount, the overall savings to the company can be substantial. If office workers cost seventy-two times that of energy costs, then "an increase of 1 percent in productivity can nearly offset a company's entire annual energy costs" (Romm and Browning 1994, p. 2).

Impressive designs exist for single-family homes as well. One of the more successful examples is the Arizona Environmental Showcase Home. It was sponsored by Arizona Public Service, or APS, Arizona's public energy utility. With a strong interest in reducing energy consumption, APS funded the research, design, and construction of this home.

Completed in 1995, the home shows how significant reduction in energy use, and other environmental goals, can be accomplished by using materials and technologies that are already widely available. The specific intention of the project was to be "state of the shelf," rather than state of the art. The design features are impressive. The structure is about 2,600 square feet in size, with four bedrooms. The environmental sustainability features are numerous: basic building materials made from recycled products (paneling made from a 50-50 mix of recycled plastic bags and waste wood products); extensive use of solar energy (to heat water, along with a roof system to send electricity back to the utility); a rainwater collection system; a graywater system, which recycles water used in flushing toilets; low-flow showerheads; and energy-efficient appliances (Build America 1996). The result is the construction of a home that has a substantially lessened impact on the environment and significantly lower resource requirements. At the same time, it is a beautiful, elegantly simple, extremely attractive and livable structure.

One of the more contentious residential design issues will be deciding on the appropriate role of the traditional "lawn." This was an issue in designing the Arizona showcase home, and a concession was eventually made to include a small, circular, turf area in the back of the house. It has been reported that in the United States there are some 80,000 square kilometers of lawn, and lawns have in many ways become the symbol of post–World War II suburban living. (Bormann, Balmori, and Geballe report there are 25 million acres, or 40,000 square miles, in turfgrass, more than 80 percent in home lawns). But as Hough notes, the lawn is also a symbol "for everything that is wrong with our relationship to the land, an expression of human control over natural diversity that extends worldwide, from Britain to California to the Far East" (Hough 1995, p. 129). There is little doubt about the significance and magnitude of the environmental impacts of lawns and of the pesticides and chemicals used in maintaining them. A study by the Yale School of Forestry and Environmental Studies systematically documents and tallies up the surprising number of these impacts (Bormann, Balmori, and Geballe 1993). They include not only the obvious pesticide and fertilizer use, but the water consumed, the air pollution created by mowing lawns (they cite the interesting statistic that in one hour, a power lawn mower emits the equivalent pollution of driving a car 350 miles), and the solid waste generated by grass clippings. The cumulative environmental impacts are impressive, to say the least. The study's authors suggest that it is time to reject the "industrial America lawn" and offer a number of alternatives. Among them are: changing lawn care practices (e.g., planting clover, using organic fertilizer), reducing the extent of a lawn, or replacing the lawn altogether (the option preferred by the authors). In a lawn's place can go trees, shrubs, and other native vegetation, which creatively, they note, could help to return a sense of place:

> A sense of place arises from our ability to recognize where we are in this world by the natural landforms and native species. Many areas of our country have lost their unique identity through the introduction of the Industrial Lawn and nonnative ornamental species. The reintroduction of native plants can help re-create a sense of place reminiscent of our predeveloped landscape. Removing the lawn and some of the nonnative plants in the yard and replacing them with native plants and native vegetation patterns is one way of reestablishing a local sense of place (pp. 145–46).

It is perhaps time, then, to encourage a different model for the spaces around our homes. These spaces could be put to much more ecologically productive and restorative uses—for example, as areas where trees and a diversity of native vegetation could be planted (with less cost and effort), as vegetable gardens, and as areas for urban wildlife. Local governments have a role to play here and can educate and provide technical assistance in exploring alternatives to the conventional lawn. Some communities have gone even further, especially in parts of the country where water is scarce. Bormann et al. cite one western community, for instance, that has started a "cash for grass" program. Under the program, homeowners who replace thirsty grass with water-conserving plants get a rebate from the local water utility. "This puts cash in the homeowner's pocket and reduces the demand on an over-tapped water company" (Bormann, Balmori, and Geballe 1993, p. 125).

Serious impediments to building environmentally friendly homes continue to exist, however. It is striking in visiting the Arizona Environmental Showcase Home, which is located in the midst of Phoenix suburbia, how few neighboring homes show any sign of use of photovoltaics. It is ironic that apparently the vast majority of homeowners in this hot, arid environment are ignoring this ubiquitous resource, the sun. One wonders why that is the case, and what obstacles exist to incorporating what seem to be extremely sensible technologies.

There are a number of reasons that may help to explain this phenomenon, as well as a number of obstacles to green building in general. One obstacle is the housing consumer. It is not at all clear that she or he is demanding such features, but it seems this is more a matter of not knowing about or understanding their availability and advantages.

It may be, then, that we must begin to find more effective ways of encouraging potential home buyers to contemplate and reflect carefully on what they actually want (and don't want) in a home. And, as Payton et al. note, the problem may often be in the way the options are posed to the buyer:

> Ironically, though a house is likely to be the largest purchase an average person is likely to make in their lifetime, most home buyers know surprisingly little about what their home is made of, the health effects of housing materials nor how much it will cost to operate the home. One home building company calls "green building" 137th on a list of "x" concerns of their home buyers. Yet, could it be that it is all in the way the question is phrased? Consumers are constantly asked to rank the things that are most important to them, e.g., jacuzzi tubs, fireplaces, etc., and such lifestyle quizzes tend to bias lifestyle responses. However, the problem is not either/or. Consumers are rarely asked, "Would you rather have kitchen cabinets made of particle board that outgas formaldehyde and thus may in the long run contribute to you getting cancer, or would you rather have cabinets of solid wood, which will be a little more expensive, but unlikely to cause you any physical harm? (Payton ed., undated, p. 12).

Clearly part of the mission behind the Arizona showcase home is to educate the public. In the short time since the house has been completed, some 15,000 people have toured it (1,000 per month are now visiting the home; Hahn, Pijawka, and Meunier 1996).

The traditional way in which architects, engineers, and other designers are paid represents another obstacle, especially to designing energy-efficient buildings. Conventionally, these fees are based on a percentage of the total cost of a building—creating a disincentive for finding ways to reduce the size of, or eliminate entirely, cooling and heating systems. (A disincentive exists as well in a fixed fee arrangement, in the sense that a designer is not rewarded for the extra effort and time needed to create a more sustainable structure.) As an alternative, architectural fees could be based on the actual performance of the building—for example, how much energy is actually used, compared with an agreed-upon base. Architects and engineers can be financially rewarded when performance targets are reached and penalized when performance falls short. This requires monitoring and evaluating the performance of a building after its construction. Payment of the final portion of a fee can be contingent upon performance evaluation.

At the very least, community officials should ensure that performance-based fee contracts are used in designing and building public structures and facilities. It is conceivable that the performance indicators could address a variety of other important sustainability goals in addition to energy efficiency—for example, the ability of a structure to withstand a natural disaster, or to provide a safe and enjoyable work environment, as perhaps measured by long-term productivity.

A significant, related obstacle is seen in the typical way that building design work is done. It is seen usually as a "linear, hand-off design and construction process—from architect to engineer to contractor to owner" (Hubbard 1997, p. 25). Sustainable buildings, however, require collaboration and teamwork among different design disciplines (something not often taught in architectural school).

Another major obstacle is that many environmental design features bump up directly against state and local laws. For health reasons, current state law in Arizona prevents the use of a graywater system in homes. And as odd as it may seem, some local ordinances forbid the placement of photovoltaic panels on roofs, as they are perceived by some to be eyesores.

Builders and financial institutions also represent obstacles in that they tend to be conservative about what design features the market will support. One enthusiastic conservationist building her own home was told by her bankers not to use a solar heating system because the bank was fearful that it would dampen the home's saleability or resale value should she default on her mortgage. Perhaps for similar reasons, builders and developers are not convinced that home buyers are interested or will care about environmental features.

And there is also the issue of cost. There is little question that at least in the short term, many of these green design features may add to the initial costs of building a home. What is increasingly more appropriate, though, when it comes to buildings is to take a longer perspective—how much energy a building will consume over its entire life, the long-term environmental costs, etc. Assuming a life-cycle analysis perspective in this case would be appropriate.

There are many promising initiatives designed to overcome these obstacles over time. One is simply disseminating information about these new techniques and technologies to architects, builders, and the general public.

Another strategy is to help housing consumers better understand the environmental implications of their home-buying decisions. One of the most impressive of these programs, and indeed the first of its kind in the United States, is Austin, Texas's, Green Builders Program. Operated by the city's Environmental and Conservation Services Department, the program rates participating homes from one to four stars according to their environmental features and systems (Austin, Texas, City of, undated[b]). Specifically, four factors are evaluated: water, energy, materials, and solid waste (see Table 4.1 for a list of star ratings). For a home to receive a four-star rating for water, for instance, the home must, among other things, have xeriscaped 75 percent of the landscape, have a computed water budget, allow roof rainwater to irrigate the landscape, and use waste/graywater for irrigation. Stars in energy are received by homes achieving a high degree of energy efficiency and utilizing solar technology, among other features. The Green Builders Program provides home buyers with a clear and straightforward sense of the environmental impacts and implications of their home choices—a clear way to connect concern about the environment with consumer decisions.

Other features of the Austin program include educating area home builders and building professionals, such as architects and engineers, about environmental features and technology, as well as providing help in marketing green building products. General environmental education of home buyers is also a goal, and the residential green builder materials distributed to the public ask (and then answer) essential questions that all residents should be able to (but often cannot) answer, such as: Where does our water come from and how does it get here? Where does our energy come from and how is it used in homes? Where does solid waste come from and how is it handled?

Green buildings and architecture represent an important way in which a

## Table 4.1
### Green Builder Program—Star Ratings

| One Star | Two Star | Three Star | Four Star |
|---|---|---|---|
| *Water* | | | |
| • Plant buffalo grass in sunny areas | • All One-Star requirements plus:<br>• Xeriscape for at least 75% of maintained landscape | • All Two-Star requirements plus:<br>• A "water budget" (an estimate of indoor and outdoor water use) | • All Three-Star requirements plus:<br>• Rainwater from the roof to irrigate the landscape, or<br>• Waste/graywater system for irrigation |
| *Energy* | | | |
| • 2 ceiling fans<br>• At least 30 Energy Star points<br>• 12.0 SEER (efficiency rating) on AC sizing by "Manual J" calculation<br>• A minimum of 600 sq. ft. of living space per ton of AC<br>• Correctly designed and installed ducts sealed with life-time materials | • All One-Star requirements plus:<br>• A third ceiling fan<br>• At least 20 more Energy Star points (50 total)<br>• Radiant barrier and continuous ridge and soffit vents<br>• Efficient water heater (0.60 Energy Factor)<br>• Shade the east and west walls (trees, buildings, etc.) | • All Two-Star requirements plus:<br>• Ceiling fans in all main rooms<br>• At least 20 more Energy Star points (total of 70)<br>• Minimum of 800 sq. ft. per ton of AC (or install minimum 14.0 SEER)<br>• Solar energy (passive or active) for 1 of the following: 40% hot water or 10% electricity or 15% space heat (earth-sheltering may substitute)<br>• Reduce health risks from electro-magnetic fields | • All Three-Star requirements plus:<br>• At least 10 more Energy Star points (total of 80)<br>• Minimum of 1000 sq. ft. per ton of AC (or install minimum of 14.0 SEER)<br>• Water heater that provides space heat ("combo" system), minimum 0.60 Energy Factor and 80% recovery efficiency |

134

*Materials*

One-Star
- 1 "recycled-content" space material
- 2 "engineered" materials
- Waste-saving concrete (at least 15% flyash)
- No ozone-depleting insulation or sheathing (no CFC or HFC foam products)
- Inside painted with low VOC products

Two-Star
- All One-Star requirements plus:
- A second "recycled-content" material
- Cabinets sealed inside and out water-based sealer, or made out of solid wood or metal

Three-Star
- All Two-Star requirements plus:
- A third "recycled-content" material
- A third "engineered" material
- One "regional" material
- Solid wood from "certified" sustainable forests only
- Low VOC products on outside
- Water-based glues
- Fiberglass out of HVAC air stream

Four-Star
- All Three-Star requirements plus:
- A fourth "recycled-content" material
- Non-toxic termite protection

*Solid Waste*

One-Star
- Build a recycling center in the kitchen or make a "holding area" in the garage or utility room

Two-Star
- All One-Star requirements plus:
- Composting system (made at the site or off the shelf)

Three-Star
- All Two-Star requirements plus:
- Make use of the trees cut at the site (for mulch, fenceposts, etc.)

Four-Star
- All Three-Star requirements plus:
- Plan for the reduction and reuse of construction waste
- Ventilated, lockable cabinet for storage of hazardous home products (e.g., paint and pesticides)

city can become more sustainable over time. Significant long-term economic benefits can also accrue to businesses (e.g., through improved productivity) and building owners (e.g., through lower heating and cooling bills). Local governments can play an important role in facilitating green building by ensuring that every new public structure or facility is designed to minimize its ecological footprint. This facilitating role also requires the elimination of unnecessary obstacles that can impede well-intentioned efforts by the private sector.

## Conclusions

Human settlements create tremendous pressures on the environment in terms of wastes generated and demands for food, electricity, water, and other resources. Communities must function with a clearer understanding of these demands and pressures, and should be planned and managed according to the principles of the natural environment in which they are embedded. Wastes can be minimized and treated as productive inputs to other activities (e.g., industrial). Cities should strive to live off of ecological interest and to protect their ecological capital, protecting and restoring diversity in the urban ecosystem.

All actions, policies, and decisions that a community makes should be examined for their environmental and resource implications, both within and outside its own bioregion. More sustainable practices, moreover, extend from regional conservation down to the ecology of neighborhoods and development projects, and indeed to the ecology of individual buildings.

*Five*

# Building a Restorative Economy

The 1990s have witnessed increased public awareness of the false dichotomy between "jobs and the environment," particularly in the wake of such high-profile issues as the northern spotted owl controversy, and also thanks to efforts on the part of industry to improve environmental performance. An array of innovative local and national initiatives are illustrating the symbiotic relationship between economy and environment. Citizens are slowly realizing that their lives can be improved through more protective environmental policies, the diversification of local economies, and greater independence from corporations that often are headquartered far from the community.

At the same time, in reaction to encroaching sprawl, increased traffic congestion, and overcrowded schools, many communities are simply halting economic development within their own borders. The challenge of this posture is that while it may be perceived to support a high quality of life, it also squelches the tax base that supports that quality of life. In areas where residential growth increases but business growth does not, there is often greater demand for schools, infrastructure, and services, but not enough funds to support those services. In such cases, either property taxes rise dramatically or bankruptcy ensues, and the rejected development simply sprawls outside local borders.

To avoid these problems, communities must undertake more strategic, forward-looking approaches to economic activity by assuming control over their own development patterns and proactively seeking out the appropriate mix of activities. For in addition to businesses providing jobs for local residents, the taxes generated from commercial activity are necessary to support the community's physical, social, and natural assets. Thus, just as a healthy environment is critical to a sound economy, a sound economic base is necessary for a healthy community.

This chapter introduces a variety of approaches to encouraging economic development that is environmentally restorative and supportive of local communities. The first section explores strategies for minimizing industry's environmental impact through protective policies and incentives, the support of ecologically restorative business activities, and conservation-based development. The latter approach, with its emphasis on local skills, assets, and cultures, is especially critical to the ongoing economic viability of rural communities. The second section considers additional strategies for investing in local labor, products, and services, including sustainable agriculture. Recognizing that a healthy environment can play a key role in a community's economic base, it also examines ways in which communities can maximize their economic potential through the recognition of natural, historic, and cultural assets.

The final section of this chapter follows up on many of the themes introduced in Chapter 3 regarding the environmental imperative to minimize sprawl through the cultivation of the compact community. Regardless of their isolated ecological impacts, businesses that are located far from downtown cannot be sustainable. Thus, the chapter concludes with ideas and examples of how to encourage business—whether retail, entertainment, or professional—to locate in downtown areas.

## Nurturing Environmentally Responsible Industry

The manufacturing-based industry of years past has fostered a perception that all industrial activity is damaging to communities, to the point that NIMBYism prevails regardless of the environmental performance of a company. From an environmental protection standpoint, perhaps the most obvious economic development strategy is to pursue only that activity which is environmentally benign or restorative. Such a strategy might involve the active support and recruitment of nonpolluting, environmentally friendly industries, especially those that manufacture nontoxic or recyclable products or that have comprehensive environmental programs or controls in place.

### Welcoming the Appropriate Mix of Activity

Rather than adopt a knee-jerk stance against economic development, communities pursuing a sustainable future must first take the time to determine the appropriate mix of economic activity for their region. Effectively implementing this vision often involves screening and recruitment approaches involving a broad coalition of businesses and related agencies and organizations. The Sierra Business Council in California, for example, is an association of more than 300 businesses that are collaborating to assess and protect the environmental and economic health of the Sierra Nevada region. The council has developed a "Sierra Nevada Wealth Index" and "Regional Balance Sheet" on which they plan to base future strategic planning for the regional economy (Sierra Business Council 1996). And in Wisconsin, the Campaign for a Sustainable Milwaukee is working to improve its regional economy by facilitating the creation of jobs and greater social equity in the central city. As just one example, they have urged a local construction project to include 25 percent minority and 5 percent female hiring goals (Sustainable America 1996).

In California's Silicon Valley, representatives of business, government, education, and local communities have joined together to promote economic vitality and community enhancement in the region. Joint Venture: Silicon Valley Network (SVN) is a uniquely collaborative effort involving not only proactive business recruitment but also efforts to address regional environmental and quality-of-life issues through public education, tax and fiscal analysis, regulatory reform (with an emphasis on streamlining), and local efforts to improve the health of communities. Recently SVN published its "Index of Silicon Valley," a holistic overview of the region's economic and "quality-of-life" indicators. The indicators cover issues of (1) education and workforce; (2) livability, including traffic delays, housing starts, and air quality; (3) community health; and (4) civic engagement, as measured by private giving and corporate contributions. A special Environmental Partnership provides pollution prevention training and is conducting a series of pilot projects demonstrating performance-based environmental strategies. The partnership has also developed the Environmental Business Cluster, the country's first business incubator for start-up environmental companies (Joint Venture: Silicon Valley Network, 1997).

The importance of first assessing the community to determine appropriate development strategies cannot be underestimated. Prince William County, Virginia, provides an instructive case study. Faced with a rapidly growing population, the county has sought to augment business taxes to fund needed services and infrastructure. With 80,000 residents working outside the county and more than 30,000 commuting at least an hour each way, they also recognized the need to reduce traffic congestion by keeping more jobs within the county. For twenty years Prince William County attempted, mostly unsuccessfully, to recruit Fortune 500 companies, developers of large shopping malls, and creators of theme parks, including the Disney Corporation. Many of these projects were vigorously opposed and defeated by area residents. In response, the county recently altered their strategic plan to recruit regional companies that make sense for the community that resides there. As part of this strategy, it is seeking ways to make it easier for smaller businesses to relocate through lower permit fees and streamlined regulations and processing (Shear 1996).

Once an appropriate business is identified, collaboration and negotiation are often required to ensure that the development is environmentally protective and a good neighbor to the community. In many cases, companies will be willing to contribute substantial environmental mitigation measures and social amenities in exchange for certainty and a streamlined permitting process.

In Berkeley, California, an area characterized by a fairly antidevelopment sentiment, the Bayer Biotechnology Corporation is building a $120 million, 120,000-square-foot plant in a traditional industrial zone. The project's approval process required Bayer's participation in more than 100 community meetings over two years. In return for such approval, Bayer has agreed to spend $12 million on environmental and community projects, including the donation of $1.4 million for the training of disadvantaged students in biotechnology, the cleanup of past contamination, and the development of a water reclamation program. The city of Berkeley facilitated the process by streamlining regulations and by creating a special "one-stop permit center" for processing building applications. In addition to obtaining the necessary zoning exemptions, Bayer has achieved certainty from the city regarding future regulations and requirements. Recognizing the importance of a diversified job base within its city limits, Berkeley is becoming more proactive about recruiting new businesses, with an emphasis on companies that offer blue-collar and entry-level jobs (McCloud 1996).

In San Bernardino County, California, business recruitment agents are using GIS to attract economic activity. Known as EDGIS (for "economic development GIS"), the system provides specialized regional data on industrially zoned sites and facilities, as well as on access to rail, airports, land use policies, building specs, and financial incentives (Environmental Systems Research Institute 1996).

## Environmentally Protective and Restorative Development

A sustainable community is one that seeks to develop and promote an economic base that has a minimal impact on the environment and is ideally restorative of it. Sustainability principles should be the cornerstone of any community employment and economic strategy. Sustainable economic development activities would be characterized by low or no pollution emissions; low energy consumption; products that contain few toxics, are designed for natural decomposition, and use sustainable materials; and a closed-loop production process for durable goods in which manufacturers design appliances and other products for disassembly and agree to maintain ownership and receive back these goods after they have been used. In short, a community's economic base should be consistent with the "ecology of commerce" reform principles advocated by Paul Hawken (1993) and others.

Localities can promote such economic activities in a variety of ways, including providing tax incentives, public investment, and financial underwriting for environmentally friendly businesses; enacting stricter environmental regulations; and offering education programs such as the Portland, Oregon, "Businesses for an Environmentally Sustainable Tomorrow" (BEST) program. Run by the Portland Energy office, BEST illustrates just how great an impact a local government can have in facilitating more environmentally friendly business practices. The BEST program serves a number of important roles, including providing educational and technical services and serving as a broker between businesses and other agencies and offices with relevant expertise. Activities undertaken by the BEST program include free energy efficiency design analysis; helping companies set up recycling programs; assisting businesses in identifying and applying for tax credits, utility rebates, and other incentives; and helping establish and run a vanpool incentives program (International Council for Local Environmental Initiatives 1994).

Moreover, communities may be able to encourage and promote business activities that not only provide jobs, income, and economic base, but are environmentally restorative in nature. Architect William McDonough has pioneered the idea of a local joint venture to produce and install superglazed windows in homes. Under the plan, several hundred workers would be employed to produce and install energy-efficient superglazed windows, thus simultaneously serving a critical local employment and economic function, generating substantial energy and cost savings for homeowners, and promoting ecological sustainability (Hawken 1993).

The idea of eco-industrial parks is one particularly potent and promising approach that local and regional governments could help to promote. The central idea behind the eco-industrial park is captured in McDonough's edict that "waste equals food." As happens in nature, we should design our economic and industrial processes so that waste becomes a useful input to some other economic activity. This more interactive and holistic approach to industrial activities offers many potential advantages. From a public perspective, it offers the potential of significantly reducing the direct and indirect costs of managing waste and pollution and of creating a more healthful environment. For the companies involved, the potential exists to lower production costs and reduce the expense associated with waste disposal.

One of the only working examples of the eco-industrial park is located in Kalundborg, Denmark. David Salvesen describes the productive dynamic and interaction between the different industrial and other activities in the park:

> There, a complex web of waste and energy exchanges has developed among the city, a power plant, a refinery, a fish farm, a pharmaceutical plant, a chemical manufacturer, and a wallboard maker. The exchange works something like this: the power company pipes residual steam to the refinery and, in exchange, receives refinery gas (which used to be flared as waste). The power plant burns the refinery gas to generate electricity and steam. It also sends excess steam to a fish farm, the city, and a biotechnology plant that makes pharmaceuticals. Sludge from the fish farm and pharmaceutical processes becomes fertilizer for nearby farms. Surplus yeast from the biotechnology plant's production of insulin is shipped to farmers for pig food. Further, a cement company uses fly ash from the power plant, while gypsum produced by the power plant's desulfurization process goes to a company that produces gypsum wallboard. Finally, sulphur generated by the refinery's desulfurization process is used by a sulfuric acid manufacturer (Salvesen 1996, p. 30).

In this way, eco-industrial parks attempt to create a closed-loop production process in which one activity's discharge and waste becomes a valuable input to another activity's production process.

This idea is still quite new, and there are currently no fully developed models in the United States. However, several parks are in the development stage, including projects in Baltimore, Maryland; Brownsville, Texas; Chattanooga, Tennessee; and Cape Charles, Virginia (Mulvihill 1996; Salvesen, 1996).

In Chattanooga, four sites in the city have been identified as locations for eco-industrial activities. The city recently sponsored a charrette to design plans for each of these sites. The results of these charrettes were interesting and forward-looking, and the process illustrates how a city can begin to closely tie together its economic and industrial development strategy, incorporating that strategy into its broader efforts to become more sustainable. In Cape Charles, a site has been purchased for the Port of Cape Charles Sustainable Technologies Industrial Park, and an international manufacturer of photovoltaic products has signed on as the first tenant; in addition to its commitment to build an assembly plant on site, the company has agreed to hire and train local workers. Two additional tenants will soon be secured for the project, and construction will begin.

There are, of course, many obstacles to the eco-industrial approach. From a planning perspective, one obstacle is the challenge of assembling the right mix of companies and industrial activities—a mix that will result in productive and useful interactions through which the wastes and production processes of some will be useful to others. In many ways, the requirements of an eco-industrial park complicate the job of a local economic development director tremendously. No longer does he or she recruit just industry, or even environmentally benign or restorative industry, but assemblages or groups of industrial activities that will fit together in significant ways.

Salvesen identifies four additional obstacles: (1) the fact that businesses have always functioned as if resources, and the ability of the environment to accommodate waste, were unlimited; (2) the conventional view that protecting the environment will involve greater economic costs; (3) a fear of disclosing trade secrets to competitors and losing autonomy; and (4) fears that a company may later be legally liable for the waste it provides for use by other companies (Salvesen 1996).

Clearly the eco-industrial park idea represents a different way of doing business, and this may be the most significant obstacle of all. Companies in an individualistic, capitalistic system may be uncomfortable in such a collaborative, coordinative arena. While it may be too early to embrace unconditionally the eco-industrial park idea, there is little question that our present environmental and ecological circumstances are pointing in that direction. And as the long-term savings in public and private costs become evident, it may be an increasingly compelling local economic development model.

Whether voluntarily or in response to regulations, companies may also take measures to enhance the sustainability not only of their own actions and practices, but also those of their employees. In response to federal Clean Air Act regulations, for example, many states and regions are requiring large employers to develop programs that reduce commuter traffic. In most cases, the stated goal is to increase the average passenger occupancy (APO) of vehicles entering and leaving the worksite each day, which will reduce the number of trips taken and vehicles on the road. Generally such programs include increased access to public transit, vanpools, on-site services, flex time, and telecommuting, among others.

In 1994, as part of a state-mandated commuter trip reduction initiative, the Educational Testing Service (ETS) surveyed all 2,200 of its New Jersey staff to determine the viability of various trip reduction options. Out of 2,098 respondents, only 15 percent indicated a willingness to carpool or vanpool. When queried as to their interest in participating in a "modified" or "compressed" work week, more than 68 percent said they would work longer hours each day in exchange for an extra day at home. In response to this clear delineation of preferences, and despite the fact that state regulations have since been lifted, ETS is now implementing a program with a heavy emphasis on a modified work week. As of December 31, 1996, some 564 of 2,316 staff work four days per week, and 49 staff work three days per week. Almost 200 staff telecommute at least one day per week and 165 are scheduled to report outside the peak morning traffic hours. In addition, approximately 13 percent of the staff carpool or vanpool to work, thanks in part to preferred parking and other incentives. Because of ETS's location on scattered greenfield sites outside of Princeton, very few staff are able to walk, bicycle, or take public transportation to work. In addition to offering subsidies for transit, ETS provides a guaranteed ride home in case of emergency, a computerized matching service for drivers searching for riders, and on-site bank machines, a dry cleaning service, and other amenities.

In California, the South Coast Air Quality Management District oversees approximately 3,400 firms—or 4,650 worksites with 1.2 million employees—that are subject to the trip reduction rule. All worksites with more than 100 employees may include old-vehicle scrapping in their mix of strategies. A company called ECO-SCRAP, formed by the Unocal Corporation, calculates air pollution/trip reduction requirements for individual companies, identifies owners of gas-guzzling vehicles, purchases the eligible vehicles, and ensures that the firm receives trip reduction credit for them. ECO-SCRAP estimates that, per worker, this approach costs less than half the cost of implementing more traditional trip reduction plans (Business and the Environment 1995).

Many communities seeking environmentally restorative development are recognizing the win–win potential of recycling and related services. While the true economic value of recycling over landfilling and other waste disposal techniques is currently a source of heated debate, the fact remains that landfills, waste-to-energy facilities, and other technologies are increasingly difficult to site. In many communities, landfills are rapidly reaching their capacity, and negotiating site locations is increasingly contentious. Meanwhile, the popularity of, and demand for, recycling as a waste disposal alternative has soared over the past several years. In 1995, for example, recycling supported more than 8,800 jobs in North Carolina (North Carolina Recycling Business Assistance Center 1995).

The area of organics recycling is particularly successful. In Boston, Greenleaf Composting, an organic materials business, manages a composting project at the 150-acre Allandale Farm involving food waste and cardboard from the Haymarket, Boston's open-air produce market, as well as feedstock from the Franklin Park Zoo, local landscapers, yard waste and wood chip haulers, and other contributors. One-half of the resulting compost is returned to the farm, which has donated the land and water in return for free disposal; the remainder is distributed to some of Boston's 120 community gardens or marketed to the public. With this experience under way, Allandale's operations have become more economically viable, and Greenleaf is expanding to other sites and negotiating more competitive tip fees (Fulford and Nash 1994).

In Minnesota, thanks to initial grant and loan support from the state Pollution Control Agency, several private companies have developed robust businesses that recycle scrap tires into tire-derived fuel, used in power plant boilers; playground safety surfaces constructed of crumb rubber; fatigue mats for assembly line workers; and soil erosion control products, among others. With a core of thriving businesses and an excess of processing capacity, Minnesota has transformed itself into a regional center for the processing of scrap tire coming from Wisconsin, Iowa, and North and South Dakota (Hvidsten 1995).

In New York's South Bronx, the Natural Resources Defense Council has teamed up with the Banana Kelly Community Improvement Association to develop a $485 million recycling mill. The mill would save sixty dollars per ton in waste transportation costs and would be powered by partially treated wastewater from a local sewage treatment plant. Low-cost financing will come from the sale of $75 million in tax-free bonds. When it is up and running, the mill will be run by the for-profit New York City Paper Mill (Greenwire 1996).

## Conservation-based Development

Led by communities in the Pacific Northwest, many localities are pursuing strategies that ultimately identify and facilitate new techniques to bridge natural resource conservation with job and community development. In rural areas this approach is called conservation-based development (CBD). It recognizes that the wealth of a region and the economic well-being of its inhabitants are inextricably tied to the health of the ecosystem, whether that health is measured in timber yields, salmon catches, or oyster harvests. In regions rich in natural resources but declining in jobs, the goal is to add value to the resource harvest as opposed to shipping raw materials out of the region.

The national pioneer in CBD is Ecotrust, an Oregon conservation group that joined with Chicago's Shorebank in 1991 to create the ShoreTrust Trading Group, thereby bridging environmental protection and economic development efforts. Recognizing that many rural entrepreneurs need advice on how to develop and market products and services, this partnership provides business advice and seed money to local entrepreneurs pursuing initiatives that are environmentally sustainable, particularly those that rely on natural resources but do not disturb the environment.

Ecotrust's first collaboration, with The Nature Conservancy, led to the formation of the Willapa Alliance, a diverse group of farmers, oyster growers, fishers, and small-business owners inhabiting the 80,000-acre Willapa Bay coastal estuary and its 600,000-acre watershed in southern Washington. After studying local markets and natural resources and interviewing local residents, Ecotrust began facilitating access to capital, markets, and credit for interested entrepreneurs. One such effort was to connect Goose Point Oysters to Nature's Fresh Northwest supermarkets, which is engaging in a variety of activities—including a video, providing recipes to chefs, and special promotions—to educate its customers on the value of a clean Willapa Bay in supporting oysters. As a result, regional demand for oysters has increased. Needless to say, the targeting of "green market" retailers is a key ingredient of Ecotrust's approach; "supporting small businesses that create new markets for socially and environmentally responsible goods and services builds the consumer base for these products, which in turn creates demand for more goods produced in a sustainable matter" (von Hagen and Kellogg 1996, p. 15).

Beyond merely establishing connections for existing products, Ecotrust provides advice on ways to add value to local natural resources—for example, cranberries. Anna Lena's, known for its cranberry relish, recently began expanding into other cranberry-based products; meanwhile, as word has spread through green market catalogs and other venues, demand for the products has increased (Maughan 1995). Finally, to assist with the development of business plans and to connect local businesses to markets outside Willapa, the ShoreTrust Trading Group offers a revolving loan fund for high-risk projects and helps to provide access to local bank loans. In 1995, ShoreTrust, The First Environmental Bancorporation was incorporated with the ultimate goal of developing a commercial bank "to complement and enhance the higher-risk credit available from ShoreTrust Trading Group" (Maughan 1995; Ecotrust 1995).

On the East Coast, the Port of Cape Charles Sustainable Technologies Industrial Park, mentioned earlier, is part of a larger, comprehensive economic development plan for the Eastern Shore of Virginia. The strategy is being implemented jointly by a group of public and private institutions, including Northampton County, the Virginia Eastern Shore Sustainable Development Corporation, and The Nature Conservancy's Center for Compatible Development. An outgrowth of Northampton County's comprehensive land use plan, the strategy involves a combination of efforts to stimulate the region's seafood industry, provide job training, foster partnerships between local farmers and urban groceries, and promote heritage tourism in the area. As a true testament to the holistic nature of this approach, Northampton County may be the first local jurisdiction in the country with its own director of sustainable development.

Formed in 1995 by The Nature Conservancy and a group of private investors, the Virginia Eastern Shore Sustainable Development Corporation has been instrumental in directly supporting economic development in the region. With more than $2 million in assets, the corporation helps develop, license, and market local products. Its Eastern Shore Venture Fund provides business loans, loan guarantees, and venture capital to local entrepreneurs.

The growth of the region's aquaculture industry, which produces clams and shellfish, provides just one example of the program's success. Between 1991 and 1995, annual sales of locally harvested clams grew from $1 million to more than $4 million, with a projection of $11 million in 1997. And employment has grown from ten full-time and ten part-time employees in 1991 to eighty-seven full-time and seventy-five part-time employees in 1995.

The Eastern Shore Sustainable Development Corporation is also collaborating with local farmers, businesses, and fishers, as well as with artisans and craftspeople, to develop food and arts and crafts products made from local resources. They have created the Eastern Shore Select brand and label, which distributes seafood chowder and sweet potatoes, among other food products; Eastern Shore furniture; and a variety of other marketable products (Center for Compatible Economic Development, undated).

## Fostering Local Self-sufficiency

Having witnessed or weathered the "boom and bust" cycles of manufacturing, military, and natural resource–based economies throughout the country, many communities are beginning to recognize the importance of a sound and diverse local economic base in maintaining long-term sustainability. The most effective strategies for sustainable economic development, therefore, revolve around ongoing investment in local labor, products, and services, including the consumption of locally grown produce and other agricultural products. As evidenced by the activities of the Eastern Shore Sustainable Development Corporation, such strategies also recognize and promote the importance of protecting a community's local heritage and ecological capital as an effective economic development strategy.

### Investing in Local Labor, Products, and Services

The past two decades have witnessed a trend in "downsizing" by large employers, both private and public, across the country. According to a 1996 study conducted by the *New York Times,* between 1979 and 1995 approximately 43 million jobs were eliminated in the United States. In 1995 alone, 3.47 million workers were laid off. During the 1990s, AT&T eliminated 123,000 jobs; Sears, Roebuck and Company, 50,000; Delta Airlines, 18,800; and Eastman Kodak, 16,800. Meanwhile, Manpower, Inc., the temporary-help agency, has become the largest employer in the country, providing approximately 767,000 substitute employees per year (Lohr 1996; *New York Times* 1996).

These statistics do not necessarily reflect the performance of the global or national economy; overall, in fact, the creation of new jobs during these time frames has far surpassed the number of jobs lost. But when a large employer goes out of business or moves away from a town in which it has been rooted for decades, the impact on the local economy and community morale can be devastating. In Dayton, Ohio, for example, the National Cash Register Company once stood as the centerpiece of community stability and pride. Today, after the loss of 20,000 jobs and a takeover by AT&T, the decline of this "hometown company" is fraying the community at its seams:

> All of this is causing a pronounced withdrawal from community and civic life. Visit Dayton, Ohio, a city fabled for its civic cohesion, and see the detritus. When Vinnie Russo left his job at National Cash Register and went to another city, the eight-five boys of Pack 530 lost their cubmaster, and they still don't have a new one. Many people are too tired, frustrated or busy for activities they used to enjoy, like church choir (*New York Times* 1996, p. 8).

In fact, with its strong sense of community and relative diversity of employment options, Dayton is faring relatively well as compared to many company towns. In the current climate of downsizing, the diversification of local economies away from dependence on one industry or paternal corporation becomes a critical strategy for ensuring community sustainability. Such a strategy requires an ongoing investment in the education, skills, and talents of the local labor force, as well as a supportive community network, affordable housing, and a healthy environment.

Corporations themselves can do far more—and, indeed, have a moral obligation—to invest in the communities they inhabit and the people they employ. In fact, in many cases, companies find that investing in local labor and other assets can work to their own benefit, particularly in terms of increased community support for potentially controversial projects, not to mention the long-term payoff that comes from having a strong base of skilled employees. As just one example, the Intel Corporation has instituted a job retraining program for employees who would otherwise be laid off due to operational or financial changes. Intel also sponsors a "redeployment program" that allows workers whose jobs are to be eliminated four months to find a new job within the company (*New York Times* 1996).

But it stands to reason that the most potentially strengthening approaches to local economic development should come from local labor and businesses themselves, as opposed to companies whose profits go elsewhere. In addition to representing the long-term economic viability of their own communities, local businesses play an important role in supporting community institutions and activities, from the sponsorship of amateur sports teams to participating in the PTA. The survival of local merchants helps to preserve the character of communities, and the personalized attention they provide is vital to maintaining not only quality service, but also the types of connections that constitute the fabric of the community.

In most cases, access to credit is the determining factor in ensuring the genesis and long-term survival of small business. Alongside the current climate of downsizing among large employers, a flurry of bank mergers and consolidations is hindering the availability of small business credit and general investment opportunities in local communities. Evidence exists that large banks, further and further divorced from local communities, are increasingly reluctant—and have little incentive—to provide smaller or nonstandardized loans. This approach results in a general disinvestment in local housing, products, labor, and services, and other local economic development projects (Fishbein 1996).

In the face of increasing bank consolidation, microcredit and other community development financing institutions (CDFIs) play a critical role in facilitating access to credit and local ownership of business as well as housing. This is particularly true among minorities, women, rural residents, and other clients to whom banks have traditionally demonstrated a reluctance to provide credit. While in-depth coverage of community development is beyond the scope of this volume, there are many examples of successful CDFIs around the country.

In North Carolina, the nonprofit Center for Community Self-Help— along with its financing affiliates Self-Help Credit Union and Self-Help Ventures Fund—provides access to loans for small businesses, nonprofits, and low-income home buyers. Self-Help loans range from several hundred dollars to $850,000. The organization also partners with business development training programs and provides technical assistance to community groups in areas seeking to become eligible for federal Enterprise Community and related funding. Perhaps most noteworthy among Self-Help's many accomplishments is its track record in purchasing, renovating, and leasing vacant, often historic buildings in downtown areas. The success of these

adaptive reuse projects stems heavily from the organization's ability to leverage public and private capital. As an example, a private donation of $1 mil-
lion enabled Self-Help to purchase and renovate the Public Service Building in Asheville; additional public funding ensured its completion. As it
does with all of the properties it renovates, Self-Help has established the
building as a center for local nonprofits and small businesses that serve the
local community (Self-Help 1995).

In communities throughout the United States, small businesses are working together to invest in their own long-term viability. In Wilson, North
Carolina, in response to learning that the chamber of commerce was working to recruit larger stores, a group of 100 small, family-owned businesses
have created an initiative called Team Wilson. In pursuing their primary goal
of staying competitive with the growing influx of chain establishments,
Team Wilson is educating the community about the importance of local
businesses as the backbone of community life. The group meets monthly,
often with invited speakers, and conducts outreach through cable TV ads, a
special discount card for shoppers, and other promotions (Yim 1996b).

Also in North Carolina, the state-sponsored Goodness Grows program is
encouraging major supermarkets to incorporate local products into their
inventories. Similar efforts are under way in Arizona, where farmers have
joined together to market local produce, including sweet corn, to large supermarkets. The Goodness Grows program has worked with Food Lion as
well as with the Hannaford chain of supermarkets. Hannaford, with owners
based in Maine, has made a concerted effort to incorporate local products
into all of its stores. Research for the Goodness Grows program has shown
that local customers prefer local products, so supermarkets are taking the
program seriously. At the same time, it is important to note that efforts on
the part of local small businesses to penetrate larger markets also require sophisticated strategies such as the development of business plans—a testament to the importance of technical assistance from organizations like
Ecotrust (Yim 1996c).

## Supporting Local and Sustainable Agriculture

As familiar as we have become with the image of the dying manufacturing
or military town, the decline of the family farm is perhaps even more familiar and disturbing to the collective psyche of this once-agrarian country.
As family farms fail while industrial agribusiness and suburban development
thrive, rural communities are withering on the vine. According to the U.S.
Department of Agriculture, as of 1995, only 556 of 2,276 rural counties in
the United States depended primarily on agriculture. From 1940 through
the mid-1980s, farm profits decreased by 10 percent and the number of
farmers decreased by two-thirds. And one recent study shows that between

1960 and 1989, in seven midwestern states, every community with a population of less than 5,200 lost businesses, and the percentage of business establishments in retail decreased from about three-fifths to about one-third (Strange 1996).

While development strategies abound in rural communities across the country, very few are sustainable, either economically or environmentally. In the Missouri Crescent, for example, the leading job growth sectors include nursing home aides, correctional officers, waste dumps, and hog factories, among others. Hence, " 'Rural development' becomes a bump-and-grind hustle to lure refugee businesses looking for a high-productivity, low-wage workforce, communities that will concede taxes in return for jobs, and state governments that will wink at regulatory infractions" (Strange 1996, p. 17). Even in areas where agribusiness is king, from Iowa to California's Central Valley, increased efficiency is sacrificing not only jobs, but also the environment and the natural resource base on which agriculture and our public health depend.

Recent studies sponsored by the Northwest Area Foundation examined the relative economic viability of sustainable versus conventional agriculture, with sustainable agriculture involving "substituting renewable resources generated on the farm for nonrenewable, purchased resources" through crop rotation, landscape management, recycling of plant nutrients and manure, and livestock waste management. The studies found that the relative proportionate debt load between sustainable and conventional farmers was similar, while sustainable farmers control fewer financial assets. Sustainable agriculture production costs are generally lower, but conventional farms have higher gross—but not necessarily net—income. In terms of their impact on local businesses, both sustainable and conventional farmers are likely to purchase goods and services in their own communities. When it comes to gaining access to markets, however, most sustainable farmers are forced to look out of state or abroad for a demand for their products (Northwest Area Foundation 1994).

The foundation also cites a study undertaken in North Dakota showing that conversion to sustainable agriculture throughout that state would increase livestock production and activity in four economic sectors: transportation, utilities, business services, and nonmetal mining. At the same time, crop production would decrease, as would activity in five economic sectors: construction, professional services, finance, retail trade, and agricultural processing. "The study concludes that gross business activity in North Dakota could decline unless an infrastructure were put in place to accommodate the changing marketing, processing, and storage needs of sustainable systems" (Northwest Area Foundation 1994, p. 19).

Clearly, we have a long way to go before such an infrastructure is in place.

However, many of the statistics cited above bode well for the viability of sustainable agriculture. Within local communities and regions, in particular, there are a variety of strategies available for providing the market that sustainable agriculture needs to stay healthy. The organic produce market in particular represents a promising outlet for local agriculture. Between 1980 and 1995, sales of organic foods increased fifteen-fold, from $178 million to $2.8 billion. Between 1994 and 1995 alone, mass-market grocery stores witnessed a 22 percent increase in sales of organic products. Ironically, however, these successes have primed the pump for big business to move in, stimulating greater interstate and international activity. Ultimately, there is the threat that large corporate interests will drive family organic farmers out of business, as happened with conventional family farms. Thus, it is important that communities promote and facilitate the local purchase and consumption of organic produce (Jones 1996).

Many of these strategies, as well as community-supported agriculture and farmers' markets, are discussed in Chapter 4. Local chefs and restaurants represent another viable market. In Washington, D.C., several noted restaurants, including Clyde's and Restaurant Nora, are known for their organic offerings. And in Boston, Chefs Collaborative 2000 is a group of prominent chefs that actively promotes the use of locally grown, seasonal ingredients within the food industry. In 1994, the collaborative signed a "Statement of Principles" for sustainable food choices. Finally, New York City's Greenmarket program publishes a directory to facilitate connections between local food producers and restaurants, caterers, and stores (Fabricant 1994).

In areas in which suburban sprawl and the enticing prospect of "selling out" to development add insult to economic injury, farmers are rethinking their operations to capitalize on citizen demand for outdoor recreation activities. In the suburbs of Washington, D.C., some farmers are experimenting with "entertainment farming" or "agri-tourism," in which they open their farms to the public for a fee. Visitors may herd cattle, pet animals, take hayrides, and simply enjoy the wide open spaces. A handful of farms serve almost as country clubs, charging members an annual fee in return for the privilege of fishing, hiking, picking-your-own berries, and other activities (Pae 1996).

## Recognizing Environmental Amenities and Cultural Heritage as Economic Assets

Increasing evidence has shown that the environment, ecological capital, and other natural assets of a region play a large role in supporting its economic base. In regions that have traditionally been highly dependent on the extraction of natural resources by industries such as timber and mining, it is the economies that have protected their natural environment and diversified away from extractive industry that are thriving. These observations were most recently documented by Thomas Power in his book *Lost Landscapes and Failed Economies* (1996), as well as in a report entitled "Economic Well-Being and Environmental Protection in the Pacific Northwest: A Consensus Report by Pacific Northwest Economists." Endorsed by more than thirty economists, the report documents increases of two to three times the national average in jobs, personal real income, total real earnings, and average real income in the four states of the Pacific Northwest between 1988 and 1994 (Association of Forest Service Employees for Environmental Ethics, undated).

In addition to diversification of industry, the report emphasizes the importance of a healthy environment in supporting the regional economy:

> As quality of life becomes more important to the region's economy and natural-resource extraction becomes less important, a shift is taking place in the economic role that natural resources play. Our natural landscapes no longer generate new jobs and incomes primarily by being warehouses from which loggers, farmers, fishermen, and miners extract commercial products. In today's world, these landscapes often may generate more new jobs and income by providing the natural-resource amenities—water and air quality, recreational opportunities, scenic beauty, and the fish and wildlife—that make the Pacific Northwest an attractive place to live, work, and do business (FSEEE, undated, p. 1).

As a testament to this perspective, companies such as Intel, Hyundai, and Hewlett-Packard claim that they have relocated to the Portland, Oregon, region to take advantage of its pleasant natural environment and compact urban area (Egan 1996a). For purposes beyond recreation and tourism, then, communities pursuing sustainable economic development would do well to protect and provide the parks, trails, waterways, waterfronts, historic districts, and other assets that constitute incentives for individuals and businesses with an appreciation for that community's heritage to locate there.

Missoula, Montana, is reviving its local economy by inviting citizens back to its Clark Fork River. A public-private partnership involving the Missoula Redevelopment Agency and the Missoula Downtown Association used tax increment financing to create a riverfront park with a piazza, river trail, and carousel. The city sponsors "Out to Lunch" concerts every Wednesday. In addition to stimulating greater economic activity, this initiative, along with a highly popular farmers' market, has provided an opportunity for citizens to meet, greet, and celebrate together (Kemmis 1995). In San Antonio, Texas, and Savannah, Georgia, entire shopping districts have sprung up around revitalized riverfronts.

In Chattanooga, Tennessee, not only is the community benefiting from a revitalized waterfront, the largest freshwater aquarium in the world, and increased economic activity throughout its downtown, it is building an economy based on the promotion of its own sustainability efforts. Drawing on the city's many successes and worldwide recognition for practicing sustainable development, the Chattanooga Convention and Visitors' Bureau is actively targeting potential delegations of visitors who would be specifically interested in holding meetings and conventions in a city known for sustainability. As just one example, in 1995 the city hosted the annual meeting of the Outdoor Writers Association of America; their conference materials and tour itinerary focused heavily on the protection of natural assets, with the hope that participants would return to the city for future visits and perhaps even write about Chattanooga. According to the Chattanooga News Bureau, the meeting did indeed generate a number of follow-up requests for information on the city and its progress. In a nation in which the convention and meeting business is a $75 billion industry, and the average individual expenditure by convention travelers is higher than for leisure travelers, such efforts constitute a wise economic development strategy (Yim 1996a).

## Heritage Tourism

In 1995, tourism in the United States generated $58 billion in tax revenues and supported 14 million jobs. Spending on food, lodging, entrance fees, and other expenses related to tourism totaled $417 billion. A large portion of these expenditures supported heritage tourism, which "affords communities endowed with a rich and attractive cultural, natural, and historical environment the opportunity to capitalize on an unparalleled economic advantage. The movement is based on the tenets of sustainable development and seeks to promote tourism in a manner that is respectful of the natural and built environments while relying on local values and beliefs" (North Carolina Heritage Tourism 1996). Beyond the simple generation of revenues, heritage tourism also nurtures appreciation of a community's heritage and efforts to protect it.

Memphis, Tennessee, is imbued with a sense of its own heritage, which includes music as well as a history largely defined by the civil rights struggle. In the years following the assassination of Dr. Martin Luther King, the city endured a bleak period, but over the past ten years, tourism in Memphis has grown by 70 percent. This success is due partially to a renewed appreciation for its music heritage, which had been largely ignored before the 1980s. Over the past two decades, the city has embraced its major asset and is capitalizing on it by actively promoting music establishments, including Graceland. These efforts have been boosted by a downtown redevelopment plan that includes the new Peabody Place development near Beale Street, the Mud Island Mississippi Museum and Park, and the National Civil Rights Museum. After having lost 36,000 residents in the 1980s, Memphis is now attracting businesses back to its downtown (Sloan 1996).

In many states, the centerpiece of the heritage tourism approach is the establishment of "heritage trails" designating historical or cultural landmarks. In honor of Tennessee's bicentennial, the state Department of Tourist Development initiated a heritage trail system that eventually will include approximately 400 signs across the state designating landmarks in the categories of history, music, and arts and crafts. In Kentucky, which ranks fourth in numbers of properties listed in the National Register of Historic Places, tourism generated $7.2 billion in 1995, and 75 percent of the state's visitors rate historical places as one of their top reasons for visiting certain destinations. And in South Carolina, a special grant provided under the Intermodal Surface Transportation Efficiency Act of 1991 (ISTEA) has funded a strategic plan—called "Southern Culture: The People and the Land"—for the state's 240-mile Heritage Corridor. The corridor will draw on the state's healthy tourist industry to expose visitors to themes of agriculture, textile industries, transportation development, and folkways in rural areas. The ultimate goal is for these rural areas to develop new tourism products that will improve local economies (North Carolina Heritage Tourism 1996).

In western North Carolina, Handmade in America was formed expressly to establish the region as the country's center for handmade objects. According to Handmade's newsletter, "These strategies focus on creating sustainable economic development opportunities that maintain our rural quality of life, providing business and financial support for craftspeople, and reinforcing a positive image of our region's craft culture through public relations and education" (Handmade in America 1996a). Handmade is an organization of several hundred craftspeople, business people, educators, and citizens working in a partnership that recognizes that regional crafts are culturally and spiritually important. The group actively supports the teaching of crafts—including a job training program for craft production—and recently began publishing a guidebook entitled *The Craft Trails of Western North Carolina*. The book includes seven scenic loop trails with more than 350 stops throughout western North Carolina. Finally, Handmade has instituted a new loan program jointly administered with the Self-Help Credit Union and the North Carolina Department of Commerce, Division of Community Assistance. The program provides loans for craftspeople to start or expand their own small businesses (Handmade in America 1996b).

While tourism can represent a healthy and sustainable approach to economic development, like the environment, it has its own carrying capacity, which should be respected and not exceeded. In planning for sustainability, communities must determine their desired level of tourist activity, with its accompanying gift shops, fast-food restaurants, and amusement attractions. Measures should be taken to protect not only the environment, but also the provision of affordable housing and other necessities for the local community.

## Bringing Business Back Downtown

Even nonpolluting or ecologically restorative business, if not well situated, can unwittingly contribute to the decline of a community and its environment. There are many examples of regions that are well populated with nonpolluting businesses, mostly situated on "greenfield" campuses, that are experiencing perpetual gridlock, long commutes, and poor air quality due to automobile exhaust. Silicon Valley, California, and the Research Triangle region of North Carolina are two such examples.

Throughout history, commerce has situated itself with easy access to the most efficient and commonly used transportation systems available (Rybczynski 1995). The development of our state and interstate highway systems has therefore lured commercial activity to the fringes of town and has even caused new "edge cities" to sprout in the exurbs (Garreau 1991). As previous chapters discuss, the auto has had a tremendous impact on our land use choices, as clearly evidenced by our office complexes and shopping centers with their large parking lots, far from downtown. In fact, according to a recent study by the Virginia-based Eno Transportation Fund, "suburb-to-suburb commuting now accounts for more than 44 percent of all work trips, while the suburb-to-city pattern holds for 38.2 percent" (Center for Livable Communities, August 1996).

As described in Chapter 3, the primary weapon against sprawl is the compact community. To promote such compactness, and to reduce traffic congestion and its attendant effects, there is a need to foster greater downtown economic activity. The nurturing of local business is also critical, not only in terms of preventing urban sprawl and excessive energy use from consumer and commuter auto travel, but also to minimize the long-distance transport of materials that fuel nonlocalized commerce. Finally, downtown economic activity is more likely to encourage a sense of place and a long-term investment in the community.

This section examines some of the forces facilitating disinvestment in downtown areas, particularly the impact of large shopping centers and megastores. Drawing from case study material from cities around the country, it explores a variety of tools, techniques, and strategies for facilitating the commercial development of downtown areas.

## "Big Boxes" and the Mall

Shopping centers and malls provide many perceived benefits, include free parking, protection from rain, cold, and heat, and, in some cases, one-stop shopping. Their centralized management and economies of scale provide the ability to support numerous establishments, simply rotating those that don't succeed out of the mix in exchange for more financially viable options. Riding the wave of these opportunities, between 1970 and 1990 there were approximately 25,000 new shopping centers built in the United States, or an average of one about every seven hours. Eventually, places such as Houston's Galleria began leasing space to hotels and banks; today, some regional shopping malls include public libraries, city hall offices, and even schools (Rybczynski 1995).

The relatively low price of land on the urban or suburban fringe, combined with economic forces within urbanized areas, have provided counterproductive incentives to local governments for recruiting various combinations of retail outlets. In Colorado, as in many areas around the country, local governments are not allowed to raise property taxes above a certain level; facing bankruptcy and the need to fund services and infrastructure, these towns claim to have no choice but to recruit outlet malls and other retail complexes that are appealing enough to compete with the large regional malls (Egan 1996b).

There is no question that there is an emerging sentiment that might best be characterized as "mall backlash" among many citizens and social commentators. In response to this sentiment, an alternative view holds that as centers of commerce, perhaps malls represent an appropriate, or at least natural, replacement for downtown commercial activity. In his recent book *City Life,* architect and social historian Witold Rybczynski describes a visit to the mall:

> The debate about whether shopping malls could or should replace or augment downtown is academic. In places like Plattsburgh, there is little doubt that the shopping mall is the new downtown . . . the atmosphere was lively, a marked contrast to the emptiness of downtown's Margaret Street. There were crowds here, excited teenagers swarming to the video arcade, parents trailing children on the way to the movie theater, young couples window-shopping, elderly people walking for exercise or sitting on park benches. On Saturdays, there were usually booths selling the sort

of mass-produced crafts that one finds at country fairs . . . The chamber of commerce occupied a stall and promoted local tourist attractions. There were even Girl Scouts selling cookies. . . . I saw people rubbing shoulders and meeting their fellow citizens in a noncombative environment. . . . As for hyperconsumerism, commercial forces have always formed the center of the American city—the old downtown no less than the new—and it is unclear to me why sitting on a bench in the mall should be considered any more artificial than a bench in the park (Rybczynski 1995, pp. 216–17).

But malls are not the same as downtowns. First, they are generally managed by one developer that strictly controls all activity. Regardless of a region's level of affluence, it is rare that any retailer that is not part of a regional or national chain can afford the high rents in malls, which require additional subsidies for common indoor space, parking, maintenance, and security. Hence, there is little opportunity for local ownership and none of the "organic" nature of downtown business activity. The individual stores in a mall, many of them nationally owned, are not subject to local market forces; nor do they usually return any of their profits to the local community.

In addition, while common gathering space is provided within the mall, this space is the creation of the private developer and not the community. The food court cannot substitute for the town square, and while free speech in malls is now protected by the U.S. Supreme Court, the atmosphere of the mall is rarely conducive to spontaneous public gathering.

As for its artificial nature, except in the rare case of the atrium-style design, it is rare to find a single element of the natural world—whether a tree or flower box, not to mention natural air or a glimpse of the sky—within the walls of a mall. In fact, the environmental impacts of large shopping malls are tremendous, with footprints in the millions of square feet, including vast expanses of impermeable parking lots. Needless to say, the mall is generally disconnected and inaccessible from any venue except the road, requiring the use of a car or bus to get there.

In the 1990s, the popularity of the regional shopping mall has been eclipsed by the emergence of "big box" megastores such as Wal-Mart, Best Buy, and Sam's. The average megastore is 110,000 square feet and generates an average of 946 car trips per hour, or almost 10,000 trips per day (Stapleton 1995) (Fig. 5.1). The irony of these stores, with their centralization and economies of scale, is that while their biggest appeal is their low prices, those citizens who most need those lower prices cannot shop there for lack of automobile transportation (Stapleton 1995).

Figure 5.1 The "big box" shopping center has a large ecological footprint.

Perhaps most disturbing, and the impetus of many anti–big box battles, is the impact of malls and big boxes on local business. Researcher Richard Stapleton reports that "Within ten years after Wal-Mart's move into Iowa, almost half of the men's and boys' clothing stores in the state disappeared and a third of all Iowa's hardware stores and grocery stores closed" (Stapleton 1995) (Fig. 5.2.)

It may be argued that the impacts described above represent nothing but the "invisible hand of the market" at work. For many citizens, it is difficult to support the local hardware store when the Home Depot down the highway offers a wider selection at half the price. Indeed, there is a very complicated combination of factors influencing the economics of the relationship between downtown and suburb, including the price of land and property in downtown areas as compared to the suburbs, as well as taxation structures. But the fact remains that our current patterns of commerce, including not only the mall but also exurban office development, are simply not sustainable, particularly from environmental and land use perspectives. Meanwhile, our downtown areas, many of which are experiencing increasing real estate vacancies, provide the existing infrastructure necessary for local business activity within walking distance of housing and civic functions.

**Figure 5.2** The proliferation of large shopping centers in suburban areas has contributed to the decline of downtown retail establishments.

### The Mall Moves Downtown

In recent years, there has been some evidence indicating that consumers—whether weary of crowds or traffic, or bored by the sameness of chain-store selections—are slowly making their way out of the malls and back to downtown to shop. According to the Center for Livable Communities (CLC), "Shoppers spent half as much time in malls in 1995 as they did in 1990" (CLC April 1996).

In response to this emerging shift in demand, and enticed by the prospect of not having to pay for mall overhead, chain stores such as the Gap and Talbots have begun occupying the main streets of affluent suburban towns. According to a 1996 *Wall Street Journal* article, to attract the major chains, downtown areas must offer ample parking and should be densely populated and affluent. In some cases, developers are buying up whole downtown shopping districts and filling them with chain and specialty stores (Pacelle 1996).

In 1995, after ardent local opposition in towns such as Williston, St. Johnsbury, and St. Albans, Vermont became the fiftieth state in the country to host a Wal-Mart store. The city of Bennington was able to convince state leaders to require that the store move into an existing 48,200-square-foot downtown building formerly occupied by F.W. Woolworth (Burge 1995). In Portland, Oregon, meanwhile, all new retail outlets must be under 60,000 square feet.

But while this type of approach does have the potential to bring life back to downtown areas, Bennington and other communities continue to fear its impact on local businesses and its general lack of contribution to the local economy. Further, because the owners of these retail establishments generally do not live anywhere near the towns in which their stores are located, there is no incentive to extend quality service or to be a "good neighbor" to the community. In short, their profits and time are not reinvested in the community.

It could be argued, however, that this scenario is still preferable to a deserted downtown and an urban fringe populated with chain stores. The recent transformation of a downtown block in San Luis Obispo, California, into a shopping district anchored by several national retailers has increased foot traffic in the neighborhood, thereby boosting the sales of existing local businesses (CLC April 1996). Similarly, Glendale, California, is renovating an enclosed shopping mall in its town center by opening it up to the street and creating a new civic park, among other improvements (CLC August 1996).

Many Americans—particularly tourists—are familiar with the type of downtown development that thrived in the 1980s through successes such as Harborplace in Baltimore, Quincy Market in Boston, and South Street Seaport in Manhattan. These areas have become prime tourist attractions for their host cities, combining extensive shopping, dining, night life, and heritage tourism. Both Quincy Market and South Street Seaport are located within a short walk from the downtown financial district, providing dining and shopping opportunities for the resident workforce. However, while both areas are popular at night as well, neither is known for its housing or resident population. In general, these are places "to be visited" rather than neighborhoods to be inhabited.

In contrast, in Baltimore and Cleveland the potential impact of this type of development approach has been far more striking. Unlike New York or Boston, these cities are not traditional tourist destinations and suffered substantial decline in the postmanufacturing days of the 1970s and 1980s. In Baltimore, the development of Harborplace in the early 1980s was largely responsible for stimulating the ongoing turnaround that city is achieving. Cleveland's downtown has been infused with $3.5 billion of investments in the 1990s, resulting in the Gateway Sports and Entertainment Center, Playhouse Square Center, Great Lakes Science Center, and the Rock and Roll Hall of Fame and Museum, among other attractions. This cultural renaissance has corresponded with and no doubt contributed to a substantial increase in retail growth in the downtown area (*Cleveland—The New American City* 1997).

## Breathing New Life into Downtown

All over the country, communities are pursuing strategic, often holistic, efforts to stimulate economic activity in their downtown areas. These approaches extend well beyond attempts to recruit large chain stores or corporations to Main Street (although the latter, in particular, can be an important element of the mix). In addition to business recruitment, downtown economic development also requires great attention to street and storefront design, a strategic tenant mix, and access to transit and parking, among other factors.

Beyond relatively small-scale efforts to incorporate corner stores or cafés into their public spaces, only a handful of New Urbanist projects have seriously connected themselves with retail activity. Perhaps the most well-known example of this approach is Kentlands, in Gaithersburg, Maryland. The housing development is adjacent to the Kentlands Shopping Center, which includes a supermarket and several big-box stores, including a Kmart and a Crown Books superstore. Writing in *Metropolis* magazine, Alex Marshall describes the development as "a typical strip mall; the only difference is that the stores have been dressed up with brick façades and white Jeffersonian columns" (Marshall 1996a). With their vast parking lots and relative lack of sidewalks and greenery, big-box developments such as the Kentlands Shopping Center require—if not invite—the consumer to drive from one store to the next. It is difficult in such an environment to picture residents of Kentlands walking from their homes to the Kmart to shop.

Recognizing this failure, the designers of Kentlands recently created a new plan for a "midtown" shopping district, designed on a more human scale, situated within the development. And Celebration, the Disney-sponsored New Urbanist development in Osceola County, Florida, does include its own downtown retail area. All commercial buildings are owned and operated by Disney, which leases only to local and regional commercial establishments. The downtown area, which includes a bank, post office, and town hall, also offers 120 apartments, most of which are located directly above the shops and restaurants (Rybcynski 1996).

In many cases, existing cities with declining downtowns simply make a conscious decision not to attempt to compete with the mall for retail activity. In the aftermath of the Oklahoma City bombing, for example, land use consultants descended on the city with advice on repairing the community, particularly the section of downtown near the Murrah building. In the end,

Oklahoma City chose not to recruit aggressively the types of stores represented in surrounding malls; instead, it is striving to become a regional entertainment center with mix of restaurants, parks, and affordable housing (Peirce 1996b).

Unfortunately, in many cases, despite the best intentions of businesses and their local champions, relocation to downtown areas is impeded due to outmoded zoning regulations originally designed to prevent noxious industrial activity from situating near residential areas. "Performance-based zoning systems" would allow business more locational flexibility, provided potential clients can satisfy certain performance standards for noise, traffic, and pollution.

Downtown development and merchants' associations can play a key role in revitalizing town centers, particularly in assisting potential tenants in securing financing and navigating the permitting process. In North Carolina, Downtown Durham, Inc. assists businesses seeking downtown office and retail property by matching clients with available space, assisting with business plan development, and providing access to loan programs. It offers a number of financial incentives including: (1) a prime-rate loan program; (2) a low-interest loan program, run by the city of Durham, enabling those enrolled in the prime-rate program to receive half the loan at 2 percent below prime (resulting in a total loan of 1 percent below prime); (3) a façade improvement and mural grant program of up to $3,000 per project; and (4) historic property tax credits of up to 50 percent. The organization also publishes handbooks and brochures on downtown investment opportunities, entertainment and shopping, and many other aspects of Durham life. It offers tours to commercial realtors and maintains databases of downtown properties for sale or lease; coordinates downtown safety programs, including bicycle police patrol and a crime database; distributes discount coupon books; and sponsors community-enhancement programs such as outdoor concerts, banners, landscaping, and graffiti removal (Downtown Durham, Inc., undated).

## Public-private Partnerships

As described earlier in this chapter, a city's choice to promote special community attributes and features—an historic streetscape, a riverfront, a musical or crafts heritage—can make all the difference in generating greater downtown activity. The most successful initiatives result from a carefully crafted combination of public and private resources and entities.

In Chattanooga, a city endowed with a remarkable amount of private wealth for a community its size, the injection of private capital into sustainable development initiatives has leveraged millions of dollars in public funds. In turn, public funds have also spawned private donations. The most striking example of such generous investment is the Tennessee Aquarium (Fig. 5.3), built in the early 1980s courtesy of a $45 million donation from a local philanthropist. The Chattanooga-based Lyndhurst Foundation has contributed millions of dollars to local initiatives, including Chattanooga Enterprise, a nationally recognized low-income housing program that also enjoys support from the city of Chattanooga and area banks. Founded in 1986 as the River City Corporation, the community's economic development organization (now called RiverValley Partners) was originally funded by eight banks and seven foundations, for a total of $10 million in grants spread over ten years. The symbiotic relationship of public and private resources, expertise, and will has come to be regarded as perhaps the most instrumental tool in Chattanooga's ongoing metamorphosis.

At the national level, the National Trust for Historic Preservation's Main Street Program is a model of public-private partnerships in downtown revitalization. The Main Street Program works with cities to identify local assets and use them to their advantage. In the 1980s, the largely abandoned town of New Bern, North Carolina, was one of the early participants in the Main Street Program. In addition to Tryon Palace, the former governor's mansion, New Bern's primary asset was its waterfront, a former seaport at the confluence of the Trent and Neuse Rivers. Citizens, local government,

**Figure 5.3** The Tennessee Aquarium, Chattanooga, Tennessee. *Source:* Chattanooga Area Convention and Visitors Bureau.

nonprofits, and businesses joined together to form a downtown development corporation called Swiss Bear, through which they obtained a $1.9 million federal urban assistance grant that helped fund the construction of a Sheraton hotel and marina. They also obtained a gift of 3.3 acres for a waterfront park. Through a number of partnerships, Swiss Bear acquired office space in a former department store that had been slated to become an adult entertainment center; four local banks made a low-interest renovation loan, and the building is now a business incubator. Downtown businesses contribute their share of redevelopment costs by paying higher taxes to fund local improvements (Twardy 1995b).

For those towns that are too small to benefit officially from the Main Street Program, collaboration and creativity can produce similar results. In western North Carolina, four towns—Andrews, Bakersville, Chimney Rock, and Mars Hill—have initiated their own collaborative program, called "Regional Heritage: A Foundation for Small Town Renewal." Working together, they plan to network with other towns in the region that have successfully revitalized their downtowns via the national Main Street Program. Drawing from their own experiences, these neighboring communities will assist with the preparation of custom-made downtown revitalization plans for the four founding towns (Handmade in America 1996c).

In the revitalization of Suisun City, California, a special effort was made to prevent the outflow of local business profits to far-flung national corporations. In the 1980s, Suisun City had a population of 26,000, a vacant Main Street, and excessive pollution, drugs, crime, and slums. The situation there was so degraded that the *San Francisco Chronicle* deemed it the "worst place to live" in the Bay Area. Again, thanks to partnerships between local government and business, today the city has turned itself around. Key elements of revitalization strategy included the designation of the entire city as a tax increment district—the extra funds paid for $50 million in bonds for inner-city development—and a master plan that makes small commercial spaces affordable to local businesses, including restaurants, shops, and offices. (The small size of those spaces also makes them less appropriate for large chain stores.) Opportunities for business owners to live above their commercial space are another important element of the mix (CLC May 1996).

Wilmington, North Carolina, represents a striking transformation from an abandoned industrial core to a thriving waterfront community. Located on the banks of the lower Cape Fear River, Wilmington's historic downtown had sunk so low in the 1970s that, in many cases, property values were considered virtually negligible. A public-private corporation called the Downtown Area Revitalization Effort (DARE) was formed in the mid-

1970s to oversee an effort that ultimately leveraged six dollars in private investment for every one public dollar toward streetscape improvement and the refurbishment of historic downtown properties.

The initial strategy took advantage of rock-bottom property values by encouraging property owners to donate buildings for a 50 percent tax gift write-off. Then DARE actively recruited businesses to purchase those properties for as little as one dollar, in return for a promise to invest in renovations and other improvements. To supplement and leverage these efforts, DARE secured a package of public funding through block grants, Small Business Administration loans, and other sources. They also made a special effort to encourage housing, restaurants, and retail downtown. The result of these efforts was a collective commitment by individual business owners of $6 million in improvements throughout the downtown area. Encouraged, the city of Wilmington committed $1 million for a riverfront park that is now the centerpiece of downtown life.

Wilmington's efforts were so successful that the film industry has claimed the city as its unofficial East Coast headquarters. Its historic, human-scale streetscape, temperate climate, and location near the coast provide a diverse array of settings for filming purposes; the increase in film-related activity over the past decade has spawned numerous new businesses, from lighting equipment to casting services to restaurants. Many of the thousands of members of the Wilmington film industry live and do business downtown. In turn, the presence of the film industry has created a demand for, and contribution to, striking enhancements in commercial development, including restaurants, shops, and nightclubs; the refurbishment of historic homes; and a general increase in downtown activity at all hours.

## The Twenty-four-hour City

To maximize its economic potential, a downtown area should be the center of community activity twenty-four hours a day. Not only does the presence of night life and round-the-clock hustle and bustle generate greater commercial activity, it also has the potential to minimize crime by ensuring a constant source of citizen "vigilance" that is lacking in vacant neighborhoods. The most powerful tool to guarantee this level of activity, not surprisingly, is the provision of a substantial mixture of housing options within a downtown area. Those who work in a particular community should have the opportunity of living there, thereby enhancing mobility between home and work and decreasing dependence on the automobile.

Unfortunately, in many downtowns, would-be residents encounter a "vicious circle" in that either housing is prohibitively expensive or the neighborhood is so degraded that, given the choice, only the most fearless would decide to move there. For this reason, in many cities it is the younger generation of risk takers, often artists, who populate "fringe" neighborhoods. Lessons from neighborhoods in Manhattan, including Hell's Kitchen, Soho, and the East Village, show that artists, writers, designers, and young people can be a key element in populating previously desolate neighborhoods. In Wilmington, North Carolina, one block of prime historic property was set aside to be marketed specifically to people who would agree to start a business or establish a residence in exchange for lower rents (Pindell 1995).

Again, outmoded zoning regulations that do not allow the mixing of uses represent another major obstacle to the "twenty-four-hour city." In Wilmington, thanks to the efforts of DARE, the city has instituted "microzoning" downtown, enabling the separate clustering of business office space, light manufacturing, residential, and retail and entertainment, all within a short walk of one another. And as described in Chapter 3, many communities are instituting programs that encourage the renovation of housing above commercial space. Cities such as Denver, Colorado; Boca Raton, Florida; and Santa Monica, Monrovia, and Pasadena, California, are all making special efforts to encourage housing as well as evening entertainment such as movie theaters downtown (CLC April 1996).

In the financial district of Lower Manhattan, one of the few areas of New York City that empties out when the business day is through, special tax incentives are encouraging the conversion of vacant skyscraper space—mostly within pre–World War II buildings—to residential dwellings. The city has also altered zoning regulations to increase the maximum allowable size of live/work spaces. The Alliance for Downtown New York, the neighborhood's business improvement district (BID), is promoting the area's historic heritage as an eighteenth- and nineteenth-century trade center, as evidenced by its supply of prewar buildings, many of which house space for which there is no longer commercial or office demand. At the same time, there remains a distinct lack of schools, parks, restaurants, and other elements of community life that other recently emerging neighborhoods, including Tribeca, have made a special effort to provide, not to mention safety features such as lighting and police bicycle or foot patrol (Vanderbilt 1996).

Richmond, California, took a holistic approach to the "twenty-four-hour city" with the creation of Memorial Park. Working through the Richmond Redevelopment Agency, the town recruited a private developer and nonprofit housing corporation to renovate a hotel into thirty-six units of senior housing, as well as sixty-four new apartments, a police substation, and townhouses for families with annual incomes between $24,000 and $40,000.

Memorial Park is adjacent to a shopping center, Bay Area Rapid Transit station, and some employment. Once vacant and blighted, this neighborhood is now a retail center with 200 new jobs and ninety-eight new households (CLC March 1996.)

## The Telecommuting Dilemma

With the increasing flexibility of work schedules offered by many companies today (e.g., flextime) and the power of the Internet, increasing numbers of people may be able to work productively from their homes for at least a portion of the work week. This has given rise to what some are calling "telecommunities." Two recent housing developments planned in Ontario, Canada (Montgomery Village and Cornell), are incorporating telecommuting features—specifically, the installation of fiber-optic cable and the incorporation of home offices (e.g., separate office areas within the home, often with their own entrances) (Warson 1995).

With the increasing accessibility of the Internet and greater locational flexibility among employers, the popularity of telecommuting is growing rapidly. In the right places (within existing urban areas, on infill sites), and integrated within existing vibrant neighborhoods and communities, telecommuting could represent a positive contribution to creating more sustainable places. It will be particularly helpful in reducing suburb-to-suburb traffic. However, telecommuting should not be viewed as a technology that justifies low-density, greenfield development, or that detracts from, or deflects energy away from, existing urban centers (e.g., Montgomery Village is some fifty miles north of Toronto). According to a 1995 report by the former U.S. Office of Technology Assessment, it is likely that telecommuting and other remote, electronically driven employment options and production technologies will facilitate the decentralization of workplaces in communities throughout the country. As such, many employees will have no reason to travel to central city areas to perform their work responsibilities. While this shift may ease the traffic burden during the rush-hour commute, it could also reduce the population mass necessary to keep downtown commercial establishments viable (Marshall 1996b).

## Variations on the Pedestrian Mall

Since the 1960s, many cities have developed pedestrian malls in downtown areas with the hope that closing the streets would lure people away from suburban malls. In the past twenty years alone, more than 200 new pedestrian malls have been created (Newman 1996). Unfortunately, most cities are finding that in their current form, pedestrian malls are not economically viable as the centerpiece of downtown commercial life, particularly as many are frequented for only a few hours of the day, usually lunchtime, when office workers emerge from their buildings for a meal.

Starting with the assumption that allowing increased auto traffic will enhance access to downtown retail, many communities—from Kalamazoo, Michigan, to Little Rock, Arkansas—are addressing this problem simply by opening portions of their pedestrian malls to traffic (White 1996). Chicago's State Street Mall will open to traffic at a cost of $24.5 million in demolition, infrastructure, and construction costs (Leager 1996). In Greenville, North Carolina, a group called Uptown Greenville is taking apart the Evans Street Mall, which was built in 1975. In an effort to encourage downtown businesses to invest in the project and make it their own, the group has instituted a "Buy a brick, bring back Main Street" campaign (Allegood 1996).

But trying to increase pedestrian-based commerce solely by emphasizing the role of automobiles is an approach that ignores the role of public transit in stimulating economic development and providing increased access to services. In Seattle, for example, a city with a commercial zone too lengthy for some to traverse conveniently, there is free bus service to support easier access to stores, restaurants, and other commercial establishments. And in St. Louis, Downtown St. Louis, Inc. is subsidizing a "free ride zone" of its light-rail system to bring people downtown.

Several cities with attractive pedestrian malls are indeed taking a more holistic approach to revamping the neighborhoods surrounding those malls. In Charlottesville, Virginia, the city council made a concerted effort to locate all major events and new attractions—including the city hall, a hotel, and a skating rink—around the pedestrian mall. The increasing integration of housing into the mall scheme—housing above most of the shops and substantial amounts of new housing on and around the mall—and the lush, green environment of the mall itself, make for a pleasant twenty-four-hour "city within a city." And in Boulder, Colorado, the city made a long-term effort to promote compact development patterns, focus all development toward downtown (all city offices are adjacent to the pedestrian mall and downtown), and resist allowing suburban shopping malls that would divert energy away from the pedestrian mall. It should be noted, however, that within the Boulder mall, limited cross-traffic is permitted in at least one place, and Charlottesville is considering the same. Both malls also benefit from having parking decks and facilities that permit shoppers from surrounding communities to visit easily.

## Conclusions

The examples and strategies explored in this chapter demonstrate in very real ways a concept that would have been unthinkable only a decade ago: that economic principles can be implemented to protect the environment and that a healthy environment can stimulate a stronger economy. Local governments, businesses, citizens, and environmental advocates are finding that it is in their best interest to work together to realize the benefits of the symbiosis of environment, economy, and community. Equally encouraging is the gradual recognition of the importance and potential of a return to downtown as the center of commercial activity and of an active community life, not to mention the primary antidote to urban sprawl.

*Six*

# The Civic Community

American society has always shown itself to be exceedingly mobile within our own borders. In the late 1800s, Frederick Jackson Turner's declaration that the frontier was closed did not stop us from uprooting ourselves and seeking out new places to stake our territory. The vast expanse of available land has shaped our development as a nation, such that our evolving pursuit of economic gain can be defined as much by the mining of natural resources and the agrarian ideal as by commerce, with only the latter requiring the presence of healthy cities. At different points in our history, and particularly in the early part of this century, Americans did indeed flock to cities as centers of commerce and culture, but as soon as suburban living became accessible and affordable, we escaped to what we thought were greener pastures.

In sum, with the exception of the early 1900s, the United States has never been a highly urbanized nation. At the same time, regardless of our patterns of development, we have always valued a flourishing community life involving face-to-face interaction with our fellow citizens. Even (or perhaps especially) in the most rural areas of this country, churches, social clubs, stores, and restaurants have always played a central role in bringing people together, whether spontaneously or on a regular, planned basis. This tendency to commune is perhaps most striking in the context of the post–World War II suburbs, where, as William Whyte observed, the compulsive joining of clubs and associations reached a frighteningly fevered pitch (as cited in Ehrenhalt 1995). One can only assume that out on the new frontier, the ardent desire to interact and conform with one's neighbors was a natural reaction to having moved far away from one's roots.

As the twentieth century comes to a close, we have consumed so much land that many of our previously wide-open spaces—from the desert surrounding Phoenix to once-rural northern Virginia—are now considered "urban" areas. Ironically, just as we have succeeded in becoming urban despite ourselves, so too have we reached the point where it has become all too easy to isolate ourselves from one another. In some cases, we are so

171

frustrated with, or frightened by, society's ills that we actively choose to wall ourselves off from our own community. In many households, long commutes and the need for two incomes leave little time for leisure or investment in community activities. Insecure about our economic future, we follow the prospect of available jobs to wherever it may lead us. Dissatisfied with the current state of our communities, we eagerly uproot ourselves for the promise of a better place to live. Television, telecommuting, and other aspects of our "information culture" are facilitating these tendencies by rendering the need for face-to-face interaction and physical proximity irrelevant.

Whether or not we claim to have actively chosen this course (and, most likely, we are ambivalent), it is not surprising that many citizens have little inclination or time to spare for participating in public life, whether such participation involves joining a civic organization or strolling in the park. Whatever the case, it seems that our transient ways and sprawling development patterns have finally taken us to the point where time, energy, and opportunity for community life have diminished significantly.

## The Erosion of Community Life

How do these tendencies affect public life, civic involvement, and the human fabric of our communities? And why should we care? In the 1990s, there seems to be a growing concern that the bonds of community are deteriorating. The 1992 Los Angeles riots and the 1995 Oklahoma City bombing are just two examples of what appears to be an increasing divisiveness among Americans and, especially in the case of Los Angeles, a lack of concern for and stewardship of our own communities. According to a 1995 *Newsweek* poll, 86 percent of people surveyed feel that we trust each other less now than we did ten years ago. In a 1996 *Time*/CNN poll, 77 percent of respondents agreed with the statement "I wish I had more contact with people in my community" (Goodwin 1997).

A national survey undertaken by the *Washington Post*, Harvard University, and the Kaiser Family Foundation echoes the *Newsweek* poll in documenting a gradual decline in personal trust among Americans from generation to generation. Two out of three Americans believe most people cannot be trusted, as opposed to thirty years ago when a majority believed most people could be trusted. Meanwhile, there has been a decline in voting and PTA membership, as well as a general lack of knowledge of such information as names of elected representatives. The study also shows that experience with crime contributes to lack of trust and that lack of economic security contributes to lack of confidence (Morin and Balz 1996).

Robert Putnam's "Bowling Alone" study is perhaps most familiar to those concerned with this problem. A professor of international affairs at Harvard University, Putnam reports that since 1980, the number of bowling leagues in the United States has declined by 40 percent, while the number of bowlers has increased by 10 percent. Over the past forty years, there has been a similar decline in the number and membership of American associations. Says Putnam, "Membership in organizations in which joining means moving a pen is rising. Membership in groups that require being someplace and knowing another member is declining" (*People* 1995, p. 128). The ultimate consequence of this shift, Putnam believes, is a decline in valuable "social capital." Examples of social capital include parental involvement in schools and neighborly interaction, which help to minimize the need for school spending and police, respectively. Putnam believes that television is largely to blame for this breakdown, particularly as the decline is uniform throughout society. He reports that the average number of hours watched per day has increased to four, and that the more hours people spend watching television, the less they vote (Edsall 1995; *People* 1995).

Putnam's assertions have generated a fair amount of debate as to whether membership in bowling leagues is a relevant indicator of civic involvement, and as to the true causes for the decline of bowling leagues. Peter Hong of the *Los Angeles Times*, for example, believes there are many possible reasons why people are bowling together less, including the availability of a wider range of activities and the fact that people have less time because women are working and fathers are helping to raise children (Hong 1996). But such arguments miss the point, which is that regardless of the root cause, we are spending less time interacting with one another face to face. Whether that interaction centers around bowling, karaoke, or a cup of coffee, it is the leisurely, casual interaction that is the relevant variable.

Regardless of the extent to which the factors cited above indicate a major breakdown in society, there are many approaches that communities can take to encourage civic involvement and to foster that undefinable but important feeling of "community." Across the country, hopeful examples abound of communities that are fostering a new civic spirit in the daily lives of their citizens. This chapter explores how and why some communities succeed in this sense while others do not.

## Articulating "Community"

There have been a number of compelling efforts in recent years to capture just what it is that we mean by "community." In *The Spirit of Community*, Amitai Etzioni refers to "the social webs that communities provide, in neighborhoods, at work, and in ethnic clubs and associations, the webs that bind individuals, who would otherwise be on their own, into groups of people who care for one another and who help maintain a civic, social, and moral order" (Etzioni 1993, p. 248). To research his book *A Good Place to Live*, Terry Pindell traveled the country searching for places offering the "Cheers factor," where "everybody knows your name" (Pindell 1995, p. 15). In *The Good City and the Good Life*, Daniel Kemmis presents a hopeful portrayal of community life that recognizes "civility" as "genius of the city" (Kemmis 1995, p. 191). And Tony Hiss, writing in *The Experience of Place*, emphasizes "connectedness" as the glue that binds natural as well as social communities (Hiss 1990, p. 126).

There are many ways in which "connectedness" to and within place can manifest itself, whether that connection is to nature, as in biophilia; to the ecosystem that one inhabits, as in bioregionalism; to special aspects of the landscape, whether rolling farmland or the Manhattan skyline; to the history of a place; or, perhaps most relevant to the themes of this particular chapter, to the human and human-made elements of the place in which one lives. These feelings of connection, in all their various forms, combine to create a "sense of place." Such feelings are important because they foster a sense of caring for place, promoting stewardship and the assumption of responsibility for others and for one's surroundings. They also remind us of the importance of preserving those special connections for future generations. In short, the stronger our sense of place, the more we care about and for it.

In 1996, *Metropolis* magazine surveyed readers regarding the definition of "community." While answers varied considerably, they also displayed a striking underlying commonality and many shared denominators. Many respondents agreed that community is founded on the ideals of participation, cooperation, and shared goals. Important, oft-cited factors and characteristics included the importance of knowing and interacting with one's neighbors, a feeling of safety, and the community's role in providing a "support network." There was a general feeling that, as one respondent put it, "suburban living is the antithesis of community." Another respondent answered, "Community is a state of mind, but it's intimately tied to public place. The sense of community flourishes when the public place provokes pride and identity" (Friedman 1996).

Whether this feeling goes by the name "community," "connectedness," "civility," or the "Cheers factor," it is clearly a concept that is difficult to articulate. The feeling is so subjective that for each individual there could be numerous definitions, many based on specific personal experiences. However varied these perspectives on community, we are certainly all too familiar with the converse. We know the feelings of fear and alienation that exist when the elements of community are absent. We are familiar with the atmosphere of apathy that pervades so many of our communities, particularly those places that pay little attention to the nuances of the built environment or that display scant regard for natural assets. We have experienced the general dulling of the senses that occurs when we feel disconnected from the landscape and from our fellow citizens. As long as we share a general sense that these feelings are no longer acceptable, we can begin to invest in those elements of place that might help restore the social fabric of our communities.

## Enhancing a Town's Special Qualities

It stands to reason that people will be more likely to invest and stay rooted in places that are worth caring about—places with a strong and appealing local identity, an ambiance of belonging, and a sense of place. Given this assumption, communities seeking to foster a sense of place or to nurture local identity might begin by identifying distinctive qualities of that place—its best natural, cultural, or physical assets—and endowing them with greater recognition. Previous chapters discuss the importance of investing in natural and cultural assets; greater attention to the scale, landmarks, and special characteristics of the built environment can be equally powerful in celebrating place. Along those lines, one respondent to the *Metropolis* survey had the following to say about the importance of scale and architecture:

> The physical environment in Greenpoint supports community. It's built on a scale which is appropriate to the population. It is consistent and contextual, and the architecture, because of the high rate of local, small-scale property ownership, reflects the aesthetic preferences of the people who live there. The community and the built environment mutually reinforce one another (Friedman 1996).

Within the sustainable community, building design can evoke a connection to the city's personality as well as to its aspirations and civic virtues. Architecture can establish and celebrate the spirit, history, and identity of a town. Buildings can be arranged so they relate to one another, and the preservation of community landmarks, particularly historic ones, can be regarded not only as a long-term investment in enhancing a community's cultural heritage and sense of place, but also as a practical and sustainable approach to ecological building design (Fig. 6.1).

In addition to enhancing a community's connection to its own heritage, historic preservation can also make a major contribution to local economic development. Throughout the country, historic battlefields, monuments,

**Figure 6.1** A civic landmark: the Chatham County Courthouse in Pittsboro, North Carolina.

settlements, and buildings are among the most popular tourist destinations. Cities and towns like Charleston; Savannah; or Woodstock, Vermont, are visited as much as for the *sense* of history they exude as for the specific sites they offer. Further, the "recycling," or adaptive reuse, of historic buildings, in addition to its ecological benefits, can result in considerable cost savings while providing additional space to house functions that serve the community. For example, while many churches across the country are thriving, others are losing their congregations due to changes in the makeup of local communities. Whether these churches are historic properties or simply represent a sacred, familiar element of community life, it is not surprising that local residents would be averse to abandoning them. As such, there is a growing trend among communities to adapt these buildings for other uses that benefit the local population. In Elizabeth City, North Carolina, with support from a community development block grant, the Antioch Presbyterian Church has become the Hugh Cale Community Center. In Metarie, Louisiana, a former church is now Christian's Restaurant. In Houston, the Sugar Grove Church of Christ was refurbished to serve as an elementary school. And many residents of New York City recognize the Limelight nightclub as a former church (Twardy 1995a).

In many communities, older school buildings are abandoned because of outmoded safety features or to make way for larger student populations. With their often elegant architecture and large size, and simply due to the fact that so many local residents have frequented them, older schools represent an excellent community landmark worthy of rehabilitation. In Raleigh, North Carolina, the Murphey School (ca. 1916) was the first integrated school in a southern capital city. It closed in the 1960s, later was used as state government offices, and then stood vacant through most of the 1980s. Through a public–private partnership dedicated to affordable housing for seniors, the school has become the Murphey School Senior Citizen Apartments. In nearby Chatham County, the EMJ computer company is inhabiting an abandoned school. When it failed to receive septic approval, the company constructed an indoor/outdoor wetland to treat wastewater. And while the property was originally zoned agricultural, EMJ received local support for the project when neighbors realized that the presence of employees during the daytime would enhance security in a neighborhood where houses stood vacant all day (Cozart 1996).

While the aesthetic appeal of local architecture is obviously important in instilling a sense of caring for the community in which it is situated, so too is its relevance and conformity to the history and culture of a place. In many communities, a landmark's visual beauty is secondary in importance to its historic or cultural value. This notion is often the focus of debate regarding public art, the appreciation of which, like all art, can be highly subjective. Fierce battles have raged over the suggested dismantling of a piece of local art or architecture that has defined a community for decades.

In his book *A Good Place to Live*, Terry Pindell offers a rather extreme example of the importance of local landmarks, however unattractive or aesthetically out of place they may seem, in establishing a sense of place. In recounting his visit to Wilmington, North Carolina, Pindell describes an ongoing debate among city residents regarding the hulking presence of the very large World War II battleship *North Carolina* directly across the Cape Fear River from Wilmington's historic downtown. As Wilmington has transformed itself into a popular tourist destination and residential community, tolerance for the presence of the *North Carolina*, to many a tacky symbol of the "old" Wilmington, has declined considerably. On his final evening after a week in Wilmington, Pindell gazes across the river at the ship:

> As the sun set, I didn't even mind the battleship. Santa Fe had its adobe, San Luis Obispo had its Madonna Inn, Charlottesville had Monticello, Burlington had Stowe. So what if Wilmington had a battleship? One look toward the river and you knew exactly where you were (Pindell 1995, p. 370).

## Designing the Community
## to Encourage Face-to-Face Contact

As Chapters 3 and 5 emphasize, a pedestrian-oriented design, particularly in a downtown setting, can serve multiple purposes. In addition to minimizing sprawl and the environmental impacts associated with the automobile, a pedestrian-oriented environment encourages face-to-face interaction as well as a greater sense of responsibility, security, and public safety. Hence, special measures to accommodate or welcome pedestrians are an integral element of planning for sustainable communities. Traffic-calming measures, ample sidewalks, and visually captivating storefronts, art, and architecture are all important aspects of this mix.

The street environment can be designed to welcome visitors to linger a while, to sit and relax as well as stroll. In addition to benches and town squares, "vest pocket parks"—small greenspaces scattered throughout downtown areas—provide opportunities not only to relax and interact with others, but also to contribute to and appreciate the more natural elements of a neighborhood.

The role of public parks cannot be underestimated, not only in terms of the natural and recreational amenities they provide, but also for their contribution to enhancing face-to-face interaction and strengthening community. Through research conducted for its Green Cities Initiative, the Trust for Public Land has determined that crime decreases in areas that incorporate parks and recreational activities. In Baltimore, a parks initiative in Gwynns Falls Valley is creating a fourteen-mile streamside trail that will traverse twenty neighborhoods before arriving at the downtown waterfront. The trail will dramatically increase access to nature and to cultural and historic sites, such as the B&O Railroad Museum, for a diversity of communities (Reardon 1996).

In large, densely populated cities such as Manhattan, public parks are among a community's most highly valued assets, not simply for their greenery, but also for the opportunity they afford for organized or spontaneous contact with other community members. A visit to Central Park or Prospect Park on a Saturday morning in the spring is uplifting not solely for the experience of running, boating, or experiencing nature, but also for the good feeling that comes with joining an impromptu Frisbee game, cheering on an amateur softball team, or gathering around a group of street musicians or expert rollerbladers. For a city that is renowned for its vast population, fast pace, busy and sometimes brusque citizens, there are countless opportunities for spontaneous, communal activity in Manhattan, thanks in no small part to its public parks.

If designed and situated carefully, elements of the built environment can also provide ample opportunity for spontaneous interaction and a sense of community. As just one example, the post office has traditionally served as a downtown location to "meet and greet," particularly in smaller towns. But throughout the country, post offices are deserting their downtown locations for new offices on the outskirts of town, where there is more room for mail-sorting operations. In some communities, including Saratoga Springs, New York, and Livingston, Montana, citizens protested vehemently when the post office announced plans to relocate to the urban fringe. As a result, in these communities, only the sorting is handled on the outskirts of town, while stamp windows and post boxes remain downtown (Robbins 1996).

In every community, there are a multitude of public buildings that serve some communal purpose. Public libraries, for example, often host lectures, make meeting rooms available to the public, and are particularly valuable in entertaining children. These important public resources must be located in areas that are accessible to all, including those who cannot afford—or are unable, due to age or disability—to drive.

In his book *The Great Good Place*, Ray Oldenburg introduces the concept of the "third place," a place beyond one's home and work—the first and second places, respectively—that occupies prominence within daily life as a place where informal public life occurs. Such places may include local coffee shops, pubs, cafés, beauty parlors, and other "hangouts" that are increasingly endangered in today's built environment. These are places where one can come and go as one pleases, and where "conversation is the main activity" (Oldenburg 1989, p. 26). In short, the third place is where spontaneous, face-to-face interaction is likely but not programmed to occur. It has played an important role in community life for generations, and with the exception of a resurgence in chain coffee houses in recent years, there is a great need for more third places in most communities, particularly in those suburban areas that tend to be dominated by fast-food franchises.

## Privatization versus the Public Realm

The concept of the "third place" also introduces the role of privatization in providing the elements necessary for more sustainable communities. The public resources discussed above are critical to efforts to build bridges between citizens and the places they inhabit. And, indeed, the appeal of the third place is that while many such places are under private ownership, they are entirely public in their orientation and make their living by welcoming community members.

Meanwhile, there are many private efforts under way that are attempting to construct the built elements of community from scratch, from the ground up. In the absence of public subsidies, these projects need to be economically viable, which means that they must be marketable. While the motives and incentives behind them may be entirely altruistic or generated solely with the goal of realizing profits—or somewhere in between—many such projects fall short because of their oversight or deliberate dismissal of the public realm.

As one example, cities and suburban areas around the country are making space for privately owned atria—either indoors or outdoors—as an alternative to public parks. In cities where greenspace is hard to come by, these areas serve as accessible areas to eat a picnic lunch or gather with acquaintances. Nevertheless, these spaces are privately owned, they close at night, and there are many limits on permissible activity within their boundaries. As Peter Katz argues, while such atria can fill a major void in areas where little open space abounds, they do not substitute for the public park in all its natural and human diversity and accessibility (Katz 1995). As Chapter 5 describes, shopping malls fulfill a similar function; they are a particularly popular hangout for teenagers, whose parents do not have to fear that their children are walking the dark streets of the town or city. In fact, in suburban areas where there is a fear of crime, some malls are opening their doors on Halloween as an alternative to house-to-house trick-or-treating; many also open early in the morning to senior citizens looking for a place to walk. Although, these are generous gestures, they beg the question of why it is not possible to find a safe place to walk outside a sterile, privatized environment.

In a new twist on urban revitalization, the city of Las Vegas recently renovated and privatized one of its most heavily trafficked streets, Fremont Street, to provide an atmosphere of greater safety and excitement. Now known as the "Fremont Street Experience," this $70 million, covered pedestrian mall—financed partially by tax dollars and mostly by hotels and casinos—offers its own light show. In return for their substantial contributions, the hotels and casinos can close the street on occasion, to hold events by invitation only or to charge admission for special events such as a New Year's celebration that previously had been accessible to all at no charge. Despite its semi-exclusivity, however, the Fremont Street Experience is succeeding in increasing pedestrian traffic and stimulating new construction by developers and casinos (Newman 1996).

## The Emergence of Gated Communities

Clearly, we are increasingly privatizing some of our more public functions, and nowhere is this tendency more striking than in the gated community. Approximately 4 million Americans live in gated communities, which are characterized by large homes on large lots, accessible only by entrance gates.

They usually provide private security, street maintenance, parks, recreation, garbage collection, and other services. Some erect electric fences to keep animals out. To maintain these features, residents willingly tax themselves heavily. A litany of codes and restrictions regulate everything from house colors to shrub height to yard and façade appearance. A gated community in Klahanie, Washington (east of Seattle), for example, allows no flagpoles, firearms, visible clotheslines, satellite dishes, streetside parking, or unkempt landscaping. Many gated communities have gun control.

These characteristics clearly illustrate the strong desire among residents of gated communities for self-governance, self-regulation, and self-sufficiency. Writing in the *New York Times*, Timothy Egan observes of a gated community, "Bear Creek is doing for itself virtually everything that local government used to do. But in place of municipal rules are a set of regulations so restrictive that many could be found unconstitutional should a city government enact them" (Egan 1995, p. 1).

The demand for homes within gated communities is rapidly increasing, and these homes appreciate in value faster than homes that are not surrounded by gates. In Southern California, one-third of new developments built in the last five years are either gated or have private governing bodies. As evidenced by their security features, the need to feel safe is clearly a big draw of gated communities. While the fear of crime is lower within gated communities, there is little evidence to show, however, that the overall crime rate within gated communities is any lower, with the exception of car theft (Blakely and Snyder 1995).

The irony of gated communities is that while their restrictions, taxation, and overall vigilance represent a remarkable effort toward self-improvement, they contribute very little to the broader community, the public realm, in which they are situated. As just one example, according to Mary Gail Snyder and Edward Blakely of the University of Southern California, a series of focus groups "found widespread disgust with the idea of paying for common space outside their own community" and less interest in participating in decisions regarding taxes, schools, and police. This tendency, they claim, "weakens the bonds of mutual responsibility that are a normal part of community living" (Blakely and Snyder 1995, p. 3).

The general retreat behind gates does not bode well for the future of community life in the United States. Not surprisingly, the exclusive nature of gated communities extends to their entrance requirements. While the U.S. Supreme Court has ruled that gated communities cannot exclude on the basis of race or religion, the price of homes alone—Bear Creek houses cost from $300,000 to $600,000—dictates this. The stringency of regulations adds to their exclusiveness.

According to Gerald Frug, professor of local government at Harvard Law

School, these communities are fooling themselves into thinking they are recreating the ties of earlier eras:

> The village was open to the public. . . . [it] did not have these kinds of restrictions. The village had poor people, retarded people. Somebody could hand you a leaflet. These private communities are totally devoid of random encounters. So you develop this instinct that everyone is just like me, and then you become less likely to support schools, parks or roads for everyone else (as quoted in Egan 1995, p. 22).

Overall, then, our public realm is being privatized. Writing in the *Atlantic Monthly*, Adam Walinsky reports that the increase in crime relative to the number of police officers has increased dramatically over the past thirty years, to the point that to return to the ratio of the 1960s would require the addition of 5 million officers. Meanwhile, there are 1.5 million private officers guarding gated communities, offices, malls, and apartment buildings. "If current trends continue, however, most of the new officers will be privately paid, available for the protection not of the citizenry as a whole . . . but of the commercial and residential enclaves that can afford them. Between these enclaves there will be plenty of room to lose a country" (Walinsky 1995, p. 40).

### New Urbanist Developments

How can we make the public realm function again? Beginning with the simple organization of our physical space, it becomes fairly obvious that the erection of gates is a movement in exactly the wrong direction. In order to circulate and interact, people need proximity, easy access, and freedom to frequent schools, public libraries, churches, playgrounds, and other community centers; they need to live near where they work in order to have more leisure time. Overall, work and home, and the privacy of home, work, and the public realm, must better reinforce one another.

Intentionally designed to encourage human contact and to foster a feeling of community, the New Urbanism offers attractive alternatives to the sprawling, sterile, fortresslike nature of gated communities. Their walkable street design, higher densities, and trademark features such as front porches are among the New Urbanism's most important contributions. However, simply by virtue of their location, most New Urbanist developments are physically disconnected from the public realm. More important, their lack of affordability immediately divorces these enclaves from the surrounding community. It is certainly true, as the New Urbanists argue, that pleasant, attractive living environments tend to command a higher price as a result of the high demand for homes there. However, there has been little demonstrated effort on the part of New Urbanist developments to provide affordable dwellings. At Kentlands (Fig. 6.2), in Gaithersburg, Maryland, single-family homes sell for approximately $220,000 and up to at least $1 million; condominiums and townhouses are priced from $175,000 to $225,000 (Marshall 1996a). At Disney's Celebration, in Osceola, Florida, downtown apartments range from $575 to $1,200 per month, with single-family homes priced anywhere from $127,000 to more than $1 million. Recent interviews with residents of both developments suggest that residents not only recognize that their neighborhoods are more expensive, but also seem to enjoy the cache that comes with living in a pricey development (Marshall 1996a; Whoriskey 1996).

Perhaps more disturbing is the fact that, all over the country, developers are latching on to the New Urbanist view and are attempting to create their own facsimiles of New Urbanist developments. Whether due to lack of perseverance, local zoning obstacles, or a combination of the two, the projects that result come up short even by New Urbanist standards. In Chapel Hill, North Carolina, for example, a self-proclaimed New Urbanist development called Southern Village has emerged just outside town (Fig. 6.3). Unlike the New Urbanist villages, its streets are not laid out on a grid, and its twisting roads are quite confusing to navigate. Situated on a large hill, Southern Village has only two access points to a road that is already so heavily trafficked that it will soon be widened to make room for more automo-

Figure 6.2 Homes of Kentlands, a New Urbanist development outside Washington, D.C., in Gaithersburg, Maryland.

Figure 6.3 One of the larger homes at Southern Village, Chapel Hill, North Carolina.

biles. Traffic lights are soon to follow. While Southern Village does offer one gourmet café and plans are under way for a larger commercial area, it is likely that all but a few of its residents will have to exit or enter the development by car more than once a day to travel to work or the supermarket. On the plus side, Southern Village is connected to a bus line, and a greenway and bicycle path lead to nearby schools.

As for affordability, homes at Southern Village range in price from approximately $220,000 to well over $400,000; an adjacent townhouse development, no different in appearance from the countless other developments scattered around the area, offers townhomes beginning at $150,000. And while Southern Village home design varies, the dwellings seem strikingly homogeneous.

### Cohousing and Intentional Communities

It seems, then, that people are fleeing the public realm regardless of whether there are gates to protect them. Indeed, even cohousing and intentional communities, designed to encourage communal activity—with shared common buildings, workshops, self-governance, and self-management—could be characterized as self-selecting enclaves divorced from the public realm.

Cohousing residents have a level of autonomy in being able to control certain aspects of their community. They have less fear of crime and neighbors to watch over their children. But while cohousing may be characterized by lower prices, it tends not to be very diverse. The fact remains that people are gravitating to these types of developments because they are dissatisfied with what current housing options and the public realm have to offer. According to one resident of Eno Commons, a cohousing development in North Carolina, "The way housing is organized right now, it's difficult to help each other in everyday life" (as quoted in Jackson 1995). And according to Don Lindemann, editor of the *National Cohousing Journal*, "There's a desire for a stronger sense of neighborhood and community. It's part of a reaction to the loss of small-town meeting places that used to be so accessible" (as quoted in Evans 1996).

## The "Participative Fabric" of Community

Gated communities, New Urbanist developments, and cohousing reflect efforts to foster or enhance community life, whatever its form. The high prices commanded by many of these housing options indicate that citizens are more than open to living at higher densities. Perhaps the most striking feature of Southern Village is that in a region where land and large lots are still abundant and relatively inexpensive, people are paying as much as half a million dollars to live in houses that are so close together. Thus, the rearrangement of the built environment constitutes an important element in the mix of approaches that might, if implemented correctly, serve to foster the connections necessary for community to occur.

Meanwhile, however, the vast majority of Americans live in areas in which large-scale redesign efforts would be infeasible, unaffordable, and wasteful. Rather than build new developments, physically retrofit existing neighborhoods, or abandon what has already been built, there are many ways in which citizens and governments can create a greater feeling of community, regardless of whether they reside in a cul-de-sac community, a declining downtown, or a rural area.

Amitai Etzioni's communitarian movement—which proposes not only a comprehensive, new paradigm, but also a specific public-policy agenda to advance it—represents one approach to instilling a new ethic of community among the general population (Etzioni 1993). And while some commentators may argue that the creation of a new movement or ethic seems about as unnatural as building entirely self-contained "insta-communities," our current disconnected tendencies seem to require no less than a major effort to change the way we interact.

A host of community-building options exist, at a variety of scales of effort and expense. Community events, for example, provide a venue for spontaneous, casual interaction in much the same way as the "third place." The farmers' market is one such ritual. In *The Good City and the Good Life*, Daniel Kemmis describes the important role of the weekly farmers' market in providing an anchor for community life:

> Moving through the market . . . I see in dozens of conversations around me an interweaving of . . . life stories, and I find delight and security in realizing once again that this fabric is Missoula, my home, my city . . . I know that one of the reasons I enjoy the Farmers' Market is because it represents for me the best of the city in microcosm (Kemmis 1995, pp. 5–6).

In addition to representing a sacred ritual for Kemmis to enjoy in the company of his son, the weekly visit to the farmers' market provides the opportunity to mingle casually with others in the community—not to mention to enjoy and support the bountiful produce provided by local farmers. Missoula's weekly "Out to Lunch" concerts provide another regular and casual venue for citizens to enjoy face-to-face interaction.

Events such as outdoor concerts and festivals are a regular fixture in communities across the country. In the warm months in Manhattan, for example, virtually every one of the north-south avenues (as opposed to cross-streets) hosts its own street festival. Given the extreme potential for traffic snarls resulting from the closing of a major avenue for an entire day, the lengths to which the city goes to support these events is a testament to the value it places on community celebrations. The New York City Marathon, Fourth of July fireworks, and extravagant parades honoring Thanksgiving, St. Patrick's Day, Chinese New Year, and Halloween are just a small sampling of community events held each year in New York City.

The extent to which these events and rituals enliven the texture of community life cannot be underestimated; nor, however, can the amount of effort and commitment they represent. Recognizing the need to orchestrate these opportunities in an organized fashion, as well as their potential for community building, many cities are incorporating events into their plans for sustainability. In Chattanooga, for example, the Riverfront–Downtown Planning and Design Center has built a pavilion and outdoor plaza in a once-vacant spot directly adjacent to its downtown headquarters (Fig. 6.4). Jazz concerts and other events are held on the plaza every Friday evening. In Charlottesville, Virginia, residents gather on the pedestrian mall for weekly "Fridays After Five" events. In Asheville, North Carolina, the town square is the site of a weekly bluegrass concert; local residents, including a great many seniors, look forward to the event regardless of the weather.

Figure 6.4 Developed by the Riverfront–Downtown Planning and Design Center, Miller Plaza is a popular downtown gathering spot for the citizens of Chattanooga, Tennessee. *Source:* Chattanooga Area Convention and Visitors Bureau.

In addition to providing a place to enjoy entertainment and mingle, these events are a way of celebrating the community, as Kemmis implies, as well as the local assets that are unique to that community. In many places, a major regional event can generate tremendous economic revenues while injecting that much-needed shot of pride that many communities are sorely lacking. As yet another element of Chattanooga's multifaceted sustainability effort, the annual Riverfront Festival (Fig. 6.5) draws visitors from all over the region to celebrate what has only recently, after decades of effort, become Chattanooga's most prized asset: the Tennessee River. In New Orleans, the annual Jazz and Heritage Festival draws visitors from around the world who come not only to hear great music, but also to sample local cuisine, appreciate local culture and history, and generally bask in the special ambiance that only New Orleans can offer.

Such opportunities for face-to-face interaction can occur at scales far smaller than the weekly concert in the park and without the physical infrastructure of the "third place." The daily visit to the "dog park," for example, is a remarkably universal ritual for urban residents across the country. Many urban dog owners, particularly those who work from nine to five, look forward to the evening visit to the park, where they are likely to meet and greet the same neighborhood dog owners on a regular basis. The dog park provides a regular but unscheduled opportunity simply to chat with other

**Figure 6.5** Chattanooga's annual Riverfront Festival draws visitors from all over the region to celebrate the city's most valuable asset. *Source:* Chattanooga Area Convention and Visitors Bureau.

members of the community. Families with children also are often likely to find reason to congregate outside of the home. In a recent editorial in the *Washington Post*, Marta Vogel describes the pleasure of gathering with neighbors in the street on summer evenings while their children play together: "We have achieved what George Washington professor Amitai Etzioni calls 'the first part to community, this warm fuzzy feeling where the postman knows your name, an interpersonal web'" (Vogel 1996, p. C1).

But Vogel stresses the fact that we cannot rely on this feeling happening spontaneously, but rather must "get to work"—through yard sales, block parties, a babysitting co-op, or a neighborhood newsletter—to foster the bonds of community. Writing in the *New Yorker*, Witold Rybczynski agrees: "Modern mobility means that the process of neighborhood creation, which previously took decades, must be 'jump-started'" (Rybczynski 1996, p. 39). On a visit to Sea Pines Plantation, on Hilton Head Island, he interviewed the Plantation's creator, Charles Fraser, who hosted a party every Saturday night for ten years to create a feeling of community there.

Local institutions can be nurtured as well. Civic groups—whether environmental organizations, the Rotary Club, or Friends of the Library—are among a community's most valuable assets. Cities and towns can support these groups by providing meeting space, or booths or tables at local events, and by generally fostering an open exchange and opportunities for partnerships. The support of community gardens can make a great difference in enhancing urban areas while providing fresh produce, employment, and a place for people to interact and work side by side toward a common goal. In Philadelphia, for example, one precinct has seen a 90 percent drop in crime as a result of its volunteer gardening programs (Reardon 1996).

Finally, the role of youth in the future of communities, and the importance of providing a stimulating environment for youth, should not be overlooked. A recent survey by the National League of Cities showed that 62 percent of city officials believe that youth crime is worsening. Teenagers need opportunities to take responsibility and to make more of their lives. Many cities have incorporated specific goals to engage youth in civic activities. Racine, Wisconsin, for example, has pledged to become "America's most youth-friendly community." The city is creating pilot projects involving a family and children's resource center, with recreation facilities, family support services, and community policing. With help from local businesses, they hold dances, a model teen court, and other activities, and the city paper, the *Racine Journal-Times*, has its own youth page (Peirce 1996). Phoenix, meanwhile, has experienced a 55 percent drop in juvenile arrests upon instituting its new late-night basketball program (Reardon 1996). And in many places, safety is enhanced and community connections fostered through community policing programs or "community watch" alliances.

## Affordable Housing and Social Equity

A principal tenet of the vision of sustainable communities is a commitment to becoming socially just, equitable, and accessible to all racial, cultural, age, and income groups. Sustainable communities work to ensure social opportunity and access to essential services for all members, to tolerate and encourage diversity, and to minimize the separation or isolation of income and racial groups.

Access to affordable housing—and, more generally, to an affordable lifestyle—is a critical element of this vision. Beyond fostering greater social equity and diversity, and alleviating the increasing segregation of our communities, the availability of affordable housing is also important from a land use perspective. As just one example, the inability of middle- and low-income workers to afford to live near their jobs—being forced, instead, to purchase less expensive property farther away—increases sprawl and adds to traffic congestion. And for those without access to transportation, mobility and employment opportunities are severely limited.

Beginning with rampant NIMBYism, a daunting range of obstacles foster disincentives and outright opposition to the adequate provision of af-

fordable housing. In part, neighborhood challenges to lower-income housing stem from the decades-old stigma of public housing "projects" that concentrated low-income residents in one isolated location. More recently, the
interspersing of affordable housing—particularly through infill development—throughout communities has provided a greater range of employment and transportation options for residents. As discussed in previous
chapters, the mixing of building types within a neighborhood can serve a
variety of purposes regardless of the income level of its residents. Throughout the stages of adult life, for example, individuals and families may encounter a series of different housing needs, from one-bedroom apartment
to four-person family home to modest retirement bungalow. The availability of all these options in one neighborhood reduces the impetus to leave
the community in search of adequate housing.

Zoning provisions and the high price of land, however, often prohibit the
most well-intentioned plans from moving forward. One of the greatest obstacles to this approach is the inability in many communities to stimulate a
mix of housing types, prices, and sizes due to zoning provisions that encourage the separation not only of uses, but also of building types. Also,
most developers are reluctant to build lower-priced housing due to a perception that to do so would minimize or even eliminate potential profit.
While this viewpoint regards higher-priced housing as the sector for greatest profit maximization, there are many approaches, particularly within the
burgeoning "green building" movement, through which alternative building methods can help lower construction costs (North Carolina Solar Center 1994).

Altering local zoning and regulatory structures, ideally through the use of
financial incentives, can help encourage greater provision of affordable
housing. Revising zoning measures to allow for multifamily and mixed-use
development is a good place to start. The use of "inclusionary zoning,"
which requires developers to incorporate a certain amount of affordable
housing into all new developments—including New Urbanist—should also
be encouraged.

In Arlington County, Virginia, the General Land Use Plan was revised in
the 1980s in order to direct high-density development toward Metro (subway) corridors. The potential for increased land value and housing demand
along those corridors posed the threat of displacement for long-time residents. Committed to the provision of affordable housing for local residents,
the county created an affordable housing overlay district. Under this provision of the plan, in order to have a site rezoned for redevelopment at high
densities, developers were required to preserve housing that traditionally
had been considered "affordable" or to replace it with new affordable housing in comparable locations. The county agreed to subsidize these efforts

given strong evidence that the developers could not afford to finance the entire replacement. Developers were able to obtain additional financing through county loans, federal low-income housing tax credits, and tax-exempt bond issues (Gallagher 1994, as cited in Porter 1997).

Tax-increment financing—which uses taxes from newly developed property to fund initiatives that are highly valued from the perspective of the entire community—has proven effective in increasing the availability of affordable housing in many communities. In many cases, developers of lower-cost homes get a short-term tax break under the condition that the savings are passed on to buyers. Or the tax increment between the value of the property before and after development can be dedicated to paying off bonds that provide lower-cost loans or mortgages. Finally, "linkage programs," in which local businesses contribute to an affordable housing fund based on the size (in square feet) of their project, can also augment available resources.

The high price of land is often regarded as a major obstacle to affordable housing. Land may be donated, either as the result of bond referenda or through the use of a community land trust (CLT), which holds and leases the land on which the houses stand to homeowners via a long-term renewable lease. A home can still be resold, but the CLT has the option of buying it back.

In many communities, nonprofit housing organizations serve as the primary catalyst in facilitating access to credit and decent homes for lower-income residents. These organizations serve as a much-needed conduit between the buyer and the bank, providing access to credit and education on everything from loan applications to home maintenance. In some cases, land is donated by the city, and the organization builds (often through the employment of minority labor) and sells the house, or arranges a lease-to-own agreement. In many communities, vacant or declining housing stock is often so plentiful that affordable housing initiatives revolve primarily around the renovation, rehabilitation, and retrofitting of existing buildings.

The most successful organizations tend to rely heavily on partnerships with private lending institutions and public agencies and are adept at leveraging financial resources from both sectors. In 1995, for example, the Chattanooga Neighborhood Enterprise (CNE) was the largest single producer of affordable housing in the country, due in large part to their ability to leverage public funding from private dollars (and vice versa) and their very thorough buyer education program. (Ironically, while CNE is one of Chattanooga's biggest sustainable development success stories, its successes are often publicly overshadowed by the city's many accomplishments in the areas of environmental protection and riverfront revitalization.)

Created in 1986, CNE receives funds from the Lyndhurst Foundation, the city of Chattanooga's general fund, numerous local financial institutions, and county, state, and federal government sources. The organization's programs stress education and access to information as the foundation for increased home ownership among lower-income communities. Thus, in addition to providing neighborhood infrastructure improvements, low-interest home loans, and affordable rental opportunities, CNE places a heavy emphasis on its home buyer education program—eight hours of training that covers loan qualification, budgeting, and access to credit, as well as home maintenance.

In its first year of operation, CNE's budget totaled under $4 million, all provided through city and foundation grants. By 1995 this figure had reached $20 million, only 25 percent of which came from grants (including $2 million from the city's general fund), with the remainder from mortgages, bank lending, and the conventional investment market. Chattanooga's ongoing willingness to support CNE's programs stems partly from the recognition that enhanced home ownership ultimately helps Chattanooga's tax base. In fact, according to Leigh Ferguson, CNE's director, an economic impact study showed a total investment in Hamilton County of $42 million in general revenues generated by real estate tax revenues from CNE projects (personal communication, November 30, 1997). Thus, through the work of CNE, the city's $2 million grant leverages both tax revenues as well as loan repayments.

Obviously these are just a few of the many policies and strategies that can serve to encourage and accommodate a greater range of housing options within the sustainable community. This brief list, however, indicates clearly that such efforts not only require but also benefit greatly from close collaboration with land use planning and economic development strategies—the very definition of the holistic approach to sustainable development.

## Beyond Housing: Other Elements of Affordability

Beyond the simple cost of construction or purchase, there are many other significant expenses associated with owning a home. As just one example, the cost of utilities—electricity, heat, and water, among others—can greatly increase monthly housing expenses. As such, energy conservation becomes an important element in ensuring affordability. Ironically, many affordable housing construction programs are so concerned with minimizing construction costs that they neglect to consider the energy costs needed to operate the home.

In some communities, in order to reduce monthly energy bills, nonprofit builders are collaborating to incorporate solar energy design into affordable housing communities. The Green Builders Program (see Chapter 4) is one such program; Jordan Commons (see Chapter 4) is another. In Greensboro, North Carolina, four nonprofit builders are collaborating on a 100-acre property that will include approximately 200 homes incorporating sustainable design as well as a neotraditional street layout. The group is hoping that the construction of such a visible project will help educate other builders and the general public about the importance and value of sustainable design in housing affordability and in general. The development of this project relies on ongoing participation from area residents and the local government (Powell 1995).

The initial cost and ongoing expense of running a home is but one aspect of affordability. Transportation costs are a key expense; therefore, access to public transportation becomes an important tool in enhancing affordability as well as in supporting environmental sustainability. Ultimately, the overall issue of "access"—to jobs, to health care, and to education—becomes more an issue of social equity rather than simply economics.

## Conclusions

There is a clear need in our country to strengthen feelings of community and to foster greater face-to-face interaction among citizens, whether by enhancing the special qualities of the built environment or encouraging greater opportunities for community participation. In our quest for a more civic city, we need to implement ideas and strategies that emphasize the importance of the public realm, diversity, and social equity above all else.

*Seven*

# Getting There from Here: Starting Points and Future Directions

The challenge of moving from the present set of conditions to a world of sustainable places and regions is a bit daunting. The previous chapters provide extensive information and ideas about what measures can be undertaken and about some of the more interesting and innovative local approaches around the country. This chapter provides some insights into how to get started at the local level and identifies some needed changes at the national level that will help to create a climate more supportive of the local and regional initiatives discussed here. It should be emphasized that this discussion is not intended to be exhaustive or comprehensive. There are undoubtedly many other ideas and approaches for beginning to move in the direction of sustainable place; these are a few of the most important ones.

## A New Ethic for Sustainable Places

We have argued that the unsustainability of current land use and development patterns reflects a crisis of values and ethics. The present built environment and the ways in which we treat the natural environment are in no small degree a result of certain dominant values in American society, among them individualism, a short moral time frame, parochialism, and anthropocentrism. It should be emphasized that these values are not always inappropriate. Balanced alongside community needs and interests, individualism can be a powerful and important value in creating a productive economy and society. Yet the extremes of individualism often have just the opposite effects. And while an emphasis on these values may have been suited to a particular time in the development of our nation, they are no longer suited to the environmental, material, and social circumstances of our country or, indeed, the planet.

One of the most significant challenges we face as a society is how to begin to shift the ethical underpinnings of our nation and culture in directions that are more supportive of sustainable development and of sustainable land use patterns and practices. The elements of a new ethic of sustainable place could certainly stimulate considerable discussion; Table 7-1 presents some of these elements as counterposed to the prevailing ethic. This volume does not advocate a choice of one value or ethic over another so much as the need to find a balance between the poles identified here. Along with individualism, for example, we need a new appreciation and ethic of interdependence. Individual or self-interest is important, but must be moderated by a greater concern than is currently expressed for the impacts of one's actions on others, in both time and space. An ethic of sustainable place, then, is composed of a number of value dimensions, including: an ethic of interdependence; respect for the interests of future inhabitants and future generations; greater respect for the needs of the broader public, and personal responsibility to that community; humility and caution in using and manipulating nature and the natural environment; and a sense of kinship with the many other life-forms that inhabit the planet and respect for the needs of the broader natural environment.

Precisely how to bring about or advance the elements of this new ethic is a question largely beyond the scope of this book. The short answer is that, as part of our efforts to create more sustainable places, we must begin to look for ways of supporting an ethic or set of ethics that will, at the same time, help to undergird such places. There are many ways to do this. Whenever we discuss policy decisions about land use and community growth, we must try to identify the underlying ethical choices involved; citizens and elected officials should be encouraged to question the moral assumptions of

## Table 7.1
### *A New Ethic for Sustainable Places*

| Current Ethic | Ethic of Sustainable Place |
| --- | --- |
| Individualism, selfishness | Interdependence, community |
| Shortsightedness, present-oriented ethic | Farsightedness, future-oriented ethic |
| Greed, commodity-based | Altruism |
| Parochialism, atomistic | Regionalism, extra-local |
| Material, consumption-based | Nonmaterial, community-based |
| Arrogance | Humility, caution |
| Anthropocentrism | Kinship |

these decisions and begin to view their choices about the future as ethical and moral choices.

Environmental education is a frequently touted antidote and, while not a panacea for unsustainable practices, is an essential ingredient in building a new ethic. The potential venues for such education range from schools to citizen advocacy efforts.

There is a growing consensus about the importance of teaching basic ecological literacy (e.g., the principles of ecology, laws of thermodynamics, concepts of wildlife biology) in schools. As David Orr has declared, "all education is environmental." In one way or another, and just as much by what we leave out of a curriculum as what we include in it, we indicate the priority and importance of the natural environment (Orr 1994). Exactly what should comprise our environmental curricula (from kindergarten through graduate school) is beyond a thorough discussion here, but there is considerable recent literature about how and what ought to be taught (e.g., Bowers 1995; Orr 1994). There are a number of ideas that merit attention: the need to take learning outside (in both urban and suburban/exurban environments); the importance of learning by doing; the need to teach citizenship and social responsibilities; and the importance of service-based learning, among many others.

Clearly, in addition to ecological facts, concepts, and principles, there must be an experiential component—the chance for students, beginning at early stages, to understand and experience the natural environment firsthand and in an emotionally direct way. In this regard, efforts in some communities to create ecology schools represent a positive step.

We should, furthermore, never miss the opportunity to incorporate an educative function into the design of school buildings. Incorporation of solar features, sustainable building materials, and recycling facilities provides chances for students to learn about sustainability and to establish a sense of personal involvement at an early age. In a way, what this means is a significant redefinition of the equipment, facilities, and other components we feel are needed for the educational mission of our schools. In addition to—or, in some cases, instead of—the asphalt playing surfaces, jungle gyms, books, desks, and blackboards, and various other conventional learning tools, we need trees on-site, wetlands and stream habitat, an active compost site, and so on. Efforts at "greening" schools, and replacing the concrete with trees and other vegetation, will serve to create a new and important set of conditions for learning.

Place-based learning is also an important element, with curricula that focus, at least in part, on what exists locally and regionally—elements within one's own bioregion (Fig. 7.1). This approach involves teaching about local flora and fauna, local history and settlement patterns, the area's landscape and topography, and the beauty and sacred places of one's home environment. The goal is to teach about the world, through the lens of one's community and region, while at the same time instilling a sense of love and caring about the places in which we actually live. Curricula should also include the active exploration of place, consistent with one's educational stage and development (e.g., whether a day visit to a local estuary for young students, or the selection of the local economy as the subject for a college or MBA accounting project).

Urban ecology programs conducted outside the context of schools can also make a significant impact. Greater attention must be paid to urban children, imparting to them a sense of the environmental wonder and complexity of cities. Again, it is important to begin this learning at an early age, building a constituency of city residents who will later passionately support the greening and protection of urban ecosystems. One model is the successful Urban Education Project instituted by Denver Audubon in the mid-1980s. The program involves trained volunteers working with small groups of children outside the classroom, exploring urban habitats and environments. The discoveries and experiences that result may seem insignificant at

Figure 7.1 Place-based learning: fourth-graders take water samples from a local river.

the time, but can have a lasting effect on the long-term development of children:

> Most of their time is spent searching for, observing, and discovering new things. Kids explore the natural world in city parks, schoolyards, rights-of-way, and vacant lots. They find different kinds of roots and creatures that live under the soil, build bird feeders to attract and observe urban wildlife, and do experiments to test the food preferences of neighborhood birds. They investigate the interrelationships between plants and animals, and have chances to compare their findings with one another . . . All participants gain a greater awareness of their surroundings, a better understanding of the natural world and our relation to it (Hollweg 1994, p. 270).

Each year the Denver program involves some 1,500 children (about 40 percent from poor families), and the effort has spawned similar programs in eight other cities (reaching 7,500 children a year nationally). The Denver program is run by 180 volunteers and one full-time coordinator and operated with a very modest budget. It effectively illustrates what can be done with volunteer labor, at a small cost, and through collaboration with the local environmental community. There is now even a national network to assist in starting these programs (VINE, or Volunteer-led Investigations of Neighborhood Ecology, based in Troy, Ohio; see Hollweg 1994).

Hands-on youth education can be applied to the built environment as well. In Washington, D.C., the National Building Museum sponsors a program called "City Vision: Community Solutions Through Design." The program provides opportunities for inner-city teenagers to shape their communities by learning sketching, model-making, photography, and other design skills and applying those skills to problems in their neighborhoods. In 1996, participants created a plan for locating trash cans in heavily trafficked areas, designed a public recycling bin with multiple compartments, and proposed the establishment of a recycling center in an abandoned building. The program, which runs for three months, culminates in a presentation before an audience of designers, teachers, family members, and friends held at the museum (National Building Museum 1997).

Education of adults is also important, of course; they must be encouraged to be "students of their places" as well (to use David Orr's term). Even residents of a city or town who have lived there many years may have a poor understanding of its environmental qualities and specialness. A unique international program called the Green Map System has recently emerged and uses visual information to provide place-based environmental education. Through the work of map-making teams composed of designers, students, environmentalists, and concerned citizens in communities around the world, the program has captured and vividly portrayed "green sites" in twenty-seven cities. Such green sites may include parks, bike paths, ecologically friendly buildings, and green businesses. Polluted sites are indicated as well, as areas that need protection or rehabilitation. The green sites are displayed on colorful maps that are printed and distributed to the public and are also accessible via the Internet. The very first Green Map was produced for New York City; its latest version includes almost 700 green sites—potentially a very powerful tool for educating citizens as to the natural and environmental features of their community (Brawer 1997).

Another challenge is to instill a sense of caring about place and environment. A recent article in the *Washington Post* is perhaps indicative of the potential here. It told the story of a "crime" committed in the community of North Beach, Maryland (Shields 1995). The crime was the cutting down, by the town, of a hundred-year-old red maple tree—an important fixture to many in the community. The action, precipitated by the fear that the tree presented a danger by hanging over a public sidewalk, unleashed a storm of criticism and complaints by neighbors and others who had loved the prominent tree. The former occupants of the house the tree fronted were reported to have cried at the news, and the current occupant put up a sign so that the community would know that he was not responsible. The irony of this story is that while the community deeply cared for this tree, there are undoubtedly a host of other environmental degradations that are far more damaging but that elicit much less protest. Still, this story illustrates a community's commitment to and love of place.

How to encourage or instill this sense of commitment to place remains uncertain, but achieving long-term sustainable places requires the development of this kind of sensibility. Some argue that what is required is for people to stop moving from place to place and to reside in and commit to a place and a home. Certainly, the increasingly mobile nature of modern society is both a cause and effect of our unsustainable patterns of development.

Another strategy is to provide opportunities for citizens to make tangible expressions of their commitment to place and to the future inhabitants of their community. One simple example is the activity of tree planting, which has become increasingly popular as a community activity in part, at least, because it represents "a demonstration of commitment to the future" (Dwyer, Schroeder, and Gobster 1994, p. 147).

We must also find ways to "rephysicalize" people, to borrow from and modify Steinberg's term. That is, we should encourage citizens to understand the fundamental ways in which their actions—regarding their homes, lawns, transportation, etc.—are tied to others and to the larger environment in which they are situated.

The physical layout and design of places can in turn help to shape the ethics that are at work within them and that can serve to undergird them. On a social level, many commentators have speculated about the role of community design. Philip Langdon argues that a street and community layout that separates and physically impedes people's movement beyond their immediate neighborhoods tends to solidify parochial outlooks. How do we encourage people to see themselves as regional citizens? One way is to make it easy to see and experience other neighborhoods. "The continuous [street] network has the virtue of not reining in a person's loyalties. It is easy for people to become acquainted with areas beyond their own neighborhood, and as they become more knowledgeable, they are likely to become more empathetic toward those places and their inhabitants" (Langdon 1994, p. 143).

Public streets and civic spaces are similarly important in instilling a broader public ethic and a sense of being part of a larger whole and in developing attachments to this broader public. Richard Sennett emphasized this in *The Uses of Disorder: Personal Identity and City Life* in 1970. In this insightful work, he argued that emerging suburban-style development, with its paucity of social "contact points," was depriving young people of learning about and dealing with other social and cultural groups, and in effect was "freezing" their moral growth and development, causing them to remain forever in emotional adolescence. In his words:

> What I envision is a restructuring of city life so that these adolescent patterns have a challenging social matrix. There are definite and workable means by which cities can become human settlements that force these coherence drives to be tested and challenged. These same city structures could confront as well older persons who have regressed to childish or adolescent indifference about the effect of their acts on the people around them (Sennett 1970, p. 139).

Constructing the "social matrix" means overcoming physical separation by creating social and civic spaces that enable and encourage people to interact: neighborhoods that promote walking and physical interaction, mixed-use development that integrates the different elements of social life, and so on. The types of cities and spaces we inhabit surely influence the kind of citizens and society we are, and the extent to which we acknowledge a broader moral community to which we owe some responsibility.

Experiential learning can be extremely important in shaping an environmental ethic and in developing a sense of kinship with, and caring for, the rest of nature. In their book *Geography of Childhood: Why Children Need Wild Places,* Gary Nabhan and Stephen Trimble argue for the importance of providing children with natural areas to explore and enjoy. They are distressed by the diminishing of these opportunities in our modern society and wonder if it bodes ill for a sense of environmental caring (Nabhan and Trimble 1994).

These factors that can help in shaping a more appropriate ethic for our time are, in fact, many of the very qualities of sustainable places. Is this circular reasoning, then, that we must have sustainable places before we can develop an ethic to support them? To some extent, yes, but there are many small ways in which actions can be taken that, over the long haul, can help to put in place a sustainability ethic. For example, protecting access to at least some wildness and nature for children during their early development will reap many benefits later in creating a more environmentally knowledgeable and caring citizenry.

It might also be argued that the task at hand is not so much creating and absorbing an entirely new ethic, but rather drawing upon and adapting values and beliefs that already exist. David Orr tells the story of a polluting oil company that felt the need to fly Old Glory (Orr 1996). Orr considered it a contradiction that the company saw itself as being patriotic, yet was engaged in a most unpatriotic act: doing serious harm to the health and environment of the community. Perhaps, as Orr pondered, we can find ways to build upon values such as patriotism that resonate well with many, to induce or encourage actions that are more sustainable. (Perhaps, for example, overusing water, buying a second car, or allowing the destruction of an irreplaceable landscape could ultimately be seen as truly unpatriotic acts.)

There is a lively debate about exactly what values, if any, all or most human beings tend to share. Perhaps that set of values might be a starting point for identifying a value foundation upon which to build sustainable place sensibilities. Rush Kidder, for instance, interviewed prominent individuals around the world to identify eight common moral values about which, he believes, there is agreement across cultures: love, truthfulness, fairness, freedom, unity, tolerance, responsibility, and respect for life (Kidder 1994). Whether or not these values are in fact common (and their precise meanings remain debatable), perhaps they offer some ideas about building a sustainability ethic. Allowing the destruction of the ecological capital necessary for future generations to have a healthful, fulfilling life would seem to violate several of these basic values, including love, responsibility, fairness, and respect for life.

There may also be certain innate ethical sensibilities that could be tapped into. The idea of biophilia suggests that humans have a "deep biological need for affiliating with life and nature" (Kellert 1996, p. 26), the result of centuries of co-evolution and symbiotic interaction with nature and other life. As Stephen Kellert notes in his book *The Value of Life,* tapping into this need may take some work:

> Unlike the "hardwired" instincts of breathing or feeding, which occur almost automatically, the biophilic values must be cultivated to achieve their full expression. They depend on repeated exposure and social reinforcement before emerging as meaningful dimensions of human emotional and intellectual life. Once learned and supported, however, they become key elements of human personality and culture (p. 26).

How to nurture these values takes us again into the realm of education, experiential learning, and opportunities to enjoy nature directly. Recent survey research suggests, however, that people are perhaps more willing to acknowledge the inherent moral worth of other forms of life than might generally be thought (Kempton, Boster, and Hartley 1995). Creating more sustainable places, though, will require a concerted effort to develop a more caring value base that builds upon our existing moral sensibilities.

It is also the case that certain groups in society that have an unusually important role in shaping our communities must begin to view their roles in more ethical terms and to acknowledge that they have ethical obligations to seek different paths. One group, much maligned in some quarters, is the development community itself. As Neal Payton observes, we must begin to work on the extent to which developers view their activities as involving certain ethical responsibilities. "Developers must see themselves not merely as initiators, but as trustees and stewards as well. Anything less is not sustainable in the long run" (Payton, undated, p. 3). The Urban Land Institute (ULI) has taken this approach through the recent publication of a set of environmentally responsible design guidelines. Also promising is the initiation by the ULI of an annual design award for the best green development.

The Haymount development, outside Fredericksburg, Virginia (see Chapter 4), while problematic in a number of ways, does exhibit the kind of ethical concern developers should be encouraged to adopt. Through their design and planning, the developers of this project have made serious efforts to address local and extra-local concerns, including affordable housing in the community (e.g., by creating a local land trust to develop and build new housing in the county and to repair existing housing) and an obligation to protect and restore the broader regional ecosystem in which it is located (e.g., by providing technical assistance on sustainability issues to farmers and landowners in the region). It remains to be seen whether the developer will be willing and able to follow through on these efforts, but it is encouraging that the project has an explicitly stated environmental ethic: "It is an ethic that accepts responsibility for the imprint and the impact of its development on the landscape and the environment" (Clark, Payton, and Tice, undated, p. 8).

## Becoming More Sustainable

Where, then, are we left, and what can be done to advance this new paradigm? Clearly, there are many different fronts on which to work. It may be necessary first to acknowledge that true sustainability may never be achievable, but that this recognition should not stop us from pursuing efforts that at least move us toward sustainability. A community that makes even one policy change in the direction of sustainability should be commended, whether it adopts an aggressive recycling program, a solar access ordinance, or a ride-share program. The difficulty or improbability of reaching sustainability should not paralyze us into complacency or nonaction. Some movement in the direction of greater sustainability is better than none.

### Understanding the Impacts of Community and Individual Decisions: Indicators and Benchmarks

One of the first things that a community can do is to begin to understand more systematically whether, and in what ways, the community is sustainable over time. More than forty communities around the country have developed some form of sustainability indicators. According to the Community Environmental Council, Inc. (CEC), which has been monitoring these initiatives, sustainable community indicators serve four main functions:

- enabling a community to identify what it values and prioritized those values
- holding individuals and a larger group accountable for achieving the results they want
- democracy building; through collaboration people engage in a community-building process
- allowing people to measure what is important and make decisions based on those results. They measure whether we are achieving what we want and whether the outcomes are improving our lives (Zachary 1995, p. 7).

Notable examples of communities that have recently developed such indicators include Santa Monica, California; Cambridge, Massachusetts; and Seattle, Washington. In Seattle, a set of forty indicators was developed through a community forum process and published by a private group called Sustainable Seattle. Two sets of indicators have now been published, the first in 1993 and the second in 1995. The 1995 report assessed the performance of all forty indicators in terms of their movement toward or away from sustainability. Fourteen indicators were determined to be moving in an unsustainable direction; eighteen remained stable; and eight showed improvement (Sustainable Seattle 1995).

In addition to its value as a measurement tool, the development of indicators can itself serve as a way to begin a structured community dialogue about the future and to educate citizens within and beyond the local community. Sustainable Seattle's reports are distributed throughout the country and serve as model documents for other communities. Perhaps more important, the dissemination of results throughout the greater Seattle region serves a valuable educational purpose.

Jacksonville, Florida, is another community that has employed the indicators process to work toward specific future goals while educating its citizenry. Beginning in 1985, the Jacksonville Community Council initiated a process that resulted in seventy-two indicators of quality of life in nine different categories: education, economy, public safety, natural environment, health, social environment, government/politics, culture/recreation, and mobility. The council assessed these indicators according to data going back to the mid-1970s and, in 1991, developed a set of priorities, targets, and goals for the year 2000. The process has involved more than 100 volunteers and has resulted in a series of educational materials on Jacksonville's quality of life (Jacksonville Community Council, undated).

Oregon's Benchmarks Program is an example of a state-level indicators approach. The state legislature created the Oregon Progress Board, which has responsibility for preparing the benchmarks. These 259 benchmarks are not simply indicators of where the state is, but statements about where the state wishes to be. The benchmarks were enacted into law in 1991, and state agencies are now required to give priority to them in their budgetary decision making.

Indicator and benchmark initiatives are promising in several ways. First, they provide a gauge, a set of indices, around which a common discussion about progress (or lack thereof) can occur. They provide an opportunity for dialogue about the range and variety of criteria that should be considered when thinking about the health, progress, and prosperity of a community. In this way, a diverse group of community members can examine such social indicators as access to health care or education and such environmental indicators as air and water quality trends or the appropriate acreage for open space and parks. Moreover, indicators represent a potentially important political tool, useful for holding the feet of local politicians to the fire for promises made and not delivered; in other words, they inject a performance measure into the political arena.

Such performance-based measures can also be useful in evaluating the cumulative effects of many discrete projects and community actions. One of the Oregon benchmarks, for example, is the percentage of new development that lies within one-quarter mile of community services, parks, and schools. This is an effective way to measure whether the advocated development and growth patterns are actually coming about. Thus benchmarks or targets, as natural extensions of indicators, provide a tangible and specific goal for sustainable places and an ability to know when a community is being successful and when it is falling short.

## Engaging the Public in a Dialogue About the Future

Creating sustainable places is very much a process of thinking about and visualizing the future. It is as much a process as an outcome. It is about soliciting the input and participation, ideally, of all individuals and groups in the community. It is about carrying on a sustained dialogue about how the community wants to grow and evolve, what it wants to look like in the future, what will likely be the results if no changes in practice and policy are made, how it will address its moral obligations (for example, to future residents and generations), and so on. One of the early steps in getting started, then, is to begin to structure a community dialogue about the future and to identify mechanisms, procedures, processes, tools, and techniques for carrying out such a dialogue.

There are a number of ideas that communities will want to consider. The word *vision* has developed a pejorative connotation of late, but it is still a useful word in describing how a community might go about thinking about its future. In recent years, dozens of communities across the United States have undertaken some form of visioning process. Usually this process involves a series of community meetings and workshops, often leading to the development of a vision statement and a set of concepts and ideas that might later be incorporated into a comprehensive plan and implementing ordinances. These processes can involve significant and sophisticated media strategies for soliciting input, including newspaper inserts, radio and television spots, video presentation, and follow-up focus group meetings, among others.

The city of Pasadena, California, for example, undertook an extensive visioning process, which it called "Imagine a Greater City" (CLC 1995c). Among the steps in this elaborate process were fifty-four community work sessions, a "city sketch plan forum," and the use of a number of public outreach methods (e.g., slide shows, speaker series, and newsletters). The process led to the preparation of a set of principles for guiding growth that have since been incorporated into the comprehensive plan. The plan, consistent with the community's vision, emphasizes walkable, mixed-use, urban villages and higher-density development in the city's downtown.

A visioning process on a regional scale has been taking place in the Portland region, under the auspices of the Metropolitan Service District (Metro). One of the most ambitious aspects of the process, "Region 2040," has focused on developing a vision and plan for what the region will look like in fifty years. It is anticipated that the region will have to accommodate another 720,000 residents, or a 65 percent population increase.

There have been a number of steps in the 2040 process so far, including community meetings, a region-wide questionnaire, and the production of a 2040 newsletter and video. The questionnaire resulted in some 17,000 responses (actually a relatively small response, given the fact that it was mailed to half a million residents) and some interesting results. Respondents were generally supportive of more compact, transit-oriented development patterns, although they were split on whether the average size of new lots should be reduced (Metro 1994).

In 1993 the Portland Metro Council appointed a Future Vision Commission, which was given the charge of coming up with a vision statement. This future vision was to be "a conceptual statement that indicates population levels and settlement patterns that the region can accommodate within the carrying capacity of the land, water and air resources of the region, and its educational and economic resources, and that achieves a desired quality of life" (Metro 1994, p. 13). The region's citizens were presented with three generalized scenarios for future growth in their region: (1) Expanding the urban growth boundary (UGB), with most growth occurring at the fringes; (2) no UBG expansion, with growth accommodated through infill and redevelopment, and new development at higher-density corridors around transit stations; or (3) some expansion of the UGB, some infill, and some growth in self-contained communities beyond UGB (Metro 1994).

A growth concept resolution was developed and adopted in December 1994. Basically, the second option was chosen, with a strong emphasis on compact development around transit lines, protection of "rural reserve areas," and the directing of public investments into already committed areas. In addition to text expression, a 2040 concept map of the region was also produced. The vision concept will then guide the development of a more detailed regional framework plan, which will be completed in late 1997.

There are a number of other participation tools that may prove useful. Many communities have undertaken some form of design or community planning charrette. Charrettes are usually one- or two-day, intensive partic-

ipation exercises often focused on the design and development of a particular site or area. Often charrettes are structured in such a way that either citizens or a panel of experts are asked to identify a variety of possible projects,
ideas, or desired changes for an area. Citizens and others may be divided
into different substantive subject areas. Chattanooga, Tennessee, has used
the charrette very successfully, and San Jose, California, has incorporated the
process into its sustainability program.

Other tools for visioning and for soliciting public input include simulation games, guided tours, and visual preference surveys. As noted in Chapter 3, the visual preference survey (VPS) may be useful in helping citizens
imagine how they would like their neighborhoods and communities to
look "on the ground." Such surveys may also be useful in dispelling concerns about the potential negative aesthetic qualities of certain types of development, such as multifamily or higher-density housing. Nelessen Associates, Inc., is best known for developing and using this technique, which
basically involves showing a series of slides of streets and development and
then asking viewers to rate the extent to which they like or dislike the images they are seeing. Based on these responses, each image is given an average score, and from these scores Nelessen is able to extract conclusions
about what features, characteristics, etc., are preferred by the respondents.

The power of geographic information systems (GIS) and computer technology can be increasingly useful in helping citizens and community leaders imagine available alternatives for future development. The California
Urban Futures (CUF) model is one recent notable example, illustrating the
power of new technologies in demonstrating the implications of different
community visions, as well as the most effective land use policies and community actions necessary to bring them about. The model has been used
creatively to show how growth patterns in the San Francisco Bay Area
would manifest themselves under different policy and planning assumptions, including a "business as usual" scenario, a "maximum environmental
protection" scenario, and a "compact cities" scenario (Landis 1995). The
CUF model allows citizens and policy makers to understand the pattern of
growth and consumption of land that would result if current trends are allowed to continue, as well as if certain sustainable place practices (e.g.,
growth containment) are implemented.

In fact, the "compact cities" scenario for the Bay Area would result in the
development of some 40,000 fewer acres of land than the "business as
usual" scenario (a 35 percent reduction in land consumption in the nine-
county area, assuming that all new growth is residential, that the density is
eighteen persons per acre or greater, and that 20 percent of new growth will
be accommodated through infill). The power of this technology is that

many other "what if" scenarios could be analyzed, depending upon the important components of a region's vision. While the "maximum environmental protection" scenario run for the Bay Area included no development in high-slope areas or on wetlands, it could be expanded, to consider other environmental constraints—for example, what would regional growth patterns look like if all 100-year floodplains were placed off-limits, as well as high-risk seismic zones (e.g., areas of high liquefaction potential, surface fault rupture zones, etc.) and other hazardous features and locations? What if a community wanted to assume higher or lower densities for new development, or wanted to incorporate certain assumptions about urban redevelopment? Computer models such as the CUF will be increasingly important in helping to visualize more sustainable places.

### Strategic Interventions

This book has identified many ways for communities to begin moving in the direction of becoming more sustainable. It is important to think strategically about what can be undertaken locally and regionally—what actions, policies, programs, and changes can make a difference. While this chapter has identified some fairly long-term changes in ethics, it is also important to identify changes and actions that can be brought about in shorter time frames.

One way to begin is to identify the range of possible intervention points in moving the community in the direction of its vision—that is, places where actions, programs, and policies might bring about important changes in the direction of sustainability. Figure 7.2 presents a simplified depiction of some of the more important points of intervention that might lead to more compact, sustainable land use patterns and lifestyles. Interventions, as the boxes in the diagram suggest, can be directed at a number of different citizens, organizations, and decision makers, including housing consumers, developers, lending institutions, local government officials, and the general public, among others.

The diagram also suggests that there are a number of different roles that could be assumed in trying to influence more sustainable development patterns. These roles may be assumed by private individuals, businesses and private organizations, or (as this book has tended to highlight) local governments. At least six roles in this intervention process might be identified: regulator, educator, analyst, facilitator/catalyst, incentive adjuster, and moralist. Each could be potentially important in bringing about a different future.

The *regulator* role might take the form of mandating certain outcomes, such as prohibiting certain unsustainable practices (e.g., building on wetlands or producing hazardous substances in local manufacturing plants).

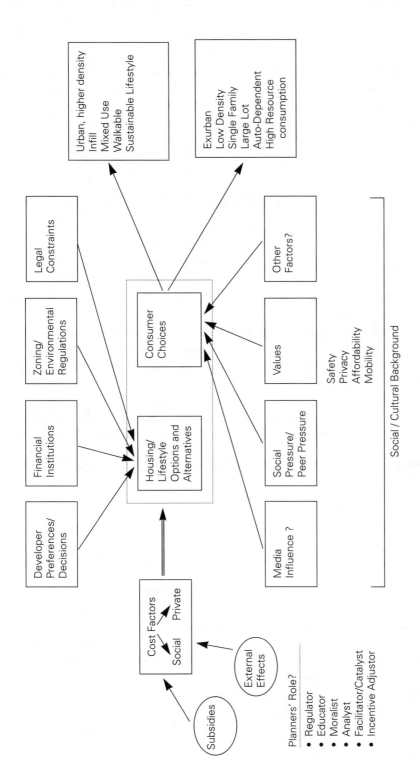

Figure 7.2 Where do we intervene to create sustainable communities?

Regulatory interventions might take the form of stipulating minimum density zoning, for instance, or modifying local land use controls so that they do not prohibit more sustainable projects and land uses (e.g., mixed-use or accessory housing units).

Still other interventions may attempt to change outcomes by *educating and informing*—for instance, attempting to modify housing consumer perceptions of the relative safety of central city housing locations, or the perceptions of developers and lenders that selling units in denser, mixed-use neighborhoods will be more difficult and less profitable.

A related role is one of *analyst* (which may precede the educator role), whereby government or private groups act to analyze and understand the environmental repercussions of decisions or the failure to make decisions. Governments often serve this function, but private groups have been extremely effective here as well. Sustainable Seattle is one such example, as is the Greenbelt Alliance.

Serving as a *facilitator/catalyst* is another role, through which actions might be taken, for example, to create the right conditions for sustainable development, or to help or push them along. A number of catalytic actions can be undertaken; an intervention might focus, for instance, on making necessary public investments.

Sometimes modest beginnings can have major long-term payoffs. Getting people to think about riding bicycles to work and to market may be as simple as pushing for demonstration bike lanes—an effort to show the potential utility and ease of riding bikes where riders feel less threatened by cars.

Still other interventions may take the form of adjustments to the prevailing system of *incentives* and disincentives. Local governments may try to make building in outlying locations more expensive, or may provide financial incentives to build in infill locations.

Finally, changes might be brought about through a *moralist* role—that is, attempting to appeal to moral suasion to convince individuals or groups that something is good or bad, or right or wrong. A frank and ongoing dialogue about whether and in what ways current patterns of development and lifestyle are or are not ethical is healthy. Planners, community leaders, watchdog groups, and others can play an important role in arguing for and defending particular future visions that may be different from conventional wisdom or the status quo. As long as there is an open and continuous process of discussion, and a democratic process of decision making, moral suasion is an available and legitimate role.

Each community must think carefully about the package of interventions that will be effective, affordable, and feasible in short-term (next year or two), medium-term (next decade or two) and long-term (fifty years or more) time frames. It is important to resist making unprioritized laundry lists of things that might be done.

## Building Partnerships

The agenda of sustainable places lends itself to building important political partnerships and alliances—partnerships that are essential for successful programs. Other recent studies have similarly emphasized partnerships. The Sustainable Use of Land Project identifies as an action agenda item the need to develop a constituency for better land use "based on new partnerships that reach beyond traditional alliances to bring together conservationists, social justice advocates, and economic development interests. These partnerships can be mobilized around natural and cultural resources that people value" (Diamond and Noonan 1996, pp. 124–125). The report of the President's Council on Sustainable Development comes to similar conclusions, calling for "community-based coalitions" that would include "businesses, employees, unions, chambers of commerce, environmental organizations, local government, and residents" (PCSD 1996, p. 90).

There are many promising types of partnerships and many recent examples of groups working together to advance common community goals. One of the most important involves the environmental community. Historically, much mainstream environmental activism has focused on legislative and policy debates at the national level, centered on important national legislation (also with obvious local and regional import), such as the federal Clean Water Act, Clean Air Act, Endangered Species Act, and the protection of national parks and forests, wetlands, and generally the preservation of nature. Increasingly, however, and by necessity, mainstream environmentalists are realizing that to protect the environment effectively requires serious involvement in the urban development process. To protect wetlands and species habitat requires not only federal environmental laws, but more compact land use and development pattern, and more attention to urban planning. Traditional environmentalists have not generally been very interested in cities, it seems, or in the agenda of cities, but this is changing. To have an effective environmental policy now requires having an effective urban policy as well.

Another potentially important partner in the pursuit of sustainable places is the historic preservation community. Important mutual concerns can be seen at both a landscape and a building scale. The destructive forces of sprawl are clearly now on the preservationists' agenda. The current president of the National Trust for Historic Preservation, Richard Moe, sees preservationists as deeply concerned with this issue and likens "current efforts to curb sprawl as the modern-day equivalent of preservationists' opposition to urban renewal in the 1950s and 1960s" (quoted in Young 1995, p. 11). Increasingly the historic preservation movement is embracing the need to protect the historic and cultural integrity of entire landscapes, in addition to single buildings or groups of buildings. Moreover, as discussed earlier, a sustainable community is one that understands its historic setting and place, and much of what makes communities attractive and possess a high quality of life has to do with the fabric of their history. Preserving the historic urban fabric also means preserving many of the qualities that we believe characterize sustainable places (e.g., walkability, sense of place, importance of the civic realm).

Furthermore, at the level of the historic building, sustainability provides a potentially potent additional argument for preservation. As the Audubon headquarters renovation project (see Chapter 4) effectively illustrates, saving buildings, rather than tearing them down, can have tremendous implications for protecting the environment; such a decision, for example, results in considerable savings in embodied energy and the averting of considerable environmental damage.

There is also no question that important new partnerships with the business community will be possible, and indeed necessary, if the vision of sustainable places is to be achieved. Increasingly, business interests are recognizing that the long-term economic productivity and success of a place will depend a great deal on its physical form, and that the heavy cost of scattered, low-density development will increasingly manifest itself as a business cost.

One of the best examples of these potential partnerships is presented in the 1995 Bank of America study *Beyond Sprawl*. One of the conclusions of that study was the importance of forming political alliances to create sustainable communities. In the words of the report: "Political alliances must be forged between environmentalists, inner-city community advocates, business leaders, government experts, farmers, and suburbanites to improve the quality of life in all our existing communities and protect our resources" (Bank of America 1995, p. 11). Gaining the leadership of the business community will be especially important in actually implementing sustainable place initiatives.

The involvement of taxpayer groups represents a powerful approach to making sustainable places and land use patterns appealing to fiscal and political conservatives. The so-called Green Scissors initiative in the 104th Congress is an example. There a coalition of environmental and taxpayer groups—organized by Friends of the Earth and the National Taxpayers Union Foundation—called for eliminating some three dozen federal subsidies (totaling $33 billion) for environmentally damaging and costly activities—activities that are not only unsustainable but financially costly to taxpayers. These programs included subsidies for mining, road building in national forests, dam projects, and overseas marketing of agricultural products (Kenworthy 1995).

The nation's churches and temples must also become more involved in creating sustainable places. In many communities the religious and spiritual sensibilities of most residents seem to end at the church or temple door; despite the occasional topical sermon on the environment, the connections between one's religious beliefs and the need to live sustainably in the world are rarely clear. Congregations and religious leaders should take a more active role in community debates about sustainability.

A recent effort to mobilize the religious community around support for reauthorizing the federal Endangered Species Act (ESA) illustrates well the potential role to be played (and the political power to be wielded) by this sector of society. The Christian Society of the Green Cross has powerfully invoked the Noah story, and the covenant between God and Creation, in defense of the ESA. An Evangelical Declaration on the Care of Creation has been drafted, which calls on "all Christians to work for godly, just, sustainable economies which reflect God's sovereignty . . . and enable men and women and children to flourish along with all the diversity of creation . . ." (Christian Society of the Green Cross 1993). Congregations are also encouraged to think about their obligations to future generations, in that the idea of "loving thy neighbor" can be seen to extend over time. And the concept of stewardship is perhaps one of the strongest spiritual imperatives for environmental protection; churches are urged to become "centers of Creation's care and renewal," an agenda that could easily be extended to sustainable places.

When it comes to risky development patterns, especially in coastal areas, the insurance industry becomes (and has become) an increasingly important player. Particularly in the wake of Hurricane Andrew, insurance groups have become increasingly active in encouraging hazard mitigation and monitoring compliance with building codes. This latter effort has involved the establishment of a new system for rating communities according to their code enforcement capabilities, with homeowners' premiums set accordingly. The Insurance Institute for Property Loss Reduction has been especially active in this area, supporting research on hazard mitigation, sponsoring industry workshops, and supporting hazard mitigation and prevention legislation. Finally, in light of the insurance industry's direct economic stake in the impacts of global climate change, insurers represented one of the strongest and earliest supporters, along with island nations, of the global climate change treaty.

The efforts of low-income housing groups demonstrate the enormous potential in combining environmental protection efforts with economic and community development, as illustrated most vividly through the example of Habitat for Humanity and its Jordan Commons initiative (see Chapter 4).

As one final example of a promising partnership, Arizona Public Service's sponsorship of the Environmental Showcase Home (see Chapter 4) demonstrates the potential power of public utilities to merge environmental and planning concerns with architectural and building standards, thereby raising the bar on home construction.

One of the advantages to forming community partnerships, and in advocating generally for more sustainable places, is that the changes sought make sense from so many different vantage points. Moving to a pedestrian- or bicycle-based society makes sense not only as a way to reduce consumption of land, but also to reduce pollution and resource consumption, and to enhance the affordability of daily life. On top of that, our overweight, underexercised society needs such activities for fundamental health reasons. Planting trees serves a similar set of interlocking benefits, providing shade and a more pleasing urban environment, fulfilling our need for natural connections, and acting as nature's carbon sinks.

## Building Support Networks

Cities and towns can also help one another in developing and implementing sustainability initiatives. Networks between and among localities are extremely important for sharing information and experiences and for creating a supportive climate, both technical and political, for undertaking creative policy changes and new directions. One function of such networks is to provide advice and guidance when specific sustainability issues or concerns arise—a sort of "sustainability mentoring" that one locality can provide to another. A city that has had several years of experience implementing a particular tool or concept can offer important expertise to other localities just embarking on similar endeavors. The issue may be a proposal to build a new light-rail system, a decision to establish a green purchasing policy, or the development of a new sustainable energy strategy for the community. Whatever the specific concern or problem area, other communities (as well as other organizations, including universities, trade organizations, or research foundations) may be able to lend important help. Such networks can help communities avoid pitfalls and prevent them from constantly having to reinvent the wheel.

Such networks of sustainable cities and towns could take many forms and could be subnetworks of already established municipal and county associations (e.g., coordinated by existing organizations such as the National League of Cities or the International City/County Management Association). These organizations are increasingly interested in sustainability issues and could play a much greater role in this area than they currently do. In addition, a number of international networks concerned with sustainability could be useful to American communities—for example, the International Council for Local Environmental Initiatives (ICLEI), based in Toronto.

An interesting potential model for building such a supportive network in the United States is Europe's Sustainable Cities and Towns Campaign, sponsored by the European Commission. This is a loose affiliation of several hundred communities, of various sizes, scattered across Europe, with common interests in sustainability. Members sign a sustainable cities charter (called the Aalborg Charter, after Aalborg, Denmark, where the first meeting of the group took place), which lays out a common agenda and vision of sustainable local development. A campaign office coordinates the program and, among other things, produces and disseminates a newsletter and other materials. A major meeting of members occurs about every two years.

One of the interesting activities of the campaign is the annual "Sustainable City Award," begun in 1996. That year, five cities out of ninety-two applicants received the award. The winning communities are proud of their awards, which seem to have a strengthening and validating effect among citizens. Among the other benefits of winning, cities may display the Sustainable Cities and Towns Campaign logo (e.g., on their stationery). There is a healthy sense of pride about these awards, and the competition has tended to encourage self-assessment (of accomplishments and deficiencies) and comparison with other communities. The awards have raised the visibility of the entire sustainable communities agenda and have certainly helped to further legitimize and buttress the efforts of the winning communities. It may be an appropriate time to start a similar campaign in the United States (or in North America) and to ask that cities and towns make a similar declaration of sustainability—perhaps a local governmental version of the AIA/UIA Declaration of Interdependence for a Sustainable Future (see Chapter 4). Adoption of a charter would help to propel and lend greater visibility to the local sustainability agenda; a network of signatories and participants would represent a significant resource base for communities to draw upon. In terms of awards, the sustainability awards given by the President's Council on Sustainable Development have certainly been helpful and represent a similar idea to their European counterpart. Still, it may be time to institute a specific, annual sustainable city/town award.

## Toward a National Policy Agenda

While this book primarily deals with local and regional strategies, it is clear that sustainability requires a number of profound and important policy changes at the national level as well. Many such initiatives would set the stage for, and support, creative sustainability initiatives at local and regional levels. This approach recognizes and draws upon the power and influence of federal policies and incentives in shaping development patterns. It is highly appropriate to think systematically about what changes need to occur at this level, in the sense that many of the development patterns and kinds of places we have today are in no small part a function of federal programs and policies, from the construction of interstate highways to the provision of extensive tax breaks for home ownership. Many states will be in an excellent position to advance some of these policies as well, and state legislatures and agencies should consider promoting a similar sustainability agenda.

What follows is not an exhaustive analysis or discussion of the elements of a national strategy for sustainable places; at best, it is a tentative listing of some of the important future changes and policy directions that must be worked on at the federal level.

### Changing the Incentive Structure

A great many changes could be made in the current home-financing system that could effectively create incentives to support more sustainable patterns of community. As Payton notes, the secondary mortgage market creates significant obstacles to funding mixed-use developments:

> Acting on federal regulations governing the key players in the market, only very limited forms of mixed use development can be underwritten. For example, while Fannie Mae, the principal underwriter, accepts mortgages for mixed use projects, its policy is to require lower debt-to-equity ratio than would be the case for mortgages used solely for housing. Furthermore, it is Fannie Mae's practice to restrict the commercial portion of a building to less than 20% of the total floor area or less than

20% rental income. Such ratios preclude the kind of small-scale mixed use development that one would be likely to find in traditional, pedestrian-oriented communities . . . Furthermore, such restrictive underwriting practices preclude live-work arrangements that allow entrepreneurs and small business people to finance housing and livelihood simultaneously (Payton, ed. undated, p. 9).

There are few financial incentives, moreover, for creating more sustainable places. One extremely promising idea is to modify the current incentive structure by adjusting the way mortgage decisions are made. Energy-efficient and location-efficient mortgages are two such promising examples.

Currently there are some provisions in place that provide mortgage incentives for choosing energy-efficient housing. Specifically, under Fannie Mae criteria, up to a 2 percent increase can be obtained in both the monthly housing expense-to-income ratio and the total obligations-to-income ratio for homes rated "high" on energy efficiency (Payton, ed., undated). This is only a modest incentive, however, and fails to take into account the total energy savings that might accrue from a decision to live in a compact city location or within close proximity to transit stations, where auto usage (and energy consumption) would be much lower. By looking at energy consumption more holistically, additional financial incentives might be offered: "Thus houses in transit friendly locations might receive an additional 1 to 2% increase in the ratios cited above, as determined by current transit ridership trends (and transportation savings) in such neighborhoods" (Payton, ed., undated, p. 11).

Another promising idea is the location-efficient mortgage, and Fannie Mae should be required to provide such. The basic premise here is that in a mortgage application, the transportation and mobility circumstances of the applicant should be taken into account. If the average two-car family spends a quarter of its after-tax income on cars, it would have much more disposable income if it chose to purchase a home near to a transit stop or in an otherwise walkable environment (a "walking home," as it is sometimes called). In a recent study of twenty-seven California communities, the Natural Resources Defense Council concluded that households in high-density neighborhoods with good access to public transit could save up to $396 per month in reduced automobile costs. Such savings should translate into lower mortgage rates or should allow applicants to qualify for higher-value mortgages (Center for Neighborhood Technology, undated).

A number of other changes to financial incentives should be considered. One way to provide auto users with incentives to reduce the amount they drive would be to reform the way auto insurance is sold. Durning proposes selling auto insurance "by the slice," whereby auto insurers would take into account the actual amount of driving done by the insured. This would be fairer and would reward those who drive fewer miles. Even better would be an "insurance-by-the-gallon" approach: "A more comprehensive and efficient solution, however, is to convert to no-fault, pay-at-the-pump insurance. Motorists would buy insurance through a flat surcharge of perhaps 40 cents on each gallon of gasoline—a charge rolled into the listed gas price just like gas taxes. Insurance-by-the-gallon would make insurance costs a factor in people's daily transportation and destination planning, even while reducing the total cost of driving" (Durning 1996, p. 53).

## Curtailing Federal Subsidies

There is considerable consensus that many of our more unsustainable land use and other practices are the results of (or are at least strongly encouraged by) the existing system of federal subsidies. This federal subsidy system extends to everything from provision of cheap water and hydroelectric energy to below-market grazing fees on public lands to a variety of price supports and agricultural subsidies (e.g., the price support for sugar production that accounts for much of the environmental destruction to the Florida Everglades ecosystem). Eliminating or severely reducing these subsidies, ensuring that resource users at least pay the market rate, and placing environmental sustainability conditions on receiving such subsidies would be a positive step. (Indeed, the President's Council on Sustainable Development strongly endorses this idea and recommends the appointment of a national commission to examine the role of federal tax and subsidy policy; see PCSD 1996.)

The federal government also provides a number of subsidies that serve to encourage development and population growth in high-risk locations. These include, most importantly, federal disaster assistance and federal flood insurance. (For a more extensive review of these programs, see Beatley, Brower, and Schwab 1994.) Under the National Flood Insurance Program, homeowners in participating communities can obtain subsidized flood insurance (at rates generally much lower than the private sector could provide) in exchange for modest mitigation and preventive measures. While the program has become more actuarially sound (rates have been increasing), it still represents a shifting of flood risks to general taxpayers and an encouragement to locate in high-hazard (and often environmentally sensitive) areas.

## Changing the Federal Tax Code

Given certain adjustments, the U.S. tax code could be a powerful instrument for encouraging more sustainable places and discouraging those that are unsustainable. There are a number of potential changes in the tax code that should be considered, and while a definitive set of recommendations for changes is not offered here, the authors believe that the future national agenda and debate about sustainable places must at least address them. Among the incentives that might be modified are tax deductions for mortgage interest and local property taxes.

Tax breaks that encourage development in hazardous locations should be corrected. The casualty loss deduction, for example, allows homeowners to deduct damages from natural disaster events from their income tax (Beatley, Brower, and Schwab 1994).

The tax code might also be modified so that certain other subsidies for low-density development and sprawl are eliminated or reduced. In particular, the provision of parking benefits to employees could be taxed, or at least considered tax-free only if employees have the option of "cashing out" (i.e., the employer gives the employee the option of having the cash equivalent of the benefit). This is currently how California treats such benefits under its state income tax. Perhaps the federal government should adopt the California rule (for a discussion of this, see Durning 1996).

The tax code could also be modified to support certain sustainable practices and technologies. The Clinton administration, for example, has proposed that a tax credit be given to companies investing in cleanup and redevelopment of brownfield sites. This would be a productive use of the power of the tax code.

### Important National Investments and Infrastructure

There are a number of investments and capital infrastructure expenditures that can only be financed and planned effectively at the federal level. The United States needs a plan for such investments, as well as for stimulating research and development of a variety of sustainability technologies.

Sustainable transportation represents one important area in which investments are needed. Given the high social, environmental, and economic costs of highway-based transportation, future investments in rail service are justified. High-speed rail is becoming a mainstay in European (e.g., the successful TGL system in France) and other countries (e.g., Japan), though it has so far had only limited application in the United States (e.g., see Eastham 1995). Development of high-speed rail here has been, in the words of one recent commentator, "frustratingly slow" (Eastham 1995, p. 99). Current conventional high-speed rail (steel wheels on steel tracks) is already providing service at speeds of 185 miles per hour and can provide environmentally friendly transportation links in a number of U.S. corridors (e.g., California and the Northwest, the Northeast, Chicago and the Midwest; see Rogers

1994). Particularly for shorter, intercity legs, high-speed rail makes considerable sense. Newer maglev (magnetic-levitation) technology presents the potential for even higher speeds and should be carefully considered (though it requires an entirely new infrastructure and cannot run on conventional rail right-of-ways). The increasing costs and congestion (airspace and airports) associated with air travel further support the importance of long-term investments in our national rail system.

The passage of the Intermodal Surface Transportation Efficiency Act (ISTEA) in 1991 was a watershed event in U.S. transportation policy. Among other features, it provides states and localities with greater discretion in how they can use federal transportation dollars, and greater ability to improve and upgrade nonautomobile modes of mobility. The act also explicitly encourages projects that enhance bicycle and pedestrian modes and has imposed (in combination with the Clean Air Act) new regional transportation planning requirements. While ISTEA has so far shown mixed results (it is not clear, for example, that many of the enhancement projects have actually improved mobility), the notion of allowing communities and regions greater discretion in using federal transportation funds is consistent with the sustainable places vision described in this book.

There are a host of other technological investments that should be considered. These include investments in renewable energy plants and technology, especially solar (and adequate funding for groups such as the National Renewable Energy Laboratory in Colorado) and technologies that support sustainable agriculture and industry, among others.

Part of the agenda of sustainability is to look critically at the current menu of public subsidies and to adjust the mix to support more sustainable development patterns and lifestyles. As noted earlier in this volume, transportation subsidies have been heavily skewed in the direction of unsustainable modes of transport, namely autos and highways. By one estimate, public subsidies for cars amount to $300 billion annually, compared to only $13 billion for public transit (Plous 1994).

## Changes in Measuring Progress

Part of the reason we are where we are today is that the guideposts we have been using to judge our progress at the national level have been misguided and wrong-headed. In particular, reliance on measures such as gross domestic product (GDP) emphasize the importance of economic transactions in the economy without a sense of whether this economic activity really improves the quality of our lives or protects the sustainability of the ecosystem upon which we all depend. There has been substantial commentary and criticism in recent years about the imperfections of the GDP.

The basic problem with the GDP is that it is simply a measure of the amount of economic activity—the amount of buying and selling—in the marketplace and fails to differentiate between what sorts of things these expenditures are going for. Perversely, the GDP counts as positives expenditures on pollution control and cleanup, crime, and natural disasters. The standard measure fails to account for income distribution and fails to acknowledge the value of the many activities that occur in the nonmarket sector, such as child care, household services, and community service and volunteer work.

Particularly alarming from a sustainability perspective is the way the GDP treats the depletion of natural resources. Depleting natural capital, whether old-growth forests or regional groundwater aquifers, is treated as income rather than capital.

A group calling itself Redefining Progress has been instrumental in bringing attention to the severe limitations of this economic measure and has produced its own creative and enlightening alternative. Called the Genuine Progress Indicator (GPI), it takes into account some twenty additional factors overlooked by the GDP (Redefining Progress, 1995). Specifically, it subtracts expenditures made to cover the costs of pollution and pollution cleanup as well as crime. It also treats as a current cost the depletion of natural ecological capital. Moreover, it factors in disparities in income and the value of nonmonetary household and community work.

The result is a different picture of recent progress. While per capita GDP has increased markedly since 1950, the per capita GPI has declined by 45 percent since 1970 (with a 6 percent rate of decline in the 1990s). "This wide and growing divergence between the GDP and GPI is a warning that the economy is stuck on a path that imposes large—and as yet unreckoned—costs onto the present and the future" (Redefining Progress 1995).

The methodological challenge of computing something like a GPI is daunting, to say the least, and any particular computational step or assumption could be challenged (e.g., is it really valid to include income disparities in this measure?). Nevertheless, the GPI is a good first attempt to provide an alternative indicator of how well our society is functioning—perhaps not to replace the GDP, but to be calculated and published (at least some version of it) alongside the GDP to provide balance and to illustrate that there are other appropriate factors to take into account.

## Placing Sustainability Conditions on Federal Funding

The federal government could begin to use the mighty power of its purse strings much more effectively to promote more sustainable local and regional development patterns than it currently does. While some planning requirements are attached to federal highway funds, for example, Calthorpe and Richmond argue that such monies should be directly tied to the creation of walkable, transit-oriented developments:

> The U.S. Department of Transportation should insist that localities use land use policy as a dynamic variable in environmental impact and transportation, instead of treating existing zone maps as a static "given." The latter approach simply compels new freeways to handle sprawl-generated traffic. Transit funds should not be given without analysis, plans, and demonstrated local commitment to use land use policy to discourage sprawl. Federal highway and transit funds should be denied to jurisdictions that do not adopt transit-oriented development land use policies (Calthorpe and Richmond 1993, p. 707).

While this may seem an extreme and politically tenuous move, it is not unreasonable to expect localities and regions to demonstrate how they plan to enhance mobility over time, presumably the purpose for such funds. A performance-based system, in which performance is measured in overall mobility (rather than vehicle miles traveled or road capacity levels), would seem reasonable. Just as with the annual progress requirements of the Clean Air Act (i.e., each community with polluted air must reduce pollution by a certain percentage annually to remain in compliance), similar performance requirements could be stipulated for mobility. The Oregon approach is one model for doing this, with modal split and VMT (vehicle miles traveled) performance standards required for each local comprehensive plan.

Calthorpe and Richmond have proposed that other federal programs, including CDBG (Community Development Block Grants) and federal open space monies, give preference to communities working to promote compact, transit-oriented growth patterns, and that housing projects receiving affordable housing credits and subsidies be required to locate in such areas (Calthorpe and Richmond 1993, pp. 708–709).

Another area of potential leverage involves the federal support and funding given to universities. David Orr proposes that our colleges and universities be evaluated not only by the usual means (e.g., publications by the faculty, the prestige and reputation of the institution), but against some measure of sustainability. He proposes a ranking that would incorporate five criteria: the per-student rate of consumption and waste production; the university's management policies (e.g., regarding recycling, energy use, etc.); whether the curriculum imparts essential environmental literacy to students (including the teaching of environmental ethics); how the university uses its financial resources and buying power (e.g., does it purchase its food locally?); and finally (and most difficult to operationalize), some measure of the cumulative environmental impacts of its graduates (Orr 1994, pp. 89–93). While politically (and operationally) difficult to implement, such a sustainability measure suggests that perhaps our nation's universities and colleges ought to be held accountable for their environmental (and social) deeds, with federal rewards meted out accordingly.

## Reforming Federal Environmental Policy

There are a number of potential reforms to the federal environmental management system that could facilitate the creation of sustainable places and landscapes. An extensive discussion of such reforms is not possible in this volume, but a number of these recommendations are proposed in the final report of the President's Council on Sustainable Development. Generally, the council recommends reforming the current environmental management system so that it is more performance-based (with companies and communities having greater flexibility in meeting national standards), making greater use of market mechanisms, and emphasizing prevention rather than end-of-the-pipe approaches (including a strong endorsement of life-cycle approaches to production and extended product responsibility). In the area of resource stewardship, the council recommends a more collaborative approach and strongly endorses the idea of ecosystem management. The final report also strongly states the importance of adjusting existing subsidies and incentives to ensure that resource users are bearing the full cost of their actions. Many of these recommendations, if implemented, would certainly do much to advance national sustainability. (PCSD 1996)

The Brownfields Initiative (see Chapter 3) represents a promising approach, and the EPA and other federal agencies must begin to identify other ways in which current environmental regulations can be modified to facilitate or encourage sustainability initiatives. Far short of endorsing a whole-sale loosening of environmental regulations, it does make considerable sense to look for ways to streamline or provide greater flexibility for local initiatives (such as infill development and redevelopment) that will have substantial long-term ecological benefits (e.g., reducing consumption of green-fields). Federal (and state) environmental laws, moreover, should not create unreasonable obstacles to the development of sustainability practices (e.g., the use of such new technologies as household graywater systems and innovative wastewater treatment systems). Indeed, not only should federal and state environmental agencies look for ways to remove roadblocks, they should actively support the development and application of such practices and technologies. A national sustainability fund should be established to provide seed funding for such initiatives.

At the national level, there continues to be a need for an agency or office that will monitor and assess environmental data and trends comprehensively and objectively. In the past, the Council on Environmental Quality has served this function to some degree. Such a monitoring agency would ideally assess environmental data on subnational and regional levels as well as on a national level, and could provide cities and regions with a better sense of how well they are meeting sustainability objectives. Recent legislative proposals to create an independent National Institute for the Environment to serve many of these functions should be supported.

Another significant environmental reform involves the concept of ecosystem management. An ecosystem management approach to environmental policy attempts to assume a much broader geographical scale of analysis and to understand changes and impacts over a considerably longer time frame. Moreover, this approach can be characterized by an effort to look carefully and thoroughly at ecological interconnections and the health and functioning of the ecosystem as a whole. Ecosystem management has received a considerable amount of attention at the federal level in the last several years. The 1995 report by the federal Interagency Ecosystem Management Task Force has strongly endorsed the concept, and the National Performance Review has suggested that ecosystem management can be an important strategy by which to coordinate and integrate federal land management decisions and planning (Interagency Ecosystem Management Task Force 1995). Furthermore, increasing experience in applying ecosystem management (e.g., in the Florida Everglades and at Balcones Canyonlands in Texas) suggests that it can be a very effective lens through which to understand and resolve difficult land use and environmental conflicts. Ecosystem management can be an important tool for integrating and coordinating the land use policies and other programs and decisions of all levels of government, as well as private sector parties.

Particularly helpful would be the development of a "national ecological network," which would create a unified and comprehensive national vision of natural areas that need protection and management. Such a system has been established in several European countries (e.g., the Netherlands), as well as for all of Europe (e.g., see Jongman 1995; van Baalen 1995). Such an idea takes the regional or bioregional network of open space and natural landscapes discussed in Chapter 4 to the next level. The system would, on both continental and regional scales, identify existing protected areas (e.g., national parks and forests, state parks, local and regional parks), as well as those areas where protection and management is still needed (e.g., corridors to link parks and important core habitat areas currently unprotected). The result would be a network of natural lands outside of, yet connecting with, urban areas. A number of advantages would be realized from such a net-

work, including greater effectiveness in protecting biodiversity, more efficient and effective use of limited acquisition and management funds at all
levels, and a landscape in which cities, towns, and urban populations are
more clearly integrated within a larger national ecological framework.

## Ecological Tax Reform: Green Taxes

Many have been critical of the current tax system because it serves to penalize "good" things, such as work and investment, and fails to penalize
"bad" things, such as pollution and resource depletion. Any long-term national sustainability agenda must seriously consider "ecological tax reform."
Green taxes, as they are commonly called, are levies placed on production or
consumption activities that create environmental hazards (e.g., pollution) or
that exhaust scarce environmental resources. Such a system can significantly
shift behavior away from destructive, short-term, unsustainable practices and
in support of sustainable practices.

As Morris describes, green taxes are different from other taxes because
their main purpose is not to raise revenue: "Property or income taxes can be
justified only because governments need money. But pollution inflicts damage. Therefore, a pollution tax is a levy that internalizes the real cost of pollution into the price of the product or service we buy. One could argue that
we should pay the costs of pollution even if we didn't need tax reform"
(Morris 1996, p.11). As discussed, the external costs of unsustainable behavior are high; so green taxes would create financial incentives to stop or
reduce such behavior.

Green taxes are not always popular, however. Proposals for a U.S. energy
tax were met with tremendous political opposition and squashed early in
the Clinton–Gore administration. The idea of a carbon tax remains a viable
one in other parts of the world, and has been adopted by several European
nations, such as Denmark and the Netherlands. Several U.S. states, including
Maryland, Minnesota, and California, have considered some sort of carbon
tax (Miller, Hoerner, and Duffy, 1996).

A significant political question is how the revenues generated by such
taxes should be used. One approach would be to use them to reduce other
taxes—for example, income and property taxes. If the adoption of green
taxes was clearly linked with reductions in other taxes, its political viability
would be enhanced. Alternatively, the revenues could be used to clean up or
otherwise deal with previous environmental degradation or to cover the
costs of critical sustainability investments (e.g., solar energy, high-speed
inner-city rail).

The President's Council on Sustainable Development stopped short of
endorsing the use of green taxes, but did recommend the establishment of

a national commission to examine tax and subsidy policies and their implications for sustainability. One of the specific tasks of the commission would be to consider opportunities for greater use of green taxes (what it calls "pollution taxes"; see PCSD 1996).

## Toward a Real National Energy Policy

The current national energy strategy seems primarily to be a nonstrategy—one that is allowing increasing dependence on foreign oil sources (and U.S. intervention when these sources are in jeopardy), tolerating contemplation in Congress of opening up pristine ecological areas that promise modest energy returns (e.g., the Arctic National Wildlife Refuge), and allowing, if not promoting, inefficient and wasteful patterns of domestic energy consumption.

For environmental, national security, and other reasons, the U.S. needs a real energy strategy—one that takes a long view and seeks to address the backsliding in energy efficiency that has occurred in recent decades. Particularly troubling are trends of increasing auto usage and declining fuel efficiency in American cars. Americans now drive an average of 8,000 miles per year (some 30,000 miles for suburban residents), a one-third increase since 1973 (*Consumer Reports* 1996, p. 9). Furthermore, auto fuel efficiency leveled out at twenty-one miles per gallon in 1991 and has been slipping ever since. There have been no new fuel-efficiency standards legislated since 1973.

What might be the elements of such a national energy policy? A number of measures should be considered, including: instituting higher gas taxes to discourage consumption; increasing federal fuel efficiency standards for new automobiles (a forty-mile-per-gallon standard is possible, technologically and economically); modifying the current tax system to further tax gas guzzlers, and providing financial rebates ("feebates") to those purchasing cars that exceed minimum efficiency standards; further supporting nonauto forms of transportation, including inter-city rail and regional mass transit, as well as regional and local programs and policies that encourage more energy-efficient land use patterns; and encouraging and supporting the development of alternative sustainable energy technologies, especially solar.

## National Demonstration Projects

One of the most effective ways to change current development practices is to point to successful examples of where development is being done differently. Some innovative projects have already emerged through the private sector. However, there is also a need for a national demonstration program to spur innovation in the area of sustainable places. This could take the form of demonstration grants (similar to the national green funds established in several other countries) or special loans and other forms of financial underwriting. What is called for, perhaps, is a new "sustainable model cities program," building on and updating that initiative from the 1960s. Among the important types of demonstration projects that could be supported are: ecological housing developments, which combine strong energy and resource conservation and other environmental features with neo-traditional design features; exemplary efforts at creating urban villages (compact, dense, transit-oriented neighborhoods with high amenity values); projects that illustrate the potential of urban infill and redevelopment of industrial and inner-city sites; urban eco-villages; and innovative local programs to "green" cities, including tree planting and urban gardening initiatives. Such a program could result in a national set of practices for sustainable planning with examples of the types of sustainable projects that traditional lending institutions are currently reluctant to finance. The Sustainable Development Challenge grants program recently created by the U.S. EPA, though financially limited, is a positive step in this direction.

Federal and state agencies could do many other things to assist communities and private developers in undertaking projects and initiatives that may be untested. The President's Council suggests stimulating innovation through the creation of "multidisciplinary design teams" that could help local governments (PCSD 1996 p. 97).

**Setting the Right Examples**

One of the most powerful things the federal government can do is to lead by example. There are a number of actions and policy changes in the area of creating sustainable places that could help to create powerful positive examples for society as a whole. One such example is the "Greening of the White House" initiative. Its aim has been to fundamentally reconfigure the White House and its operations to reduce energy and resource consumption and to dramatically reduce its overall environmental impacts.

It has also been suggested that greater attention be given to putting the White House grounds to uses that are more ecologically sustainable and appropriate to the times in which we are living. Among the suggestions for "more appropriate symbols of power and authority": ". . . a meadow that includes so called 'weed' species and a once a year mowing; a wetland, expressing one of the richest and most important of habitats; a vegetable garden that could make the White House self-sufficient, or feed Washington's poor; and an apple orchard, productive, beautiful and the American fruit" (Hough 1995, p. 129).

There are many other ways in which the federal government can take the lead—for example, by ensuring that any federal building project incorporates community sustainability principles. Whether a post office or a federal courthouse complex, such facilities should incorporate a mixing of uses (including housing) and contribute in positive ways to the street life, vitality, and attractiveness of the communities in which they are located. The new framework plan for the monumental core district in Washington, D.C., contains proposals illustrating this kind of thinking. The plan suggests a new kind of government building, "with a public life and an invigorating street and neighborhood presence" (National Capital Planning Commission 1995, p. 17). Existing buildings, the plan notes, could be retrofitted and improved over time to incorporate these same kinds of features (e.g., mixed-uses, housing, and neighborhood-oriented functions).

There are many locational decisions that could substantially help in promoting more sustainable urban patterns. Sustainability goals can be supported, for instance, by ensuring that major federal projects and buildings are located at or near key public transit stations and are designed in ways that encourage nonautomobile forms of mobility.

## Population and Immigration

One of the most politically controversial issues in this nation today is the question of immigration. Legal immigration has grown to 1 million per year (Ruben 1994). There are many differences of opinion on the topic with some of the environmental community believing that we must curtail immigration to protect our environment. This is troubling in that it exposes us to the same criticism we direct at communities that are "forting up" to keep certain people and income groups out. Yet any national agenda of sustainable places must at least begin to confront and talk about this issue and to address the thorny questions raised by it. Determining the amount of immigration permitted, and over what time frame, has tremendous implications for how easy or difficult it will be for communities to develop sustainably.

While this book does not advance a definitive position on this topic, it seems that immigration policy and decisions should be closely linked to community sustainability. Specifically, continued immigration should perhaps be conditioned or accompanied by a quantifiable national commitment to advancing more sustainable urban forms and community development patterns. We can and should accommodate immigration, but only if we also continue to move in the direction of a net reduction in resource consumption. Our population cannot continue to grow at the same time that we consume ever greater amounts of resources. We cannot accommodate increasing numbers of immigrants, for example, if vehicle miles traveled continues to rise and the energy efficiency of cars continues to decline.

Precisely what form such a linked approach would take is uncertain, but at minimum, some consideration should be given at a national level to where, geographically, immigration should occur—which cities, regions, and states can best support future growth from immigration, and how places can be modified to accommodate such growth.

As many environmentalists have argued, concerns over population and resource consumption also support the need to address the problems in other countries that give rise to pressures to immigrate in the first place. Ultimately, we need to move beyond merely treating the symptoms and work to promote sustainable places and conditions in other nations as well. The concept of sustainable places should thus be incorporated into our foreign as well as national policies.

It is distressing, in fact, that many developing countries appear to be aspiring to the dominant model of development used in the United States. China, for example, recently announced a major new initiative to expand its road and highway system and appears to have embraced the principles of the American car culture. Its latest five-year plan envisions the paving of some 93,000 miles of new roads, and it has completed preliminary work on developing four new national expressways that will "crisscross the Chinese landscape like a giant tic-tac-toe grid" (Wong 1996). American foreign policy should seek to help other countries investigate and put in place a different human settlement model based on sustainable practices of community building.

## The Role of Planners and the Planning Academy

Planners clearly have a critical role to play in promoting the dialogue about sustainability and in conceiving public policy solutions that promote community sustainability. Planners must become better at pointing out the unsustainability of conventional planning and development policy and at putting forth (or helping to put forth) an alternative vision of a future that is more in line with the ethical imperatives outlined above. Planners are often in a position to initiate important first steps, such as developing a series of indices to act as benchmarks of a community's current (un)sustainability and its subsequent progress. Planners can also encourage the formation and growth of grassroots community groups like Sustainable Seattle and Eco-City Cleveland, groups that may eventually help to shape the local political agenda.

There is also much that can and should be done to integrate sustainability concepts into the planning academy. Surveys of college planning programs suggest that formal attention to sustainability is limited (Martin and Beatley 1993). At the University of Virginia, a number of promising initiatives have been undertaken, including the creation of new courses in sustainable communities that have exposed graduate planning students to both theory and current practice at a number of scales and jurisdictional levels. Sustainability perspectives are also beginning to be incorporated into other topical course areas, including courses on housing and transportation. The lens of sustainability leads students to question conventional ways of responding to such topical subjects. And throughout the curriculum, students are encouraged to view planning as a holistic process and to understand the critical and essential interconnections among different planning specialties or subfields. The Virginia program's emphasis on sustainable community has generated an extremely useful dialogue among faculty and students and has encouraged a new and more integrated perspective on the different concentration areas within the department (e.g., environmental planning, housing and community development, land use planning, historic preservation).

Planning scholars also have an important role to play in pursuing research subjects that aid in promoting sustainability. Among the important research topics are a more comprehensive understanding of the environmental, social, and economic costs associated with sprawl and land-consumptive development, and documenting (quantitatively and otherwise) the experiences of communities, from Amsterdam to Curitiba to Portland, that have sought to implement an alternative development vision. The elements of such comparatively successful visions remain poorly understood.

Planning academicians must also look closely at what is being taught in planning programs to ensure that future practitioners are adequately equipped with the theory, tools, and methods they will need to face the challenge of creating sustainable places. In some cases, this simply means revising the way traditional skills and knowledge areas are taught (e.g., rethinking the ways in which traditional land use controls can be used to better promote sustainability). In other cases, there are new methodologies and analytical techniques that planning students must begin to understand and master (many of which have been described in the preceding chapters), including ecological footprint analysis, eco-auditing, and life-cycle analysis, among others. In addition, planners must become even more proficient at process skills, learning to organize, structure, and facilitate community visioning processes, for instance, and other processes by which the community seriously and systematically imagines and charts its future. And while not to the same degree as architects and designers, planners must be better able to deal in the realm of the visual—to be able to present alternative futures visually and graphically (through a variety of visual media, including computer simulations and graphics, GIS, drawing and sketches, street and neighborhood plans, photography, etc.), or at least be able to interface with and effectively guide designers, artists, and others in preparing such images. The visual realm will be especially important in inspiring and motivating the public about alternative future paths, and its power and influence should not be underestimated in the planning academy.

Along these lines, more progress must also be made in training design students (and others) to work collaboratively. The agenda of sustainable places will require that planners work together with other professionals—architects, engineers, city managers—to put into place the holistic, integrative solutions that have been suggested here. Architecture schools, within which many planning programs are located, must themselves do a better job of promoting interaction and collaboration among and between their students and faculty (e.g., through joint studios), as well as with other schools and disciplines (e.g., business schools, engineering departments) on campus.

As has been argued above, some of the most important sustainability issues will require action at national and international levels in such areas as population, immigration, and foreign trade policy. While the sustainable communities movement is extremely promising, it must be recognized that long-term global sustainability will be next to impossible without effectively addressing population growth. Planners can and should be actively involved in national and international debate about this and other sustainability-related issues; they also have an important role to play in educating the public about these concerns.

To be sure, there are many obstacles to achieving sustainability, including an existing economic system founded on assumptions of unlimited expansion and growth, a political system that represents special interests but does not deal effectively with the interests of future generations and the environment, and a cultural context that has historically venerated private property rights. Planners have an important role to play in overcoming such obstacles and in helping elected officials and citizens understand why the vision of a sustainable future is a desirable and compelling one and how they can lead society toward that future.

# A Final Note: Advancing a Comprehensive and Compelling Vision

There is a pressing need for a fundamental shift in the ways in which we build and develop in the United States, and in the shape and form of our communities. The costs of the current approach—whether measured in terms of ecological damage, unnecessary infrastructures, health care needs, or less time with one's children—are too high. These costs create places that are socially dysfunctional and lacking a sense of connectedness to nature and to one's neighbors. These are not the inspirational places that people need. The current model is not working and must be replaced by a more comprehensive and compelling vision.

While the precise contours of that vision are a matter of debate, at minimum it should assume a willingness to adopt a longer temporal frame of reference than that to which we are accustomed. The vision requires a continual effort to integrate aspects of environment, economy, and community in mutually reinforcing ways—a perspective that draws strength from the dynamic, interconnected nature of its citizens and natural assets. In this way, the vision of sustainable communities considers the "ecology of place" in all its many forms.

As this book has shown, the path toward sustainability is a long one. It requires a whole host of incremental, individual efforts that are coordinated and advanced through their connection to a broader vision. It is not about "quick fixes." Thus, while there is a certain sense of urgency to the need for new methods of place building, the complexity of the task at hand demands a holistic and very carefully considered approach.

Many communities around the country have risen to this challenge. In cities, towns, and villages throughout the United States, citizen groups, business leaders, planners, and elected officials are joining together to work principles of sustainability into the design and management of their communities. Their efforts are encouraging and, at times, inspirational.

At the same time, our collective attempts to achieve sustainability are often hindered by the image that many have in their heads of a spartan, materially limited life of less. Countering these negative images involves increasing the effort to call attention to the very real, very high costs of continuing present patterns. A more positive, hopeful approach requires advancing the vision of the many attractive qualities of sustainable places, and the many different ways and arenas in which that vision may be realized.

# Bibliography

Ahern, Jack, and Jestena Boughton. 1994. "Wildflower Meadows as Sustainable Landscapes." In *The Ecological City,* edited by Rutherford H. Platt, Rowan A. Rowntree, and Pamela C. Muick. Amherst: University of Massachsuetts Press.

Allegood, Jerry. 1996. "Greenville Takes Aim at Mall." *News & Observer,* 27 March, p. 3A.

ALT-TRANS: Washington Center for Transportation Alternatives. 1995. "How Do Americans Subsidize Driving?" Fall newsletter, p. 1.

American Institute of Architects (AIA). 1996. *AIA Environmental Resource Guide.* Washington, DC: AIA.

Andruss, Van, Christopher Plant, Judith Plant, and Eleanor Wright, eds. 1990. *Home! A Bioregional Reader.* Philadelphia: New Society.

Aplet, Gregory, Nels Johnson, Jeffrey T. Olsen, and J. Alaric Sample, eds. 1993. *Defining Sustainable Forestry.* Washington, DC: Island Press.

Arax, Mark. 1995. "Sprawl Threatens Central Valley, Study Says." *Los Angeles Times,* 26 October, p. 3.

Arrington, G.B. 1994. Newsletter on the MAX system. Portland Metropolitan Service District.

Austin, Texas, City of. 1995. Press release on wind project. 28 February.

Austin, Texas, City of. Undated (a). *Appliance Efficiency Program.* Austin: Environmental and Conservation Services Department.

Austin, Texas, City of. Undated (b). *Green Builder Program: A Sustainable Approach.* Austin: Environmental and Conservation Services Department.

Baker, Gina Lynn. 1996. "Ecovillage Development in Urban Areas: Opportunities and Barriers." Master's thesis, Department of Urban and Environmental Planning, University of Virginia, Charlottesville.

Baldwin, A. Dwight, Judith DeLuce, and Carl Pletsch, eds. 1993. *Beyond Preservation: Restoring and Inventing Landscapes.* Minneapolis: University of Minnesota Press.

Bank of America. 1995. *Beyond Sprawl: New Patterns of Growth to Fit the New California.* Executive summary. San Francisco: Bank of America.

Barnett, Dianna L., and William D. Browning. 1995. *A Primer on Sustainable Building.* Snowmass, CO: Rocky Mountain Institute.

Barton, Hugh, and Noel Bruder, eds. 1995. *A Guide to Local Environmental Auditing.* London: Earthscan.

Beatley, Timothy. 1995a. "Planning and Sustainability: The Elements of a New (Improved?) Paradigm." *Journal of Planning Literature* 9(4): 383–393.

Beatley, Timothy. 1995b. "The Many Meanings of Sustainability: Introduction to a Special Issue of JPL." *Journal of Planning Literature* 9(4): 339–341.

Beatley, Timothy. 1994a. "Creating Sustainable Communities." *Colonnade* X (i) (Spring): 7–13.

Beatley, Timothy. 1994b. *Ethical Land Use: Principles of Policy and Planning.* Baltimore: Johns Hopkins University Press.

Beatley, Timothy. 1994c. *Habitat Conservation Planning: Endangered Species and Urban Growth.* Austin: University of Texas Press.

Beatley, Timothy. 1993. "Urban Policy and Fair Equality of Opportunity," In *Shaping a National Urban Agenda,* edited by Gene Grigsby and David Godschalk. Los Angeles: University of California, Los Angeles Center for Afro-American Studies.

Beatley, Timothy. 1989. "Environmental Ethics and Planning Theory." *Journal of Planning Literature* 4 (1): 1–32.

Beatley, Timothy, and David J. Brower. 1993. "Sustainability Meets Mainstreet: Principles to Live—and Plan—By." *Planning* 59(5): 16–19.

Beatley, Timothy, David J. Brower, and Anna Schwab. 1994. *An Introduction to Coastal Zone Management.* Washington, DC: Island Press.

Beatley, Timothy, David J. Brower, and Lou Ann Brower. 1988. "Managing Growth: Small Towns and Rural Communities." Report prepared for the Office of State Planning, State of Maine.

Becker, William J. 1994. "The Case for Sustainable Redevelopment." *Environment and Development* (American Planning Association), November, pp.1–4.

Blakely, Edward J., and Mary Gail Snyder. 1995. "Fortress Communities: The Walling and Gating of American Suburbs." *Land Lines* 7(5): 1, 3.

Bormann, F. Herbert, Diana Balmori, and Gordon T. Geballe. 1993. *Redesigning the American Lawn: A Search for Environmental Harmony.* New Haven, CT: Yale University Press.

Bouvier, Leon F., and Lindsey Grant. 1994. *How Many Americans? Population, Immigration and the Environment.* San Francisco: Sierra Club Books.

Bowers, C. A. 1995. *Educating for an Ecologically Sustainable Culture.* Albany: State University of New York Press.

Brawer, Wendy E. Green Map Sysytem [online]. [New York, NY]: *Modern World Design,* Feb. 1997 [cited March 17, 1997]. Available from Internet: <URL: http://www.greenmap.com>. E-mail: mwd@greenmap.com.

Brown, Lester R., and Hal Kane. 1994. *Full House: Reassessing the Earth's Population Carrying Capacity.* New York: Norton.

Brown, Lester, A. Durning, C. Flavin, H. French, N. Lenssen, M. Lowe, A. Misch, S. Postel, M. Renner, L. Starke, P. Weber, and J. Young. 1994. *State of the World 1994.* Washington, DC: Worldwatch Institute.

Browning, William. 1991. "Green Development: Determining the Cost of Environmentally Responsive Development." Master's thesis. Massachusetts Institute of Technology, Cambridge.

Build America. APS Environmental Showcase Home [online]. Build America Radio, April 1, 1996 [cited July 2, 1996]. Available from Internet: <URL: http://www.buildamerica.com/old/4-1-96/wkshow.htm>.

Burchell, Robert W., and David Listokin. 1995. *Land, Infrastructure, Housing Costs and Fiscal Impacts Associated with Growth: The Literature on the Impacts of Sprawl Versus Managed Growth.* Cambridge, MA: Lincoln Institute of Land Policy.

Burchell, Robert W., et al. 1992. "Impact Assessment of the New Jersey Interim State Development and Redevelopment Plan." Report II, research findings.

Burge, Kathleen. 1995. "Vt. Makes it Complete Set for Wal-Mart in America." *Boston Globe,* 17 September, pp. 40–41.

Business and the Environment. 1995. "Unocal Spinoff to Help Southern California Companies Cut Air Pollution." *Business and the Environment,* August, p. 11.

Cairncross, Frances. 1992. *Costing the Earth.* Cambridge, MA: Harvard Business School Press.

Calthorpe, Peter. 1993. *The Next American Metropolis: Ecology, Community and the American Dream.* Princeton, NJ: Princeton Architectural Press.

Calthorpe, Peter, and Henry Richmond. 1993. "Sustainable Growth: Land Use and Transportation." In *Changing America: Blueprints for the New Administration,* edited by Mark Green. New York: Newmarket Press.

Carley, Michael, and Ian Christie. 1993. *Managing Sustainable Development.* Minneapolis: University of Minnesota Press.

Center for Compatible Economic Development. Undated. *A Citizen's Guide to Achieving a Healthy Community, Economy & Environment.* Leesburg, VA: The Nature Conservancy.

Center for Livable Communities. August 1996. "Resources to Bring Us Back to the Center." *Livable Places Update.* Sacramento, CA: Local Government Commission.

Center for Livable Communities. July 1996. "Transit-Oriented Development Steams Ahead." *Livable Places Update.* Sacramento, CA: Local Government Commission.

Center for Livable Communities. May 1996. "Suisun City—A Cinderella Story." *Livable Places Update.* Sacramento, CA: Local Government Commission.

Center for Livable Communities. April 1996. "Superstore Versus Community Core." *Livable Places Update.* Sacramento, CA: Local Government Commission.

Center for Livable Communities. March 1996. "Transit-Oriented Development

Revitalizes Richmond's Downtown." *Livable Places Update.* Sacramento, CA: Local Government Commission.

Center for Livable Communities. 1995a. *Model Projects: The Crossings.* Sacramento, CA: Local Government Commission.

Center for Livable Communities. 1995b. *Model Projects: Village Homes, Davis, CA.* Sacramento, CA: Local Government Commission.

Center for Neighborhood Technology. Undated press release. "Location Efficient Mortgages: A Summary Explanation." Chicago.

Cervero, Robert. 1994. "Transit Villages: From Idea to Implementation." *Access.* (University of California, Berkeley, Transportation Center) 5 (Fall): 8–13.

Chesapeake Bay Foundation. 1993. "Feeding the Auto Habit with Hidden Subsidies." Transportation Resource Book 1(4) (September): 1–4.

Christian Society of the Green Cross. 1993. "Evangelical Declaration on the Care of Creation." Wynnewood, PA.

Clark, John A., Neal I. Payton, and David A. Tice. Undated. "Haymount—A Sustainable Community on the Banks of the Rappahannock." Unpublished paper.

Cleveland—The New American City [online]. [Cited June 30, 1997]. Available from Internet: <URL: http://www.cleveland.oh.us/visit/>.

Cobb, Clifford, Ted Halstead, and Jonathan Rowe. 1995. "If the GDP is Up, Why is America Down?" *Atlantic Monthly* 276(4): 59–78.

Cohn, D'Vera. 1996. "Population Loss Puts D.C. in Company of Other Cities." *Washington Post,* 4 February, pp. A10–A11.

Colborn, Theo, John Peterson Myers, and Dianne Dumanoski. 1996. *Our Stolen Future: Are We Threatening Our Own Fertility, Intelligence, and Survival?* New York: Dutton.

Collins, Beryl Robichaud, and Emily W. B. Russell. 1988. *Protecting the New Jersey Pinelands: A New Direction in Land Use Management.* New Brunswick, NJ: Rutgers University Press.

Collins, Richard C. 1994. Lecture notes on sustainability, Environmental Choices class, University of Virginia, School of Architecture, Charlottesville.

*Consumer Reports.* 1996. "Newswatch: Does America Have an Energy Strategy?" *Consumer Reports,* July, p. 9.

Cozart, Elizabeth. 1996. "Old Schools Learning New Tricks: Rehabilitation Can Make Financial, Historical, and Emotional Sense." *News & Observer,* 3 March, p. 1D.

Crosbie, Michael J. 1993. "Audubon Society Opens Green Headquarters." *Progressive Architecture* 19(March): 19–20.

Culliton, Thomas J., M. A. Warren, T. R. Goodspeed, D. G. Remer, C. M. Blackwell, and J. J. McDonough. 1990. *Fifty Years of Population Change Along the Nation's Coasts, 1960–2010. A Special Earth Week Report.* Silver Spring, MD: National Oceanic and Atmospheric Administration Office of Ocean Resources Conservation and Assessment.

Daly, Herman E., and John B. Cobb. 1989. *For the Common Good*. Boston: Beacon Press.

Daly, Herman E., and Kenneth N. Townsend, eds. 1993. *Valuing the Earth: Economics, Ecology and Ethics*. Cambridge, MA: MIT Press.

DeGrove, John. 1984. *Land, Growth and Politics*. Chicago: APA Planners Press.

Diamond, Henry L., and Patrick F. Noonan. 1996. *Land Use in America*. Washington, DC: Island Press.

Dillon, David. 1994. "Fortress America: More and More of Us Are Living Behind Locked Doors." *Planning* 60(6):10–12.

Dinsmore, Clement. 1996. "State Initiatives on Brownfields." *Urban Land,* June, pp. 37–42.

Dodge, Jim. 1990. "Living by Life: Some Bioregional Theory and Practice." In *Home! A Bioregional Reader,* edited by Andruss, Plant, Plant, and Wright. Philadelphia: New Society.

Downs, Anthony. 1994. *New Visions for Metropolitan America*. Washington, DC: The Brookings Institution.

Downtown Durham, Inc. Undated. *Financial Incentive Programs*. Durham, NC: Downtown Durham.

Duany, Andres, and Elizabeth Plater-Zyberk. 1991. *Towns and Townmaking Principles*. New York: Rizzoli.

Durning, Alan. 1996. *The Car and the City*. Northwest Environment Watch Report #3. Seattle: Northwest Environment Watch.

Dwyer, John F., Herbert W. Schroeder, and Paul H. Gobster. 1994. "The Deep Significance of Urban Trees and Forests." In *The Ecological City,* edited by Platt, Rowntree, and Muick. Amherst: University of Massachusetts Press.

Easley, Gail V. 1992. *Staying Inside the Lines*. PAS Report 40. Chicago: American Planning Association.

Eastham, Tony R. 1995. "High-speed Rail: Another Golden Age." *Scientific American,* September, pp. 100–101.

Ecotrust. 1995. *Fiscal Year 1995 Annual Report*. Portland: Ecotrust.

Edsall, Thomas B. 1995. "TV Tattered Nation's Social Fabric, Political Scientist Contends." *Washington Post,* 3 September, p. A5.

Ehrenhalt, Alan. 1995. *The Lost City: The Forgotten Virtues of Community Life in America*. New York: Basic Books.

Egan, Timothy. 1996a. "Portland's Hard Line on Managing Growth." *New York Times,* 30 December, p. 1.

Egan, Timothy. 1996b. "Urban Sprawl Strains Western States." *New York Times,* 29 December, pp. 1, 14.

Egan, Timothy. 1995. "Many Seek Security in Private Communities." *New York Times,* 3 September, pp. 1, 22.

Ehrlich, Paul R., and Anne H. Ehrlich. 1991. *Healing the Planet: Strategies for Resolving the Environmental Crisis*. Reading, MA: Addison-Wesley.

Environmental Systems Research Institute. 1996. "The County of San Bernardino Economic Development GIS." *ESRI ARC News,* Spring, p. 34.

Erdmenger, Christoph, Birgit Dette, and Konrad Otto-Zimmerman. 1997. *Local Environmental Budgeting.* Freiburg, Germany: International Council for Local Environmental Initiatives.

Etzioni, Amitai. 1993. *The Spirit of Community: The Reinvention of American Society.* New York: Touchstone.

Etzioni, Amitai. 1988. *The Moral Dimension: Toward a New Economics.* New York: Free Press.

Evans, Judith. 1996. "Co-Housing, a Neighborly Thing to Do." *Washington Post,* 27 January, pp. E1, E4.

Fabricant, Florence. 1994. "Restaurant Chefs Create Partnerships with Local Growers." *In Business,* January/February, pp. 30–32.

Fishbein, Allen J. 1996. "The New Redlining: Community Credit in an Era of Bank Consolidation." Paper presented to the CDFI Leadership Forum, New York, September 16.

FOCUS Kansas City. 1997. "Building the New American City—Making Connections for the 21st Century." Working draft, January 1997.

Forest Service Employees for Environmental Ethics (FSEEE). Undated. "Economic Well-Being and Environmental Protection in the Pacific Northwest: A Consensus Report by Pacific Northwest Economists." Executive Summary. Eugene, OR: FSEEE.

Frank, Peter. 1995. "The Making of Harmony." *Conde Naste Traveler,* May, pp. 24–25.

Friedman, Diana. 1996. "Community: Just What Is All the Talk About?" [online] [New York]: *Metropolis,* Nov. 1996 [cited March 5, 1997]. Available from Internet: <URL: http://www.metropolismag.com/nov96/survey.html>.

Freund, Peter, and George Martin. 1993. *The Ecology of the Automobile.* Montreal: Black Rose.

Fulford, Bruce, and Brooke Nash. 1994. "Agricultural Composting in Boston." *Bio-Cycle* 35 (12): pp. 76–79.

Furuseth, Owen, and Chris Cocklin. 1995. "An Institutional Framework for Sustainable Resource Management: The New Zealand Model." *Natural Resources Journal* 35(2)243–273.

Gallagher, Mary Lou. 1994. "Arlington County's Affordable Housing Protection District." *Planning* 60(4): 12–13.

Galston, William A. 1991. *Liberal Purposes: Goods, Virtues and Diversity in the Liberal State.* New York: Cambridge University Press.

Gangloff, Deborah. 1995. "The Sustainable City." *American Forests,* May/June: 30–33.

Garbarine, Rachelle. 1996. "A New Incentive for Upstairs Housing Downtown: State Program Offers $10 Million in Loans to Store Owners." *New York Times,* 29 September, Sec. 9, p. 9.

Garreau, Joel. 1991. *Edge City: Life on the New Frontier.* New York: Doubleday.

Girardet, Herbert. 1992. *The Gaia Atlas of Cities: New Directions for Sustainable Living.* New York: Anchor.

Godschalk, David R., and Francis Parker. 1975. "Carrying Capacity: A Key to Environmental Planning?" *Journal of the Soil and Water Conservation Society* 30(4): 160–165.

Godschalk, David R., David J. Brower, Larry D. McBennett, Barbara A. Vestal, and Daniel C. Herr. 1979. *Constitutional Issues of Growth Management.* Chicago: APA Planners Press.

Goldsmith, William W., and Edward Blakely. 1992. *Separate Societies: Poverty and Inequality in U.S. Cities.* Philadelphia: Temple University Press.

Goleman, Daniel. 1992. "A Rising Cost of Modernity: Depresssion." *New York Times,* 8 December, p. C1.

Goodwin, Robert. 1997. "Coming Together: Volunteerism Is Vital Element to Saving Communities." *NonProfit Times,* January, p. 50.

Gordon, David, ed. 1990. *Green Cities: Ecologically Sound Approaches to Urban Space.* Montreal: Black Rose.

Greenwire. 1996. "New York: Bronx Paper-Recycling Mill Gets State Approval." 12 June.

Grove, Noel. 1994. "Greenways." *Land and People* 6(2): 2–8.

Gurwitt, Rob. 1994. "The Urban Village War." *Governing,* November, pp. 50–56.

Habitat for Humanity. Undated. *Jordan Commons: A Homestead Habitat for Humanity Neighborhood.* Homestead, FL: Habitat for Humanity.

Hahn, T., D. Pijawka, and J. Meunier. 1996. "Project Report: Environmental Showcase Home, Phoenix, AZ." In *AIA Environmental Resource Guide.* Washington, DC: American Institute of Architects.

Hamilton, Martha M. 1995. "A Cottage for Sale: Low-cost Granny Flats Combine Proximity with Privacy," *Washington Post,* 31 October, Special Health Section, p. 9.

Handmade in America. 1996a. Promotional brochure.

Handmade in America. 1996b. "Partners: Explorations in Community." Newsletter. No. 7 (October).

Handmade in America. 1996c. "Partners: Explorations in Community." Newsletter. No. 6 (April).

Hart, Stanley I., and Alvin L. Spivak. 1993. *The Elephant in the Bedroom.* Pasadena: New Paradigm.

Hawken, Paul, 1993. *The Ecology of Commerce: A Declaration of Sustainability.* New York: HarperCollins.

Hawthorne, Richard. 1996. Lecture given to the Sustainable Communities Forum, University of Virginia, School of Architecture.

Herd, Milton, and Vladimir Gavrilovic. 1995. "Willis Wharf Citizens Define Their Future Using a Creative Planning Process." *Economic Development and Planning,*

March/April, Virginia Review, Review Publications, Inc. Hiss, Tony. 1990. *The Experience of Place.* New York: Vintage Books.

Hollweg, Karen S. 1994. "Ecology Education for City Children," In *The Ecological City,* edited by Platt, Rowntree, and Muick. Amherst: University of Massachusetts Press.

Hong, Peter. 1996. "Lack of Bowling Leagues as Civic Collapse? Gutter Ball." *News & Observer,* 24 March, p. 6E (reprinted from the *Los Angeles Times*).

Hough, Michael. 1995. *Cities and Natural Process.* London and New York: Routledge.

Houghton, J. T., G. J. Jenkins, and J. J. Ephrams, eds. 1990. *Climate Change: The IPCC (Intergovernmental Panel on Climate Change) Scientific Assessment.* New York: Cambridge University Press.

Hubbard, Gunnar. 1997. "Performance-Based Fee Contracts: Doing It Right the First Time." *Solar Today,* January/February, pp. 24–26.

Hvidsten, Scott. 1995. "Pumping Up Tire Recycling Markets: A State Perspective." *Resource Recycling* 14(10): 36–42.

Iannone, Donald T. 1996. "Sparking Investment in Brownfield Sites." *Urban Land,* June, pp. 43–45, 64.

Ingerson, Alice E., ed. 1995. *Managing Land as Ecosystem.* Cambridge, MA: Lincoln Institute of Land Policy.

Interagency Ecosystem Management Task Force. 1995. "The Ecosystem Approach: Healthy Ecosystems and Sustainable Economies." Washington, DC, June.

International Council for Local Environmental Initiatives. 1994. *Promoting Sustainable Business Practices, Portland, OR.* Case study 26. Toronto: ICLEI.

International Council for Local Environmental Initiatives. Undated(a). *Greening the City: Chicago, U.S.* Case study 37. Toronto: ICLEI.

International Council for Local Environmental Initiatives. Undated(b). *Environmental Auditing: Lancashire County, UK.* Case study 6. Toronto: ICLEI.

International Union for the Conservation of Nature. 1991. *Caring for the Earth: A Strategy for Sustainable Living.* Gland, Switzerland: IUCN.

Jackson, Deirdra. 1995. "Cooperative Community Has Spirit to Share with Close-Living Neighbors." *News & Observer,* 2 July, pp. 1A, 14A.

Jackson, Kenneth. 1996. "America's Rush to Suburbia." *New York Times,* 9 June, p. E15.

Jackson, Kenneth T. 1985. *Crabgrass Frontier: The Suburbanization of the United States.* Oxford, UK: Oxford University Press.

Jacksonville Community Council Inc (JCCI). JCCI's Quality of Life Project and Replication Kit [online]. JCCI undated [cited Feb. 10, 1997]. Available from Internet: <URL:http://www.unf.edu/~clifford/jcci/qip.htm>.

Jacobs, Allan B., 1993. *Great Streets.* Cambridge, MA: MIT Press.

Jacobs, Jane. 1961. *The Death and Life of Great American Cities.* New York: Random House.

Jacobs, Michael. 1991. *The Green Economy: Environment, Sustainable Development, and the Politics of the Future.* London: Pluto Press.

Jensen, Deborah B., Margaret S. Torn, and John Harte. 1993. *In Our Own Hands: A Strategy for Conserving California's Biological Diversity.* Berkeley: University of California Press.

John, DeWitt. 1994. *Civic Environmentalism: Alternatives to Regulation in States and Communities.* Washington, DC: CQ Press.

Joint Venture: Silicon Valley Network. [online] Index of Silicon Valley 1997 [cited March 1, 1997]. Available from Internet: <URL: http://www.jointventure.org/index/toc.html/>.

Jones, Teresa B. 1996. "Boom Market Now a Growing Concern: Organic Farming Pays Off, But Too Few Farmers Planting." *News & Observer,* 14 July, pp. 1B, 5B.

Jongman, Rob H. G. 1995. "Nature Conservation Planning in Europe: Developing Ecological Networks." *Landscape and Urban Planning* 32: 169–83.

Jordan, William. 1993. " 'Sunflower Forest': Ecological Restoration as the Basis for a New Environmental Paradigm." In *Beyond Preservation: Restoring and Inventing Landscapes,* edited by Baldwin, Deluce, and Pletch. Minneapolis: University of Minnesota Press.

Judd, Dennis R. 1995. "The Rise of the New Walled Cities." In *Spatial Practices: Critical Explorations in Social/Spatial Theory,* edited by Helen Liggett and David C. Perry. Thousand Oaks, CA: Sage Publications.

Kansas City, Missouri, City of. Undated. "FOCUS: Project Overview."

Katz, Peter. 1995. "What Makes a Good Park?" *Trust for Public Land* 7(1): 7–9.

Katz, Peter. 1994. *The New Urbanism.* New York: McGraw-Hill.

Kellert, Stephen. 1996. *The Value of Life.* Washington, DC: Island Press.

Kelley, Chris. 1996. "In Search of New Life for Smaller Cities." *Land Lines* 8(2): 1, 3.

Kemmis, Daniel. 1995. *The Good City and the Good Life: Renewing the Sense of Community.* New York: Houghton Mifflin.

Kempton, Willett, James S. Boster, and Jennifer A. Hartley. 1995. *Environmental Values in American Culture.* Cambridge, MA: MIT Press.

Kennedy, Patrick. 1995. "An Infill Developer Versus the Forces of No." *Urban Ecologist* 2: 11.

Kenworthy, Jeffrey, Felix Laube, Peter Newman, and Paul Barter. 1996. "Indicators of Transport Efficiency in 37 Global Cities." Report prepared for the World Bank.

Kenworthy, Tom. 1995. " 'Green Scissors' Coalition Seeks $33 Billion in Cuts." *Washington Post,* 31 January, p. A13.

Kenworthy, Tom. 1994. "GOP Plan to Broaden Property Rights Could Cost Public Dearly." *Washington Post,* 13 December, p. A7.

Kidd, Charles V. 1992. "The Evolution of Sustainability." *Journal of Agricultural and Environmental Ethics* 5 (1): 1–26.

Kidder, Rushworth. 1995. *Shared Values for a Troubled World: Conversations with Men and Women of Conscience.* San Francisco: Jossey-Bass.

Knapp, Gerrit, and Arthur Nelson. 1992. *The Regulated Landscape: Lessons on State Land Use Planning from Oregon.* Cambridge, MA: Lincoln Institute of Land Policy.

Kopp, Raymond J., and V. Kerry Smith, eds. 1993. *Valuing Natural Assets: The Economics of Natural Resource Damage Assessment.* Washington, DC: Resources for the Future.

Kunstler, James Howard. 1993. *The Geography of Nowhere.* New York: Touchstone.

Kunstler, James Howard. 1996. *Home from Nowhere.* New York: Simon & Schuster.

Lancaster, California, City of. Undated. "Urban Structure Program: A New Approach to Urban Development Financing."

Landis, John D. 1995. "Imagining Land Use Futures: Applying the California Urban Futures Model." *Journal of the American Planning Association* 61(4) (Autumn): 438–56.

Landrigan, P. J. and H. L. Needleman. 1994. *Raising Children Toxic Free.* New York: Farrar, Straus and Giroux.

Langdon, Philip. 1994. *A Better Place to Live: Reshaping the American Suburb.* Amherst: University of Massachusetts Press.

Larmer, Paul. 1994. "Boulder's Ingenuity Has a Few Drawbacks." *High Country News* 26(16): 11.

Leager, Andrew. 1996. "Tear Down Downtown's Mall." *News & Observer,* 18 April, p. 19A.

Ledebur, Larry C., and William R. Barnes. 1993. *All in It Together.* Washington, DC: National League of Cities.

Leinsberger, Christopher B. 1996. "Metropolitan Development Trends of the Latter 1990s: Social and Environmental Implications." In *Land Use in America,* edited by Henry L. Diamond and Patrick F. Noonan. Washington, DC: Island Press.

Leopold, Aldo. 1949. *A Sand County Almanac.* New York: Oxford Press.

Lester, Chris, and Jeffrey Spivak. 1995. "Suburbs Can't Escape the Cost of Separation." *Kansas City Star,* 17 December, p. A1.

Little, Charles E. 1995. *Greenways for America.* Baltimore: Johns Hopkins University Press.

Local Government Commission. 1995. *Participation Tools for Better Land Use Planning.* Sacramento, CA: Local Government Commission.

Lohr, Steve. 1996. "Though Upbeat on the Economy, People Still Fear for Their Jobs." *New York Times,* 29 December, p. 1.

Lowe, Marcia. 1994. "Reinventing Transport." In *State of the World 1994,* edited by Lester Brown. Washington, DC: Worldwatch Institute.

Lowe, Marcia. 1990. "Alternatives to the Automobile: Transport for Liveable

Cities." Worldwatch Institute Paper No. 98. Washington, DC: Worldwatch Institute.

Lucy, William H. 1995. *Danger of Traffic Fatalities and Homicides by Strangers in Metropolitan Areas.* Charlottesville: University of Virginia, Department of Urban and Environmental Planning.

MacDonald, Randy. 1996. "Can We Catch a Ride on the Cascadia Express?" *Oregon Quarterly* (University of Oregon), Autumn, pp. 16–19.

Malin, Nadov. 1995. "Restoring the Tall-Grass Prairie." *Environmental Building News,* (September/October) 4(4): 9–11. Malin, Nadov. 1993. "Embodied Energy— Just What Is It and Why Do We Care?" *Environmental Building News* 2(3) (May/June): 8–9.

Martins, Lauren. 1996. "CEC Plans Drive on Metro Growth." *Colorado Environmental Report,* July/August.

Marsh, William M. 1991. *Landscape Planning: Environmental Applications.* New York: John Wiley.

Marshall, Alex. 1996a. "Suburb in Disguise." *Metropolis* (July): 70–97.

Marshall, Alex. 1996b. "Technology Transforms the Places We Live." *Metropolis* (March): 21–101.

Martin, Evelyn, and Timothy Beatley. 1993. "Our Relationship with the Earth: Environmental Ethics in Planning Education." *Journal of Planning Education and Research* 12 (2): 117–26.

Mathews, Jessica. 1996. "We'll Have to Put the Brakes On." *International Herald Tribune,* 2 October, p. 6.

Maughan, Janet. 1995. "Beyond the Spotted Owl: Investing in 'Green Market' Enterprises Can Be Good for Both Business and the Environment." *Ford Foundation Report,* Winter.

McCamant, Kathryn, and Charles Durrett. 1989. *Cohousing: A Contemporary Approach to Housing Ourselves.* Berkeley, CA: Ten Speed Press.

McCloud, John. 1996. "Berkeley Hopes $120 Million Plant Erases an Image." *New York Times,* 29 September, Sec. 9, p. 1.

McDonough, William. 1993. "Design, Ecology, Ethics and the Making of Things." A centennial sermon, Cathedral of St. John the Divine, New York, 7 February.

McHarg, Ian. 1969. *Design with Nature.* Garden City, NY: Anchor.

McKenna, M. A. J. 1997. "Americans 9 Percent Fatter Since '80: Minority Women are Heaviest of All." *Atlanta Constitution,* 7 March, pp. D3–4.

McPherson, E. Gregory. 1994. "Cooling Urban Heat Islands with Sustainable Landscapes." In *The Ecological City,* edited by Platt, Rowntree, and Muick. Amherst: University of Massachusetts Press.

Meadows, Donella. 1994. "Can Los Angeles Learn to Live with Limits?" *Utne Reader* 66 (November/December): 136–38.

Meadows, Donella H., Dennis L. Meadows, and Jorgen Randers. 1992. *Beyond the Limits.* Post Mills, VT: Chelsea Green.

Meadows, Donella H., Jorgen Randers, and William W. Behrens III. 1972. *The Limits to Growth.* New York: Universe.

Metropolitan Service District (Portland). 1994. "Metro 2040 Growth Concept." Region 2040 Decisions for Tomorrow, 8 December.

Mohney, David, and Keller Easterling, eds. 1991. *Seaside: Making a Town in America.* Princeton, NJ: Princeton Architecture Press.

Moll, Gary. 1995. "Urban Ecosystems: Breakthrough for City Green." *American Forests,* Autumn, pp. 23–27, 70.

Morin, Richard, and Dan Balz. 1996. "Lowered Expectations: Fewer and Fewer Americans Say They Trust Strangers, Government Leaders or Societal Institutions." *News & Observer,* 11 February, pp. 23A–24A (reprinted from the *Washington Post*).

Morris, David. 1996. "Pollution Taxes." *Coop America Quarterly,* Spring, p. 11.

Muller, Frank, J. Andrew Hoerner, and John Duffy. 1996. *State Carbon Tax Model* (Model and User's Guide). College Park, MD: Center for Global Change.

Mulvihill, David A. 1996. "Inquiry: What Is an Eco-industrial Park?" *Urban Land,* January, p. 80.

Myers, David, and Ed Diener. 1996. "The Pursuit of Happiness." *Scientific American,* May, pp. 70–72.

Nabhan, Gary, and Stephen Trimble. 1994. *The Geography of Childhood: Why Children Need Wild Places.* Boston: Beacon Press.

Nadis, Steve, and James J. Mackenzie. 1993. *Car Trouble.* Boston: Beacon Press.

National Building Museum. 1997. "How and Why We Build: Outreach and Scout Programs." *Blueprints* 15(2): 6.

National Capital Planning Commission. 1995. *Extending the Legacy: Planning America's Capital for the 21st Century.* Washington, DC: National Capital Planning Commission.

National Commission on the Environment. 1993. *Choosing a Sustainable Future.* Washington, DC: Island Press.

Nelessen, Anton C. 1994. *Visions for a New American Dream.* Chicago: APA Planners Press.

A. Nelessen Associates Inc. 1993. *Picture This... The Results of a Visual Preference Survey.* Survey done for Portland, Oregon, region. Princeton, NJ: A. Nelessen Associates, Inc.

Nelson, Arthur C. 1994. "Oregon's Urban Growth Boundary as a Landmark Planning Tool." In *Planning the Oregon Way: A Twenty-Year Evaluation,* edited by Carl Abbott, Deborah Howe, and Sy Adler. Corvallis: Oregon State University Press.

Nelson, Arthur C. 1988. *Development Impact Fees.* Chicago: APA Planners Press.

Nelson, Arthur C., and Terry Moore. 1996. "Assessing Growth Management Policy Implementation: Case Study of the United States' Leading Growth Management State." *Land Use Policy* 13(4): 241–59.

Newman, Morris. 1996. "What Happens to a Street When it Becomes an Experience?" *Metropolis* (April): 23.

Newman, Peter, and Jeffrey R. Kenworthy. 1992. *Winning Back the Cities.* Leichart, Australia: Pluto Press.

Newman, Peter W. G., and Jeffrey R. Kenworthy. 1991. "Transport and Urban Form in Thirty-two of the World's Principal Cities." *Transport Reviews* 11(3): 249–72.

Newman, Peter W. G., and Jeffrey R. Kenworthy. 1989. *Cities and Automobile Dependence: An International Sourcebook.* Aldershot, England: Gower.

Newman, Peter W. G., and Jeffrey R. Kenworthy. 1988. "Gasoline Consumption and Cities: A Comparison of U.S. Cities with a Global Survey." *Journal of the American Planning Association* 55(1): 24–37.

Newman, Peter W. G., and Jeffrey R. Kenworthy. 1988. "The Transport Energy Tradeoff: Fuel Efficient Traffic Versus Fuel Efficient Cities." *Transportation Research* 22(3): 163–74.

*New York Times.* 1996. *The Downsizing of America.* New York: Times Books.

North Carolina Heritage Tourism. 1996. "Heritage Tourism and Sustainable Development." *Heritage Tourism,* no. 3 (Winter): 7.

North Carolina Recycling Association. 1995. "Should We Go for 'Pay-as-you-throw?" *T R-Word* 7(4): 1, 6.

North Carolina Recycling Business Assistance Center. 1995. *The Impact of Recycling on Jobs in North Carolina.* Raleigh: North Carolina Department of Environment, Health, and Natural Resources, Office of Waste Reduction.

North Carolina Solar Center. 1994. "Center Awarded Grant for Affordable Housing Program." *Carolina Sun,* Fall, pp. 7–8.

Northwest Area Foundation. 1994. *A Better Row to Hoe: The Economic, Environmental, and Social Impact of Sustainable Agriculture.* St. Paul, MN: Northwest Area Foundation.

Norwood, Ken, and Kathleen Smith. 1995. *Rebuilding Community in America: Housing for Ecological Living, Personal Empowerment, and the New Extended Family.* Berkeley, CA: Shared Living Resources Center.

Noss, Reed F., Edward T. LaFoe III, and J. Michael Scott. 1995. *Endangered Ecosystems of the United States: A Preliminary Assessment of Loss and Degradation.* Washington, DC: U.S. Fish and Wildlife Service.

Nowlan, David M., and Greg Stewart. 1991. "Downtown Population Growth and Community Trips: Recent Experience in Toronto." *Journal of the American Planning Association* 57(2): 165–82.

Oldenburg, Ray. 1989. *The Great Good Place.* New York: Paragon House.

1000 Friends of Oregon and the Home Builders Association of Metropolitan Portland. 1991. "Managing Growth to Promote Affordable Housing: Revisiting Oregon's Goal 10." Portland, OR: 1000 Friends of Oregon.

Orr, David. 1996. Lecture in Environmental Choices class, University of Virginia, School of Architecture.

Orr, David W. 1994. *Earth in Mind: On Education, Environment and the Human Prospect.* Washington, DC: Island Press.

Pacelle, Mitchell. 1996. "More Stores Spurn Malls for the Village Square." *Wall Street Journal,* 16 February, p. B1.

Pae, Peter. 1996. "Farmers Milking a New Cash Cow: City Slickers Charged Top Dollar for a Taste of Life in the Fields." *Washington Post,* 30 September, pp. B1, B3.

Patton, Ann. 1993. *From Harm's Way: Flood Hazard Mitigation in Tulsa, Oklahoma.* Tulsa: City of Tulsa Public Works Department.

Pattonsburg Sustainable Economic Development Council (PSEDC). Undated. *Pattonsburg Constructed Wetland Project,* Pattonsburg, MO: PSEDC.

Payton, Neal I., ed. Undated. "AIA/Nathan Cummings Roundtables on Sustainable Architecture and Development."

Pearce, David, Anil Markandya, and Edward B. Barbier. 1989. *Blueprint for a Green Economy.* London: Earthscan.

Peirce, Neal R. 1996a. "Teenagers Need Responsibility, Opportunities to Make More of Their Lives." *News & Observer,* 31 March, p. 23A.

Peirce, Neal R. 1996b. "How Tragedy Renewed a Downtown's Spirit." *News & Observer,* 24 March, p. 25A.

Peirce, Neal R. 1995. "Once-Crumbling California Town Revives Itself the 'Smart' Way." *News & Observer,* 3 September, p. 27A.

Pendall, Rolf. 1994. "Land Availability and Zoning: Implications from a National Survey." *On the Ground* 1(1) (Fall):.19–20.

*People.* 1995. "In His Own Words: Our Separate Ways." *People,* 5 September, pp. 125–28.

People for Open Space. 1983. *Room Enough: Housing and Open Space in the Bay Area.* San Francisco: People for Open Space.

Pepper, David. 1996. *Modern Environmentalism: An Introduction.* London: Routledge.

Perciasepe, Robert. 1996. "The Watershed Approach." *Urban Land* June, pp. 26–30.

Pimental, David, and Mario Giampietro. 1995. "Food, Land, Population and the U.S. Economy," Study prepared for Carrying Capacity Network, Washington, DC.

Pindell, Terry. 1995. *A Good Place to Live: America's Last Migration.* New York: Henry Holt and Company.

Platt, Rutherford H. 1996. *Land Use and Society: Geography, Law, and Public Policy.* Washington, DC: Island Press.

Platt, Rutherford H., Rowan A. Roundtree, and Pamela C. Muick. 1994. *The Ecological City: Preserving and Restoring Urban Biodiversity.* Amherst: University of Massachusetts Press.

Plous, F. K. 1994 "Off the Road, Vehicles." *Planning,* September, pp. 8–12.

Population Reference Bureau. *1997 World Population Data Sheet* [online]. [Washington, DC]: Available from Internet: <URL: http://www.prb.org/info/97wpds. html>.

Poracsky, Joseph, and Michael C. Houck. 1994. "The Metropolitan Portland Urban Natural Resources Program." In *The Ecological City,* edited by Platt, Rowntree, and Muick. Amherst: University of Massachusetts Press.

Porter, Douglas. 1989. *Understanding Growth Management.* Washington, DC: Urban Land Institute.

Porter, Douglas R. 1997. *Managing Growth in America's Communities.* Washington, D.C.: Island Press.

Portland, Oregon, City of. 1993. "Carbon Dioxide Reduction Strategy." Portland Energy Office, November 10.

Portland, Oregon, City of. Undated. *Traffic Calming Program: Keeping Our Neighborhoods Safe.* Bureau of Traffic Management educational brochure.

Powell, Bob. 1995. "Solar Energy Design in Affordable Housing Communities." *Carolina Sun* 18(1): 1–2.

Power, Thomas Michael. 1996a. *Lost Landscapes and Failed Economies: The Search for a Value of Place.* Washington, DC: Island Press.

Power, Thomas Michael. 1996b. "The Wealth of Nature: Environmental Quality, Not Mining, Logging or Ranching, Is Driving Local Economic Development in the West." *Issues in Science and Technology* 12(3) (Spring): 48–54.

President's Council on Sustainable Development. 1996. *Sustainable America: A New Concensus for Prosperity, Opportunity, and a Healthy Environment for the Future.* Washington, DC: U.S. Government Printing Office.

Previtti, Laurel. 1995. "Planning a More Sustainable San Jose." *Urban Ecologist* 4:.11, 22.

Public Technology Inc. 1993. *Local Government Sustainable Buildings Guidebook: Environmentally Responsible Building Design and Management.* Washington, DC: Public Technology Inc.

Rabinovitch, Jonas. 1992. "Curitiba: Towards Sustainable Urban Development." *Environment and Urbanization* 4(2):62–73.

Real Estate Research Corporation. 1974. *The Costs of Sprawl.* Washington, DC: Council on Environmental Quality.

Reardon, Christopher. 1996. "Whose Woods These Are." *Ford Foundation Report* 27 (1): 18–23.

Redwood, Tavoh. 1994. "Tree Time." *Planning,* September, pp. 13–15.

Rees, William E. 1995. "Achieving Sustainability: Reform or Transformation?" *Journal of Planning Literature* 9(4): 343–61.

Rees, William E. 1992. "Ecological Footprints and Appropriated Carrying Capacity: What Urban Economics Leaves Out." *Environment and Urbanization* 4 (2):121–30.

Rees, William E., and Mark Roseland. 1991. "Sustainable Communities: Planning for the 21st Century." *Plan Canada* 31(3): 15–26.

Robbins, Jim. 1996. "Mont. Town Fights to Save Post Office." *News & Observer,* 3 December, p. 10A (reprinted from the *New York Times*).

Rogers, Bill. 1994. "Making Rail Competitive with Highways and Airports." *Place Matters* (Center for Neighborhood Technology, Chicago), Fall, p. 3.

Romm, Joseph J., and William D. Browning. 1994. *Greening the Building and the Bottom Line: Increasing Productivity Through Energy-Efficient Design.* Snowmass, CO: Rocky Mountain Institute.

Roseland, Mark. 1992. *Toward Sustainable Communities.* Ottawa, Ontario: National Round Table on the Environment and the Economy.

Roy, Kimberley. 1996. "Pinelands of New Jersey: An Experiment in Achieving Sustainable Development Through a Combination of Land Use Management Strategies." Independent research project, Department of Urban and Environmental Planning, University of Virginia.

Ruben, Barbara. 1994. "Coming to America: Immigrants and the Eenvironment," *Environmental Action,* Summer, pp. 23–24.

Rybczynski, Witold. 1996. "Tomorrowland: Living in a Community Planned by Disney Has to Be a Nightmare, Doesn't It?" *New Yorker,* 22 July, pp. 36–39.

Rybczynski, Witold. 1995. *City Life.* New York: Scribner.

Sale, Kirkpatrick. 1991. *Dwellers in the Land: The Bioregional Vision.* Philadelphia: New Society.

Salvesen, David. 1996. "Making Industrial Parks Sustainable." *Urban Land,* February, pp. 29–32.

Salvesen, David. 1990. *Wetlands: Mitigating and Regulating Development Impacts.* Washington, DC: Urban Land Institute.

San Francisco League of Urban Gardeners. 1996. *SLUG Update,* Fall/Winter.

Schneider, Devon M., David R. Godschalk, and Norman Axler. 1978. *The Carrying Capacity Concept as a Planning Tool.* PAS Report 338. Chicago: American Planning Association.

Schoonmaker, Peter K., Bettina von Hagen, and Edward C. Wolf, eds. 1996. *The Rain Forests of Home: Profile of a North American Region.* Washington, DC: Island Press.

Seattle, Washington, City of. 1994. "Seattle's Comprehensive Plan: Toward a Sustainable Seattle. A Plan for Managing Growth 1994–2014."

Self-Help. 1995. *Self-Help Biennial Report 1993/1994.* Durham, NC: Self-Help.

Sennett, Richard. 1970. *The Uses of Disorder: Personal Identity and City Life.* New York: Norton.

Shaw Homes, Inc. 1995. "Environmentally Responsible Development at Prairie Crossing." Background materials distributed at Urban Land Institute symposium on environmentally responsible development, 2–3 June, Chicago.

Shaw Homes, Inc. Undated. *Prairie Crossing: A Natural Landscape for Living.* Grayslake, IL.

Shear, Michael D. "Pr. William Shifts from Big to Small: County Downsizes Its Ideal Business Targets." *Washington Post,* 30 September, pp. B1, B6.

Shields, Todd. 1995. "Tree Trimming Sparks Fury in Md Town." *Washington Post,* 7 December, Metro section, p. C1.

Shirley, Larry. 1997. "Utility Restructuring Roars Down the Track." *Solar Today,* January/February, p. 4.

Sierra Business Council. 1996. *Sierra Business Council News.* March/April 1996.

Sit, Mary. 1992. "Creating a Neighborhood: Cohousing Takes Root." *Washington Post,* 24 October, p. 11.

Sloan, Gene. 1996. "Memphis: Rebirth of Blues City. Music and Museums Bring Tourists Back." *USA Today,* 26 April, p. 7D.

Smeloff, Ed, and Peter Asmus. 1996. *Reinventing Electric Utilities.* Washington, DC: Island Press.

Smith, Daniel S., and Paul Cawood Hellmund, eds. 1993. *Ecology of Greenways.* Minneapolis: University of Minnesota Press.

Souder, William. 1996. "Don't Panic, But Look at Those Frogs." *International Herald Tribune,* 2 October, p. 1.

Spirn, Anne Whister. 1984. *The Granite Garden.* New York: Basic Books.

Stapleton, Richard. 1995. "The Superstore Syndrome: A Small Town Stands Up to Megastore Sprawl." *Land and People* 7(2): 12–17.

Stead, Dominic. 1995. "The Purchase Audit." In *A Guide to Local Environmental Auditing,* edited by Hugh Barton and Noel Bruder. London: Earthscan.

Steinberg, Theodore. 1995. *Slide Mountain: Or the Folly of Owning Nature.* Berkeley: University of California Press.

Steiner, Frederick. 1991. *The Living Landscape: An Ecological Approach to Landscape Planning.* New York: McGraw-Hill.

Strange, Marty. 1996. "Transforming the Rot Belt: Sustainable Rural Communities." *Northwest Report* 19 (January): 16–21.

Surface Transportation Policy Project. 1997. "Highways No Longer Lone Star in Texas." STPP weekly e-mail newsletter, 28 February.

Sustainable America. 1996. "Grassroots in Bloom—The Campaign for a Sustainable Milwaukee." *SA Talks* 1 (2) (October): 9–10.

Sustainable Seattle. 1995. *Indicators of Sustainable Community: Sustainable Seattle 1995.* Seattle: Sustainable Seattle.

Swezey, Blair G. 1997. "Utility Green Pricing Programs: Market Evolution or Devolution?" *Solar Today,* January/February, pp. 21–23.

"Tax Reform Fights Sprawl." Undated. Briefing memo, Honorable Hilda Mason, Council of the District of Columbia.

Thurow, Charles, William Toner, and Duncan Erley. 1975. "Performance Controls for Sensitive Lands." PAS Report 307/308 Chicago: American Planning Association.

Todd, Nancy Jack, and John Todd. 1994. *From Eco-cities to Living Machines: Principles of Ecological Design,* Berkeley, CA: North Atlantic.

Tonn, Bruce E. 1986. "500-year Planning: A Speculative Provocation." *Journal of the American Planning Association* 52(2): 185–93.

Tulsa, Oklahoma, City of. 1994. "From Rooftop to River: Tulsa's Approach to Floodplain and Stormwater Management." Tulsa Stormwater Management Advisory Board and Public Works Department.

Tustian, Richard E. 1984. "TDRs in Practice: A Case Study of Agriculture Preservation in Montgomery County, Maryland." In *1984 Zoning and Planning Law Handbook,* edited by J. B. Gailey. New York: Clark Boardman.

Twardy, Chuck. 1995a. "Saving Grace." *News & Observer,* 22 September, pp. 1D, 3D.

Twardy, Chuck. 1995b. "Renaissance on the Neuse." *News & Observer,* 2 July, pp. 1G, 9G.

Ulrich, Roger S. 1981. "Natural Versus Urban Scenes: Some Psychological Effects." *Environment and Behavior* 13: 523–56.

*Urban Ecologist.* 1995. "Ecological Rebuilding: Bay Area." *Urban Ecologist* 4(1): 22.

*Urban Ecologist* 1994. "Ecological Rebuilding Around the World." *Urban Ecologist* 3: 12–13, 17.

Urban Land Institute. 1989. *The Costs of Alternative Development Patterns: A Review of the Literature.* Washington, DC: Urban Land Institute.

U.S. Office of Technology Assessment. 1993. *Preparing for an Uncertain Climate.* Washington, DC: U.S. Government Printing Office.

van Baalen, J. 1995. "Towards Nature Development and the National Ecological Network for the Netherlands," In *Nature Restoration in the European Union.* Copenhagen: Danish Ministry of Environment and Energy.

Vanderbilt, Tom. 1996. "The New Wall Street" *Metropolis* (November): 22–26.

Van der Ryn, Sim, and Peter Calthorpe. 1991. *Sustainable Communities.* San Francisco: Sierra Club Books.

Vogel, Marta. 1996. "The Lonely Heart of the Suburbs." *Washington Post,* 16 June, pp. C1–C2.

von Hagen, Bettina, and Erin Kellogg. 1996. "Entrepreneurs and Ecosystems: Building Sustainable Economies." *Northwest Report* 19 (January): 10–15.

Wackernagel, Mathis, and William Rees. 1996. *Our Ecological Footprint: Reducing Human Impact on the Earth.* Gabriola Island, BC: New Society Publishers.

Walinsky, Adam. 1995. "The Crisis of Public Disorder." *Atlantic Monthly* 276(1): 39–54.

Walter, Bob, Lois Arkin, and Richard Crenshaw, eds. 1992. *Sustainable Cities: Concepts and Strategies for Eco-city Development.* Los Angeles: Eco-home Network.

Warson, Albert. 1995. "Building Telecommunities." *Urban Land,* May, pp. 37–39.

*Washington Post.* 1996. "Paying Through the Hose." *Washington Post,* 11 May, p. A-21.

White, Ed. 1996. "Cars May Return to Another Mall." Associated Press, August 21.

White, Rodney R. 1994. *Urban Environmental Management: Environmental Change and Urban Design.* New York: John Wiley.

Whoriskey, Peter. 1996. "Disney Builds a Town and, Surprise, It's Full of Good Ideas." *News & Observer,* 28 November, p. 15E.

Williamson, David. 1995. "Study: More Walking and Biking Would Help U.S." *Chapel Hill Herald,* 19 March, p. 8.

Wilson, E. O. 1992. *The Diversity of Life.* Cambridge, MA: Harvard University Press.

Wong, Yu. 1996. "Getting Goods to Market Remains a Major Headache." *International Herald Tribune,* 26 October (sponsored advertisement section).

World Commission on Environment and Development. 1987. *Our Common Future.* Oxford, UK: Oxford University Press.

World Resources Institute. 1996. *World Resources, 1996–97.* New York: Oxford University Press.

World Resources Institute. 1995. *World Resources, 1995–96.* New York: Oxford University Press.

World Resources Institute. 1994. *World Resources, 1994–95.* New York: Oxford University Press.

Worldwatch Institute. 1995. *State of the World, 1995.* Washington, DC: Worldwatch Institute.

Yaro, Robert D. 1996. Lecture in Environmental Choices class, University of Virginia, School of Architecture.

Yaro, Robert D., and Tony Hiss. 1996. *A Region at Risk: The third regional plan for the New York–New Jersey–Connecticut Metropolitan Area.* Washington, DC: Island Press.

Yim, Su-Jin. 1996a. "Renovation to Spur Renewal." *News & Observer,* 13 January, p. 1D.

Yim, Su-Jin. 1996b. "Community Spirit to Foster Community Backing: Wilson Firms Team Up to Fight Back: Small, Family-owned Concerns Look After Own Interests." *News & Observer,* 7 February, pp. 1D, 6D.

Yim, Su-Jin. 1996c. "N.C. Flavor on Grocery Shelves: Stores Making Space for Local Products." *News & Observer,* 25 May, pp. 1D, 6D.

Young, Dwight. 1995. *Alternatives to Sprawl.* Cambridge, MA: Lincoln Institute of Land Policy.

Youngman, Joan. 1996. "Local Property Tax Reform: Prospects and Politics." *Land Lines* 8(July): 1, 6–7.

Zachary, Jill. 1995. "Sustainable Community Indicators: Guideposts for Local Planning." Santa Barbara: Community Environmental Council, Inc.

Zero Population Growth. Undated. "Frequently Asked Questions: Things You Ought to Know About Population."

Zuckerman, Wolfgang. 1992. *End of the Road: From World Car Crisis to Sustainable Transportation*. Post Mills, VT: Chelsea Green.

# Index